From the Chickasaw Cession to Yoknapatawpha

Historical and Literary Essays on North Mississippi

To Margaret and Tom —
Hope you enjoy these stories
of the 19th and mid-20th centuries
about our home region in
Mississippi — *J Wilson*

Compiled and Edited by
Hubert H. McAlexander

From the Chickasaw Cession to Yoknapatawpha: Historical and Literary Essays on North Mississippi © copyright, 2017, Hubert H. McAlexander

ISBN: 978-1-936946-78-5

The Nautilus Publishing Company
426 S Lamar Blvd. Suite 16
Oxford, MS 38655
Tel: 662-513-0159
www.nautiluspublishing.com

First Edition

Front cover design by Le'Herman Payton

Cover images clockwise from top left: Jacob Thompson; Walter Place; Sherwood Bonner; Holmes Teer, Oxford Courthouse surrounded by Federal army tents; Green Pryor.

Library of Congress Cataloging-in-Publication Data has been applied for.

Printed in the USA

10 9 8 7 6 5 4 3 2 1

TABLE OF CONTENTS

PART I: THE CHICKASAW CESSION

Part II: High Cotton

PART III: FLAMES OF WAR

PART IV: POST-WAR LIFE

PART V: HISTORY, RACE, YOKNAPATAWPHA

To Ruff Fant,
friend from childhood, with many connections since Cession days,
who has made my last years productive and who is responsible for this book.

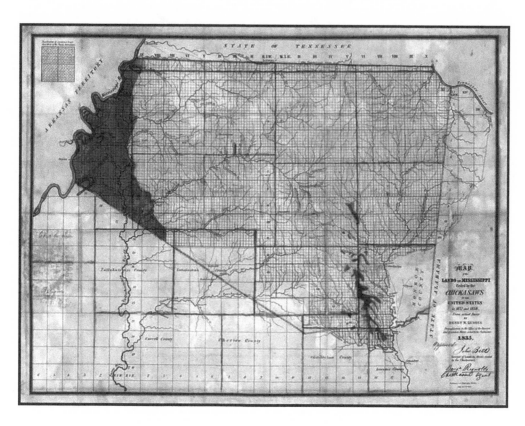

Henry M. Lusher's map of the Chickasaw Cession as it was plotted
Barry Lawrence Ruderman Antique Maps Inc.

PART I:
THE CHICKASAW CESSION

THE PONTOTOC LAND OFFICE

JACK D. ELLIOTT, JR.

By the 1832 Treaty of Pontotoc Creek, the Chickasaw tribe ceded to the United States their domain. This action came just two years after the Choctaw Cession. Now the attention of both pioneers and speculators focused upon north Mississippi. As the details of Andrew Jackson's Choctaw initiative were being settled and the Choctaw people removed from their land, attention shifted to the block of land relinquished by the Chickasaws. An essential step was the creation of a land office.

The area initially claimed by the Chickasaw tribe included much of north Mississippi and extended north to the Ohio River. Beginning with the British Proclamation of 1763 and continued as a cornerstone of American Indian policy, Indian lands west of the Appalachians were put under a political-legal distinction termed "Indian Territory," designating these lands under the jurisdiction of the central government and outside that of the governments of colonies and later of states and territories. Within the Indian Territory only tribal laws and laws of the central government held. When the Mississippi Territory was established in 1798 and the State of Mississippi in 1817, most lands were in Indian Territory, so territorial and state laws had no bearing there. By implication there were also no local governments (counties or municipalities) within the Indian Territory, nor was land owned privately. This was about to change.

As tribal lands were ceded to the United States, they were removed from the Indian Territory designation and placed under the laws of the territories or states in which they were located; the land was surveyed and sold by the federal government. By 1829, the year in which Andrew Jackson came into office as president, the Indian Territory had been whittled down to several large islands of tribal lands, each several million acres, with the last remnants of Chickasaw and Choctaw territory constituting most of north Mississippi. In anticipation of Jackson's move to force the cession of these lands, the state passed an act on February 4, 1829 — one month before his inauguration — extending legal process across those remnants while extending the boundaries of counties adjacent to the Indian

Territory to bring the area into the system of county government. Most of the Chickasaw territory was placed under the jurisdiction of Monroe County, which had been established in 1821, originally on the east side of the Tombigbee River. The extension of state law across a federally-defined Indian Territory — apparently illegally — might have been contested had the political atmosphere not been so favorable to Indian removal. After the Jackson administration came into office in March 1829, the new Secretary of War noted that the federal government was unable to stop the extension of state jurisdiction over the Indian Territory. State jurisdiction effectively prevented chiefs from exercising authority, thus undermining tribal solidarity and placing tribes under unfamiliar laws. Furthermore, it brought a rush of white settlers into the Chickasaw lands. Bowing to the inevitable, the Cherokees, Chickasaws, Choctaws, and Creeks soon agreed to cede their lands and move west.

The Choctaws ceded the last of their lands at the Treaty of Dancing Rabbit Creek on September 28, 1830, and agreed to move west to a newly established Indian Territory in what is now Oklahoma. On October 20, 1832, the Chickasaws followed suit by signing a treaty at their council house near Pontotoc Creek (several miles southeast of the present town of Pontotoc, and now known as Chiwapa Creek). The treaty was known as the Treaty of Pontotoc Creek, or as the Treaty of Pontotoc. Two days later, supplementary articles to the treaty were signed at the same location.

The preamble to the treaty reads: "The Chickasaw Nation find themselves oppressed in their present situation; by being made subject to the laws of the States in which they reside. Being ignorant of the language and laws of the white man, they cannot understand or obey them. Rather than submit to this great evil, they prefer to seek a home in the west, where they may live and be governed by their own laws. And believing that they can procure for themselves a home, in a country suited to their wants and condition, provided they had the means to contract and pay for the same, they have determined to sell their country and hunt a new home."

In the treaty the Chickasaws agreed to cede all their land lying east of the Mississippi River and to move west of the river as soon as adequate land could be located. The U.S. agreed in turn to have the land surveyed and offered for sale at public auction with all the proceeds to be paid to the Chickasaws after deducting the cost of surveying and selling the land. The area to be surveyed and sold was vast, constituting about 6,700,000 acres in Mississippi and Alabama, with a small strip in Tennessee.

This was certainly no small task given the area involved, and it required an agency to be located in the area. The sixth article of the treaty provided for the appointment of three officials, surveyor general, register, and receiver, all appointed by the president with "the advice and consent of the Senate." The surveyor general was allowed a clerk and draftsman while supervising a number of deputy surveyors contracted to survey various parts of the grid system. The register and receiver were each allowed one clerk. The three officials were standard for land offices, which were thereby divided into three separate but symbiotic units. In general, the office of the surveyor general was referred to as the "surveyor's office," while the offices of the register and receiver were known collectively as "the land office." A site for the three offices would be established, according to the treaty, "somewhere central in the [Chickasaw] nation, at such place as the President of the United States may direct."

On March 27, 1833, five months after the treaty signing, Elijah Hayward, commissioner of the General Land Office (hereafter GLO), transmitted a commission from President Andrew Jackson to John Bell, a merchant from Cotton Gin Port, Mississippi, appointing him surveyor general for the Cession lands.[1] Appointments would also soon go to Robert Tinnin as register and William Forbes Savage as receiver.[2] However, there was little that the latter two officials could do until land sales began, and that couldn't occur until at least part of the lands had been surveyed.

On April 10, Hayward requested that Bell investigate possible locations for the site of a land office.[3] After several exploratory trips, Bell drafted a report on May 27 that examined the comparative advantages of various sites for the land office, recommending in the end a site he called "Love's Old Place,"[4] apparently referring to the former farmstead of Thomas Love,[5] a British trader who had sired several mixed-blood children who became a dominant force within the Chickasaw tribe. The site was authorized by the president on June 11, 1833.[6] On August 30, Register Robert Tinnin reported to Washington that the land office would be called "Pontotoc," obviously borrowing the name from the site of the

---

1 Letter, Elijah Hayward, Commissioner GLO, to John Bell, March 27, 1833, RG49, Entry 13 (Copies of letters sent by the GLO pertaining to the Pontotoc Land Office), vol. 1, page 1.

2 Letter, Elijah Hayward, Commissioner GLO, to Robert Tennin, May 20, 1833, RG 49, Entry 13, volume 1, page 16.

3 Letter, Elijah Hayward, Commissioner GLO, to John Bell, April 10, 1833, RG 49, Entry 13, volume 1, pages 3-4.

4 Abstract of letter received by the GLO from John Bell, May 27, 1833. RG 49, Entry 8 (Abstracts of letters received by the GLO pertaining to the Pontotoc Land Office). The one volume that constitutes Entry 8 is not paginated.

5 "There was a small farm nearby which embraced the region now used as a grave yard. This farm was owned by Thomas Love, a refugee loyalist." Rev. Frank Patton, "Reminiscences of the Chickasaw Indians" No. XV, Old and New Pontotoc, from an unidentified newspaper. Internal evidence strongly suggests that it was a Pontotoc newspaper from late 1876.

6 Abstract of letter received by the GLO from the President of the U.S.A., June 11, 1833, RG 49, Entry 8.

treaty signing.[7] The name was further institutionalized when, on October 14, 1833, a post office named Pontotoc was authorized.

On July 18, the GLO commissioner instructed the newly appointed, but not yet working, Robert Tinnin to arrange for the construction of three office buildings at the site to serve as the offices of the surveyor general, register, and receiver. All were to be constructed according to identical specifications: log construction, 32 x 34 feet in plan, one-and-a-half stories, with three rooms on each floor.[8] A contract was soon made with a James White[9] and the buildings constructed over a period of months. In the meantime John Bell presumably had to operate out of his own newly constructed home.[10]

By the stipulations of the Treaty of Pontotoc, the offices were constructed on a 640-acre section of land, that was to be reserved for federal use. Of course, when the site was selected, no section lines had been surveyed. On February 10, 1834, Bell informed the GLO that the reserved section had been selected.[11] The two townships within which the parcels lay had been surveyed early so the reserved section could be defined with reference to the survey grid.[12] Once defined, the boundaries of the reserved section would be used as the boundaries against interlopers, whose intrusion would be met by the force of the law. In 1835, reference was made to "the grog shops established over the line of the office section," implying that to obtain maximum exposure to customers, these merchants located themselves as closely as possible to the boundary of the reserved section.[13]

---

7 Abstract of letter received by the GLO from Robert Tinnin, August 30, 1833, RG 49, Entry 8.

8 Letter, Elijah Hayward, commissioner GLO, to Robert Tinnin, register, Florence, AL, July 18, 1833. RG 49, Entry 13, volume 1, page 27-28.

9 Abstracts of two letters received by the GLO from Robert Tinnin, both dated November 7, 1834 that allude to James White's contract for the erection of the office buildings along with White's account for the same. RG 49, Entry 8.

10 By January 1834, Bell reported having taken possession of his office. Abstract of letter received from John Bell, January 24, 1834. RG 49, Entry 8.
All the offices were completed by early September 1834. Letter, John M Moore, acting commissioner GLO, to Lewis Cass, secretary of war, September 10, 1834. Moore noted that, "These buildings have been completed under his [Tinnin's] superintendence." RG 49, Entry 13, volume 1, pages 71-72.

11 Abstract of letter received by the GLO from John Bell, February 10, 1832, RG 49, Entry 8. The reserved section consisted of the southeast one quarter of Section 32 and the southwest one quarter of Section 33 in Township 9 Range 3 East, along with the north one half of Section 5 Township 10 Range 3 East. While this was not one single section, the combined parcels were contiguous and constituted the same acreage as a section.

12 Letter, Elijah Hayward, GLO commissioner, to John Bell, March 24, 1834, RG 49, Entry 13, volume 1, pages 55-56 refers to the survey of Townships 9 & 10 Range 3 East as being completed.

13 Abstract of letter received by the GLO from register and receiver at Pontotoc, May 29, 1835, RG

On August 17, John Bell wrote to the GLO informing them that he would commence building his private residence in a few days. Additionally, he urged the federal government to authorize the opening of a tavern on the reserved section.[14]

On September 6, the president issued approval for the opening of a tavern. However, it was to be built and operated at the owner's expense, and the owner had to be a person of good character approved by all three of the officials at that land office.[15] The person selected for the job was John L. Allen, who came highly recommended.[16] He was the Chickasaw sub-agent (June 1, 1829-March 31, 1835) and was married to Margaret Colbert, apparently the daughter of General William Colbert, the mixed-blood Chickasaw chief whose family was a major power in the Chickasaw Nation. Allen was authorized to operate the tavern in July 1834.[17]

Before the land could be sold it had to be surveyed, and the survey would follow the pattern that had emerged from its first implementation in the 1780s in Ohio by the federal government. The developed plan entailed subdividing the land into six-mile square units called townships, with each township subdivided into 36 one-mile square "sections." However, townships were not laid out willy-nilly. They were surveyed as part of a grid-system based on an east-west axis termed the base line and a north-south axis termed the principal meridian.

The survey of the 1832 Chickasaw Cession used the Winchester Line as the east-west Chickasaw base line. This line had been surveyed by General James Winchester in 1819 to define the northern boundary of Mississippi. The north-south Chickasaw Meridian had not yet been determined, and without that designation the survey of townships and sections could not be conducted. The surveys were conducted by "deputy surveyors," who worked under federal contracts and the supervision and coordination of the surveyor general and employed crews of flagmen, markers, and chain carriers. Deputy Surveyor John Thomson signed a contract on August 7, 1833, to begin the survey of the Chickasaw Meridian at the intersection of the Winchester Line and the Wolf River, and on August 29, drove the stake that established the initial point, thereby determining the layout of

---

49, Entry 8.

14 Abstract of letter received by GLO from John Bell, August 17, 1833, RG 49, Entry 8.

15 Abstracts of letters received by GLO from the president of the U.S.A. and Lewis Cass, secretary of war, both dated September 6, 1833, RG 49, Entry 8. Letter, John M. Moore, acting commissioner GLO, to John Bell, September 9, 1833. RG 49, Entry 13, vol. 1, pages 31-32.

16 Abstract of letter received by GLO from John Bell, June 9, 1834, RG 49, Entry 8.

17 James R. Atkinson, *Records of the Old Southwest in the National Archives*, 1997, 11; James R. Atkinson, *History of the Chickasaw Indian Agency East of the Mississippi River*, 1998, note 186, page 70.

the entire grid system.[18] Subsequent surveys expanded the grid delineating township and range lines, while other surveys laid out the interior section lines within townships.[19]

As the land was surveyed it was transferred to private individuals. There were two types of transfer: (1) allotments or reservations to individual Chickasaws and their families and (2) private sales to individuals. Approximately one-third of the area was allotted, while the remaining two-thirds were sold at public sale to the highest bidder.[20]

During the summer and fall of 1834, and long before the allotment or sale of land, speculators were operating through middlemen who provided money or store accounts to Chickasaws in exchange for title bonds obligating them to convey title to their lands once they obtained them.[21] As the surveys were proceeding, Chickasaw Agent Benjamin Reynolds, along with Sub-Agent John L. Allen, began working with the Chickasaws to locate their allotments. The Chickasaw Agency at that time was located in northwest Alabama near the Tennessee River a considerable distance from the land office and from the center of Chickasaw activity. Consequently, Reynolds was compelled to increasingly conduct his operations from Pontotoc beginning in early fall 1834.[22] Within a few months it became

18 "Field Notes of the Basis Meridian of the Chickasaw Cession Mississippi Surveyed by John Thomson, Deputy Surveyor 1833," online at the BLM website; notes at the bottom of the "Plat of Township 1 Range 1 East of the Chickasaw Meridian," online at the BLM website.

19 Letter, Thomas H. Blake, commissioner GLO, to Walter Forward, secretary of the treasury, January 6, 1843, RG 49, Entry 13, volume 2, pages 250-261. Surveys continued for the most part from August 1833 through late 1837.

20 Letter, Richard M. Young, commissioner GLO, to Jefferson Davis, U.S. Senate, February 10, 1848, Tables A and B, RG 49 Entry 13 Volume 3, pages 238-241.

21 Mary Elizabeth Young, *Redskins, Ruffleshirts, and Rednecks: Indian Allotments in Alabama and Mississippi 1830-1860*, Norman: University of Oklahoma Press, 1961, pages 116-117.

22 Reynolds began paying for board and accommodations usually with Thomas C. McMackin, the leading hosteler, who was located close to the land office, but just outside the reserved section. According to Patton, "Gen. McMackin opened a house of entertainment on his own purchase south of Allen [the tavern operated by John L. Allen, which was adjacent to the land office buildings] but on the same hill." Rev. Frank Patton, "Reminiscences of the Chickasaw Indians" No. XV, Old and New Pontotoc. McMackin's locating "south of Allen but on the same hill" apparently meant that he was on the southern tip of the ridge south of Allen and the land office and just across the southern section line and thereby outside the reserved section.
A list of government expenditures includes a representative entry that illustrates the use of McMackin's establishment with $125.25 paid to McMackin "For board of B. Reynolds, interpreter, servant, and horses, and furnishing them with provisions for the camp when making locations of reservations, from March 19 to June 4, 1835, while engaged in locating reservations." *Expenditures from the Chickasaw Fund: Letter from the Secretary of War, Communicating a Detailed Statement of All the Expenditures Made from the Chickasaw Fund between the 2d Day of March, 1833, and the 1st Day of January, 1843*, Document no. 65. Originally published 1843, reprinted Aberdeen MS: Chickasaw Publishing Co., 1982, pages 50-54.

necessary to establish a branch office of the Chickasaw Agency at Pontotoc.[23]

As Chickasaw reservations were located and assigned to their claimants, an influx of land buyers and Chickasaws with land to sell converged on Pontotoc. Some of the new arrivals had interests beyond merely purchasing land. By the summer of 1835, a church and academy were established, and the New York and Mississippi Land Company and other land companies began to establish permanent offices. By 1835, Pontotoc had become a cluster of federal offices — land offices, post office, and branch Chickasaw Agency — along with a growing populace of non-government personnel, many involved in the transfer and acquisition of land and others providing services.

With allotments to the Chickasaws in full swing, public land sales at auction began. Announced well in advance, the first sale ran from January 4-31, 1836, with 960,023 acres offered to the highest bidders.[24]

Days after the land sale, legislation provided the basis for transforming the Pontotoc settlement. On February 9, 1836, the state legislature created new counties for the Cession lands using the survey grid to define the boundaries, with one being called Pontotoc County.[25] On the 14th, another bill was passed that appointed commissioners to organize and hold elections in the new counties. Among the six appointed for Pontotoc County were two land office officials: John Bell, the surveyor-general, and Robert Tinnin, the register.[26] After the county government was organized, a site for a county seat town to be called—not surprisingly, Pontotoc — was selected on land owned by Thomas McMackin that lay to the south of and adjacent to the reserved section. A block in the town was donated to the county for a courthouse square. McMackin soon erected a new and grander

---

23 This branch office closed in September 1837 following the beginning of Chickasaw emigration to what is now Oklahoma in June 1837. James R. Atkinson, *History of the Chickasaw Indian Agency East of the Mississippi River*, 1998, pages 44-45. See expenditure of $200 paid by Reynolds to Thomas C. McMackin "For rent of a house used as an office by agent at Pontotoc, from September 1, 1835, to June 15, 1836." *Expenditures from the Chickasaw Fund: Letter from the Secretary of War, Communicating a Detailed Statement of All the Expenditures Made from the Chickasaw Fund between the 2d Day of March, 1833, and the 1st Day of January, 1843,* published 1843, reprint of Document no. 65, 1982, page 52. James R. Atkinson, *Splendid Land, Splendid People: The Chickasaw Indians to Removal,* University of Alabama Press, 2004, 232-233.

24 Letter, John M. Moore, principle clerk public lands GLO, to Thomas H. Benton, U.S. Senate, December 26, 1838, "Statement exhibiting the Sales in the Chickasaw Cession of 1832," RG 49 Entry 13 vol 1, pages 306-307.

25 "An Act to define the boundaries of certain counties therein named, and for other purposes," Laws of Mississippi, 1836, 2-14.

26 "An Act to organize certain new counties therein named, and for other purposes," Laws of Mississippi 1836, 46-49.

hotel on the block east of the court square.[27]

The second public sale ran from September 5 through November 20, 1836, with 2,601,130 acres offered for sale, more than twice that offered in January. On November 23, the young Edward Fontaine arrived in Pontotoc for the first time and recorded an interesting sketch of the place:

> Pontotoc is a flourishing embryo town in the centre of the Chickasaw Nation; it is located in a fine salubrious region.... The first house was built here in June 1835; now there are 40 Stores and near 2000 inhabitants. Its present prosperity is entirely ephemeral. The extensive mercantile establishments and expensive taverns are supported almost exclusively by the crowd of speculators and adventurers who attend the land sales, and the Indians who have sold their reservations and received their value. Hundreds of these are now in the streets. Many drunk and most of them wasting their money as fast as they can. It is amusing to see their displays of finery. The dress are all of the most fanciful kinds — of every variety of cut and colour. Some of them are ridiculously gaudy, while others are rich and tasty—giving the wearer a martial and splendid appearance. As soon as the land sales are over and the money of these [Indians] is expended the glory of Pontotock will fade, and its wild novelty vanish — and it will appear but as the other respectable inland towns of our country. At present it resembles a Methodist Camp ground. Its buildings are a collection of rude ill constructed huts, with the exception of a few neat little framed painted dwellings. These are tenanted by a collection of people from every State, and from many foreign countries. In this collection is centered perhaps more shrewdness and intelligence than can be found in any other congregation of the same size.[28]

By the end of 1837 the major survey was completed and on November 17, 1840, the office of surveyor general was closed.[29] Land sales continued but inevitably declined. By the early 1850s, the expense of operating the land office had exceeded its revenues and in 1853 the order to close was sent down from Washington.[30] A list was prepared of the remaining lands offered for sale while the reserved section on which the office was located was surveyed and sold. Because of its proximity to the town of Pontotoc, this parcel was

---

27 Pontotoc County Deed Book 1, pages 340-342.

28 Journal of Edward Fontaine, entry for Nov. 23, 1836, Edward Fontaine Papers, 1809-1879, folder 1 (reel 1), Special Collections, Mississippi State University.

29 Letter, James Whitcomb, commissioner GLO, to Levi Woodbury, secretary of the treasury, January 2, 1841, RG 49, Entry 13, volume 2, page 98.

30 Young, *Redskins, Ruffleshirts, and Rednecks*, page 168; Letter, John Wilson, commissioner GLO, to Robert McClelland, secretary of the interior, March 29, 1853, RG 49, Entry 13, volume 3, pages 401-403.

surveyed into streets and city lots. The final sale was held in May 1854, after which the last business was wrapped up.[31] On September 30, 1854 — the end of the third quarter — the offices of the register and receiver were closed, with business and archives transferred to R.W. Edmondson, the clerk of the federal court in Pontotoc who handled any remaining business through the outbreak of the Civil War.[32] When the doors closed, an institution which had once been at the center of activity in north Mississippi came to an end.

---

31 Letter, John Wilson, commissioner GLO, to Robert McClelland, secretary of the interior, September 20, 1854, RG 49, Entry 13, volume 4, pages 40-42.

32 Letter, John Wilson, commissioner GLO, to A.J. Edmondson & J.W. Drake, register & receiver, September 26, 1854, , RG 49, Entry 13, volume 4, page 44-45; abstract of letter received by GLO from A.J. Edmondson, October 14, 1854, RG39, Entry 8.

Appendix: Land Office Officials

Surveyor General

John Bell	7 May 1833—31 December 1837
James McLennan (Acting)	1 January 1838—31 January 1838
P.H. Fontaine	1 February 1838—17 November 1840
Office closed November 17, 1840	

Register

Robert Tinnin	1833—1841
Andrew Jackson Edmondson	1841—1849
J.T. Brooks	1849—1853
Andrew Jackson Edmondson	1853—1854
Office closed September 30, 1854	

Receiver

William Forbes Savage	1833
William Edmondson	1834—3 February 1838, the day he died in office
Solomon Clark	1838—21 September 1842, the day he died in office
John F. Wray	1842—1845
William S. Taylor	1845—1848
William W. Leland (1813-1881)	1848—1849
James W. Drake (1803-1888)	1849—1854
Office closed September 30, 1854	

THE COLBERTS

Hubert H. McAlexander

The Colberts are central to any work on the Chickasaw Cession. Settling in the domain in the 1730s was James Colbert, who became a trader and later a military leader of the tribe. By some accounts, he accumulated as many as 150 slaves. By his three Chickasaw wives he founded an important dynasty. According to the primary student of the southeastern Indians, Don Martini, "In no other tribe did one family exercise the power and control that the Chickasaw Colberts held over their people."[1]

In the last few years, there has been controversy about Colbert's nationality, whether he was born in Scotland or America, and even his given name(s), and there is some genealogical disagreement about precise lines issuing from him. We will only note such debate. The dramatic facts of his life are not subject to question, and letters fix his death in late 1783 or early 1784. Furthermore, the importance of the dynasty is beyond question.[2]

At the time of the Chickasaw Cession in 1832, the tribe had a king — Ishtehotopa. Below him were a ranked group of chiefs. According to Harry Warren, writing in 1904, immediately below Ishtehopopa was Chief Itawamba Mingo, or Levi Colbert, son of trader James Colbert.[3]

We will try, in general, to treat the children of James Colbert sequentially, though there is even controversy about the order. We begin with Warren's statement that "Four of his sons became chiefs of the tribe." The consensus is that the oldest son by the first wife was the famous warrior General William Colbert. In 1794, he followed Piamingo as principal chief of the Nation. Given the title major general in the treaty of 1816 with the United States, he died at Tockshish, about four miles from Monroe Mission, in what is now Pontotoc County, Mississippi. Rickey Butch Walker's 2012 study, *Chickasaw Chief George Colbert: His Family and His Country*, cites agency records for an 1824 death date for William Colbert.[4]

---

1 Arrell M. Gibson, *The Chickasaws* (Norman, OK: University of Oklahoma Press, 1971), 65. Don Martini, *Southeastern Indian Notebook: A Biographical and Genealogical Guide to the Five Civilized Tribes: A Biographical and Genealogical Guide to the Five Civilized Tribes*, 1685-1865 (Ripley, MS: Ripley Printing Company, 1986), 37.

2 Richard A. Colbert, "James Logan Colbert of the Chickasaws: The Man and The Myth," *North Carolina Genealogical Society Journal*, 22 (May 1994), 82.

3 Harry C. Warren, "Some Chickasaw Chiefs and Prominent Men," *Publications of the Mississippi Historical Society* (1904), 8:562.

4 Warren, 8:555. Rickey Butch Walker, *Chickasaw Chief George Colbert: His Family and His Country* (Killen, AL: Bluewater Publications, 2012), 52.

The son that Warren and Walker treat second (and Martini third) is Col. George Colbert. Walker notes that genealogy is not an exact science, but one wishes that the tracing of the Colbert line were more scrupulous, clearer, and more consistent in regard to sources and citation. Warren describes George Colbert as "perhaps the most prepossessing of the Colbert brothers in appearance and manners." Walker obviously finds him the most important of the sons, devoting a book to him. He became a very rich man through operating, from 1797 until 1817, Colbert's Ferry on the Tennessee River, where the Natchez Trace crossed it in present-day Colbert County, Alabama.[5]

When the importance of the Trace declined after the official postal route was changed, George Colbert moved to a place near the center of the nation, on Wolfe Creek, west of the site of Tupelo. He married two daughters of Doublehead, a Cherokee Chief. The first wife, Tuskiahooto, was "reputed to be the fairest of all the Indian princesses" (Walker, 92). The second wife was Saleechie. "In 1836," reads a much-quoted statement, "I attended the land sales at Pontotoc. The first night in the nation I stayed at Saleechie Colbert's four miles west of where Tupelo now stands. She was a woman well-fixed up, had a good house, and gave good fare" (quoted by Warren, 557). Col. George Colbert moved to Indian Territory and died in 1839.[6]

Already remarked upon earlier is the next son, Maj. Levi Colbert, named Itawamba Mingo or Bench Chief. Harry Warren calls him "the most celebrated of the brothers." In 1796, Levi Colbert gained fame by leading a party of Chickasaws against the Creeks, and, after 1825, he was considered the principal chief of the tribe. Four years later Thomas McKenney wrote from the Bureau of Indian Affairs that Levi Colbert was "to the Chickasaws what the soul is to the body." Levi Colbert died in the summer of 1834 en route to Washington in a delegation aiming to amend the 1832 treaty.[7]

Levi Colbert's home was a mile west of Cotton Gin Port on the Tombigbee, which was made the eastern border of Chickasaw lands in 1816. As the 2003 history of the extinct town comments:

> From his residence at the top of the bluff overlooking the Tombigbee, he possessed an awe-inspiring view to the east across the bottomlands and terraces, from which he could observe the beginnings of the town of Cotton Gin Port (57).

For two decades, this house became virtually the seat of Chickasaw government. Levi

---

5 Warren, 557; Walker, 61, 46; Martini, 39-40.

6 Walker,114, 92-93; Martini, 39.

7 Warren, 558-559; Martini, 38-39

Colbert had many children, including a son, Martin, who lived near Horn Lake in the extreme northwestern part of the Cession, near Memphis, Tennessee, and died in 1840.[8]

After Levi Colbert come two less distinguished sons. According to Walker, Samuel Colbert was killed by northern Indians shortly after 1780. He was married and perhaps left children. The next son was Joseph Colbert, who served as interpreter for the Chickasaw Nation in 1799 and died at Colbert's Ferry on the Tennessee River.[9]

Maj. James Colbert was the youngest son of the trader James Colbert. According to Don Martini, "He was a delegate to Philadelphia in 1795, captain in the Chickasaw detachment against the Creeks in 1813-14, and a party to all the treaty negotiations between 1801 and 1832." In 1810, he moved to present-day Houlka in Chickasaw County, near the agency headquarters. His first wife was Susan James, designated a Choctaw by Martini. They separated in the 1830s, and she moved to the village of Chulahoma in Marshall County. Maj. James Colbert immigrated to Indian Territory in 1838, and died four years later.[10]

According to nearly all listings, the Colbert trader had only two daughters. By his first wife, he had a daughter, "the girl is said to be Sally Colbert, later wife of Thomas Love." Every source puts at least a "probably" before this identification, but all name the girl, Sally, as wife of Thomas Love. Love was the patriarch of another mixed blood dynasty, next in power to the Colberts. See my essay on the Loves in this volume, and note the strange connection between Sally Colbert Love's younger sister Susan Colbert — and that sister's niece Elizabeth (Betsy) Love Allen later in this present essay.[11]

Both Martini (38) and Walker (81-83) list the final Colbert child as a daughter, Susan. She married, first, a white man, James Allen. Martini has this to say about him in *Southeastern Indian Notebook* (1986):

> James Allen, a native of North Carolina and reputedly at one time a lawyer in Nashville, Tennessee, arrived in the Chickasaw Nation sometime before 1793. In 1797, he was married to Susan

---

8 Jack D. Elliott, Jr., and Mary Ann Wells, *Cotton Gin Port, A Frontier Settlement on the Upper Tombigbee* (Jackson: Mississippi Historical Society, 2003), 57. Martini, 39.

9 Walker, 75-76. Martini, 39-40.

10 Martini, 40.

11 "Most Colbert researchers say she was Sally Colbert, the sister of Gen. William Colbert and the daughter of [the founder]," writes Marie Garland, on page 2 of her compilation, *The Chickasaw Loves and Allied Families* (Ardmore, OK: Ardmore Photocopy Co., c1970). I did not know of this book until after my essay on the Loves had been accepted by the *Journal of Mississippi History*. I telephoned the publication with the discovery, but staff members did not make the changes and the inclusion of this source. The identity of Sally Colbert Love is always treated as only probable (see Martini, 37), but Walker makes her far too old (likely his mistake) to be the mother of the Love children as Marie Garland presents them (see Walker, 57-60).

Colbert, the youngest daughter of trader James Logan [sic] Colbert. (14-15)

Confusion has been generated by the next fact. Rather soon, James Allen married again. The second wife of James Allen was his first wife's niece, Betsy Love, daughter of trader Thomas Love and (supposedly) Sally Colbert. We will not go into the additional mix-up between this James Allen and one John Allen, also an active figure in the Nation.

Betsy Love Allen's grave is located in Toccopola in western Pontotoc County. She is an important figure in Mississippi history. The lawsuit over her estate established a woman's right to property in her own name. But Betsy Love Allen is often confused with or conflated with Susan Colbert, the first wife of James Allen. James Allen's simultaneous multiple marriages were sanctioned by Chickasaw custom. Ignorance of that custom must be in part responsible for this mix-up. Thus, in this instance as well as in other matters, confusion still goes on regarding the Colberts.[12]

---

12 Two important sources—*Mississippi: A Guide to the Magnolia State* (Jackson : Mississippi Agricultural and Industrial Board, 1938), 487, and Keith A. Baca, *Native American Place Names in Mississippi* (Jackson: University Press of Mississippi, 2007), 118—make the mistake. In her Love genealogy, Marie Garland states that the James Allens lived at Toccopola and mentions controversy over Mrs. Allen's estate. But she did not realize how important the ruling on the estate was in cultural history.

Chickasaw County:
Local Government on the Frontier

Jack D. Elliott, Jr.

On February 9, 1836, Chickasaw County was legislated into being by the Mississippi Legislature.[1] This was not an isolated event, for the same act also established eleven other counties which together covered most of the lands that were ceded by the Chickasaws to the United States by the Treaty of Pontotoc on October 20, 1832. The creation of these counties represented a fundamental step in the transition from Chickasaw-federal sovereignty to state and local governmental rule. From a larger perspective, it was part of a process of establishing local governments that began in 1634 when the Virginia Colony created the first counties, with *county*, a name derived from English tradition, becoming a popular form of local government in other colonies and later in states and territories.[2] Events associated with the founding of Chickasaw County are both idiosyncratic and universal, in sum a microcosm of the establishment of local government on the western frontier.

The area of Chickasaw County had been part of a vast area claimed by the Chickasaw tribe that included much of north Mississippi and extended north to the Ohio River. Throughout most of the eighteenth century, the tribe, consisting of about 5,000 people, was concentrated in the "Chickasaw Old Fields," located in what is now Tupelo. During the late 1700s-early 1800s, the Chickasaws began to disperse from the Old Fields, settling onto scattered farmsteads. Many settled on the Pontotoc Ridge that runs from north to south through the center of what became Pontotoc and Chickasaw counties, with the Natchez Trace—the great highway that connected Natchez and Nashville — passing through the area. The southern part of this area became known as Houlka after nearby Houlka Creek. Its population consisted of a mixture of Chickasaws, mixed-bloods, whites, black slaves, and a few Choctaws who had settled in the Chickasaw lands.[3] The Houlka area would form the earliest population core for Chickasaw County.

Beginning with the British Proclamation of 1763 and carried on as a cornerstone of

---

1 "An Act, to define the boundaries of certain counties therein named, and for other purposes," *Laws of Mississippi* 1836, pages 9-14.

2 Edward T. Price, "The Central Courthouse Square in the American County Seat," *Geographical Review*, vol. 58, 1968, 36-37.

3 James R. Atkinson, *Splendid Land, Splendid People: The Chickasaw Indians to Removal* (Tuscaloosa: University of Alabama Press, 2003), 183-187.

American Indian policy, Indian lands west of the Appalachians were placed under a political-legal distinction termed "Indian Territory," which placed them under the jurisdiction of the central government and outside that of the governments of colonies and later of states and territories. Within the Indian Territory only tribal laws and laws of the central government held. When the Mississippi Territory was established in 1798 and the State of Mississippi in 1817, most of these lands were in Indian Territory, so territorial and state laws had no bearing there. By implication there were also no local governments (counties and municipalities) within the Indian Territory, nor was land owned privately. As part of its Indian policy, the United States established the Office of Indian Agency to provide liaisons between the central government and the respective tribes. In 1797 Samuel Mitchell was appointed Chickasaw agent, the first to actually reside in the nation.[4] He established the Chickasaw Agency on the Natchez Trace in the Houlka area where it served as the major point of contact between the U.S. government and the tribe for almost three decades before being moved to near the Tennessee River in late 1825-early 1826.[5]

As tribal lands were ceded piecemeal to the United States, they were removed from the Indian Territory designation and placed under the laws of the territories or states in which they were located. By 1829, the year Andrew Jackson became president, the Indian Territory had been whittled down to several large islands of tribal lands, each several million acres in size with the last remnants of Chickasaw and Choctaw territory constituting most of north Mississippi. In anticipation of Jackson's move to force the cession of these lands, the state passed an act on February 4, 1829 — one month before his inauguration — extending legal process across those remnants while extending the boundaries of counties adjacent to the Indian Territory to include large chunks of the area.[6] However, these counties were far too large to produce effective county governments. Most of the Chickasaw territory was placed under the jurisdiction of Monroe County, which had been established in 1821, originally on the east side of the Tombigbee River.

The extension of state law and the resulting loss of their autonomy demoralized the

4 Jack D. Elliott, Jr., "Historical Overview," chapter 2 in John W. O'Hear, James R. Atkinson, Jack D. Elliott, Edmond A. Boudreaux III, and John R. Underwood, *Choctaw Agency, Natchez Trace Parkway: Archaeological and Historical Investigation, Madison County, Mississippi* (Tallahassee FL: Cobb Institute of Archaeology, Mississippi State University in Cooperation with Southeast Archeological Center, National Park Service, 2000), 17-24.

5 James R. Atkinson, *History of the Chickasaw Indian Agency East of the Mississippi River* (Starkville MS: privately published), 1998.

6 "An Act to extend legal process into that part of the state now occupied by the Chickasaw and Choctaw tribes of Indians, Feb. 4, 1829," in A. Hutchinson, *Code of Mississippi: Being an Analytical Compilation of the Public and General Statutes of the Territory and State* (Jackson MS: Price and Fall, State Printers, 1848), 135.

tribes. Bowing to the inevitable, the Choctaws ceded the last of their lands to the United States at the Treaty of Dancing Rabbit Creek on September 28, 1830, and agreed to move west to a newly established Indian Territory in what is now Oklahoma. The Chickasaws followed suit two years later with the Treaty of Pontotoc Creek.

Before the Chickasaw lands could be sold, they had to be surveyed, and the surveys began on August 29, 1833, with the establishment of the initial point, the intersection of the two axes — the base line (east-west) and the principal meridian (north-south) — that defined the survey grid.[7] The survey permitted the efficient location and sale of parcels while providing a convenient grid by which the boundaries of the new counties could be defined. By 1835 the survey had sufficiently progressed that land sales began bringing a rush of settlers into the area.

The increasing population required a structure of local governments closer to the citizenry than that of the counties extended in 1829 across the Indian Territory. The legislation of February 9, 1836, remedied this by the creation of the 12 new counties. However when these counties, including Chickasaw County, were established, they existed only on paper. To rectify the situation, five days after, on February 14, the legislature appointed commissioners for each of the new counties with the responsibility of organizing the first elections for the new counties. Five were appointed for Chickasaw: John Delashment, Richard Elliot, Thomas Ivy, Thomas Gates, and Benjamin D. Anderson.[8] They met at the home of a mixed-blood Chickasaw Mila McGee in the Houlka area where, as recalled years later, they used a tree stump for a writing table. Their task was to establish the basis for a county government by holding an election on April 20 to supply members for a Board of Police (equivalent to the present-day Board of Supervisors), a five-member body that would constitute the core of the new government as prescribed by the state's 1832 constitution, which stated that board members "shall have full jurisdiction over roads, highways, ferries, and bridges, and all other matters of county police; and shall order all county elections." The five elected were Asa Braddock, Benjamin Bugg, Thomas Gates, Litttleberry Gilliam, and Thomas D. Woolridge. Their first duties included holding additional elections to fill out the county government, establishing public roads, and establishing a county seat to be located within five miles of the geographical center of the county. Because there was no designated county seat, the board met itinerantly at various stores and houses. The first meeting was at the store of Reuben H. Grant, apparently located in the Houlka vicinity. The order of business was to divide the county into five police districts

---

7 "Field Notes of the Basis Meridian of the Chickasaw Cession Mississippi, Surveyed by John Thomson, Deputy Surveyor, 1833," in the online Records of the General Land Office.

8 "An Act to organize certain new counties therein named, and for other purposes," *Laws of Mississippi*, 1836, page 46.

and appoint inspectors and officers for an election to be held on May 6-7 for sheriff, coroner, probate court judge, clerk of the probate court, clerk of the circuit court, assessor and collector, treasurer, and surveyor and for each of the districts two justices of the peace and one constable. With this election the county government was fully established. However, it was a government without a single courthouse or office building.[9]

On June 20 the board met at an unnamed Indian house and received four proposals for the donation of land on which a county seat town would be located from four potential donors. They then adjourned to examine the proposed sites. Meeting two days later at Gates's store, they had not decided on a site, but voted to provide a right-of-way through the county for the New Orleans and Nashville Railroad, an act of optimism, in a time when railroad mileage in the region was almost nonexistent.[10] It would be over two decades before Chickasaw County would get its first railroad in 1859, the Mobile & Ohio, passing only through the northeastern corner of the county and the town of Okolona. [11]

On July 2, the board accepted the proposal of land speculator Joel Pinson of Pontotoc for a donation of 80 acres, a parcel that, while lying south of the Houlka area, was centrally located in the county and adjacent to the Natchez Trace. On July 8, the Board officially designated the site as the county seat to be known as "Houston," after Maj. General Sam Houston, commander-in-chief of the Army of Texas, who had gained fame following his decisive defeat of the Mexican Army at the Battle of San Jacinto on April 21 of that year.[12]

On July 8 the board made arrangements to establish public roads connecting Houston to other centers. They first appointed commissioners to review and lay out a road running northwards from the site of the county seat in the direction of Pontotoc in neighboring Pontotoc County, where the U.S. Land Office and the newly established county seat of Pontotoc were located. A similar group was appointed to establish a road running eastward from Houston toward the town and port of Aberdeen on the Tombigbee River in Monroe County. The routes were approved at a later meeting with residents appointed to oversee and maintain the roads in a time before the existence of maintenance crews. Among the residents appointed were several Chickasaws.[13]

9 James R. Atkinson (ed.), "A History of Chickasaw County, by Tim Turpentine." *Journal of Mississippi History* 41, no. 4 (Nov. 1979): 319-33.

10 Atkinson, "A History of Chickasaw County, by Tim Turpentine."

11 "Change of Schedule," news item, provides a time for daily departures of the train from Okolona, indicating that railroad construction which had been progressing northward to the town had reached the town by late October 1859. *Southern Broad-Axe*, newspaper, West Point MS, October 26, 1859.

12 Atkinson, "A History of Chickasaw County, by Tim Turpentine."

13 Atkinson, *Ibid.*

From July into early August, the site donated by Pinson was surveyed into a town plat consisting of 49 blocks—seven by seven—with the central block set aside for county use as the courthouse square. On August 15, with a crowd of prospective purchasers, Sheriff Richard L. Aycock began the auction of town lots, following which businesses and homes were established. Temporary county buildings were erected, followed by a brick court-house on the square, which served as the home of county government and as a symbol of law and justice.[14] Houston gained the trappings of municipal government with a state charter granted on May 9, 1837, and a post office authorized on December 5, 1837.[15] By this time Chickasaw County had been transformed from a mere legal entity into a social and political reality, the foundations of which were established in 1836.

---

14 Atkinson, *Ibid.*

15 National Archives, RG28, Records of the Post Office Department, M841 Appointment of Postmasters, 1832 - September 30, 1971, Roll 67: Mississippi: Adams—Itawamba Counties, page 106.

The Saga of a Mixed-Blood Chickasaw Dynasty

Hubert H. McAlexander

Published first in *Journal of Mississippi History*, 49 (November 1987) 288-300.

At the end of the Revolutionary War, a Tory named Thomas Love fled into the hills of northern Mississippi, found refuge among the Chickasaws, and married into the tribe. He became the founder of a remarkable mixed-blood dynasty. Pragmatic and adaptable, his descendants made their way successfully in the worlds of both the white man and the Chickasaw during an era of great social change. The saga of the Loves not only reveals a dramatic aspect of the frontier experience in Mississippi, it also presents an interesting facet of the struggle for ethnic survival and identity in the history of the American Indian.

During the course of the eighteenth century, a number of influential mixed-blood families emerged in what were called the Civilized Tribes of Southern Indians: the Cherokees, Chickasaws, Choctaws, Creeks, and Seminoles. The earliest and most prominent of these among the Chickasaws was the Colbert family, founded by the Scotsman James Logan Colbert, who settled among the tribe in 1729 and during the remaining forty years of his life established himself as a rich planter with 150 slaves. A model of success in the Chickasaw Nation, he left his descendants by three Indian wives wealthy and powerful. The Loves lived always in the shadow of the Colbert dynasty, but they were not mere followers of the Colbert example. They left their own mark.[1]

Though the fact that Thomas Love and his Chickasaw wife were soon numbered among the ranks of the emergent mixed-blood aristocracy led by the Colberts is documented by accounts of the period, no details of Love's life have survived. His marriage brought him into the tribe, but membership descended in the female line; and the offspring of the union were counted Chickasaws of the house of In-cun-no-mar, their mother's line. There were 10 children (see genealogical chart). Seven were sons: Henry, Isaac, Slone, Benjamin, Samuel, Robert, and William. Most of these married mixed-bloods. Of the three daughters — Elizabeth Love Allen, Delilah Love Moore, and Nancy Love Boyd — the first married a mixed-blood and the latter two, white men. This is the generation that firmly established the family's fortunes, both economic and political.[2]

---

1 Arrell M. Gibson, *The Chickasaws* (Norman, Okla., 1971), 65.

2 Harry Warren, "Some Chickasaw Chiefs and Prominent Men," *Publications of the Mississippi Historical Society*, VIII (1904), 560-61; H.F. O'Beirne, *Leaders and Leading Men of Indian Territory* (Chicago, 1891). i-ii, 276.

By the 1820s, most of the family were living in a prosperous farming community centered some six miles southwest of the present town of Holly Springs. The bulwark of the substantial settlement was Henry Love, evidently the oldest son of Thomas the Tory and the one considered by whites the "most enlightened." In 1826, Presbyterian missionaries located a station that they named Martyn a mile from Henry Love's house, which stood at the crossing of two Indian trails near Pigeon Roost Creek. Love, his wife, Sally, and several other family members joined the Presbyterian Church at the mission; the children of the family attended school there. For many years, the community that flourished for a radius of several miles from Martyn Station and Henry Love's log homestead was one of the important centers of mixed blood influence in north Mississippi.[3]

It was only after President Andrew Jackson began the drive to move the Chickasaws west of the Mississippi, however, that the Love family gained great power within the tribe. Their rise to positions of leadership was remarkably swift. During the negotiations for the first of the removal agreements, the 1830 Treaty of Franklin, Henry Love's younger brother Benjamin acted as official Chickasaw interpreter. Benjamin Love, who had been educated in Washington, held this post for the rest of his life. In October of 1833, when twenty-one chiefs set out to locate western land on which to settle, one of the leading members of the expedition was Henry Love. By the next year, these two Love brothers had attained a place of eminence in Chickasaw affairs. In the spring of 1834, the tribe selected five men to travel to Washington and seek modifications of the 1832 Treaty of Pontotoc ceding the Chickasaw estate — two Colberts, one full-blood Chickasaw, and Henry and Benjamin Love.[4]

The changes that these delegates were instrumental in effecting through the Treaty of Washington altered the nature of the approaching sale of Chickasaw lands and made the Loves and other mixed-blood families wealthy. The entire tribe held in common the Chickasaw domain, and by the terms of the Pontotoc treaty, proceeds from the land sales were to go into a general fund from which individuals received payment according to a formula based on the size of the family and the number of slaves owned. Though satisfied with the formula, the mixed-blood leaders wanted over one-third of the six million acres allotted directly to members of the tribe, who could then sell the land themselves. The Chickasaw representatives to Washington had the best interests of the tribe at heart, and they sought to protect those not competent to handle their own affairs. By the new treaty,

---

3 Dawson A. Phelps, "The Chickasaw Mission," *Journal of Mississippi History*, XI II (1951). 230; E.T. Winston, *"Father" Stuart and the Monroe Mission* (Meridian, 1927), 31-39; Map of Township 4, Range 3 West, dated September 8. 1834, Marshall County Chancery Clerk's Office; "Sketch of the Chickasaw Cession by Erasmus P. McDowell—to Samuel McCorkle, 1835, Nov" in possession of Thomas C. Stewart, on loan to Marshall County Library, Holly Springs.

4 Grant Foreman, *Indian Removal: The Emigration of The Five Civilized Tribes of Indians* (Norman, 1932), 193, 199-200.

such tribesmen could dispose of their allotments only with the approval of two Chickasaw leaders from a list of six that included King Ishtahotapa and the five delegates to Washington. But while protecting the less worldly members of the tribe, the Love brothers and the other negotiators also put themselves in a position to make a great deal of money.[5]

When Henry and Benjamin Love returned from Washington, they acted immediately to secure choice allotments for their family. The most promising town site in all the Chickasaw Cession was a bluff on the Tallahatchie River 12 miles south of Martyn Station. Thinking that the location would be the farthest navigable point on the river, a small group of squatters and speculators led by one Wyatt Mitchell had already settled there and built cabins. Many held high hopes for the future of this village, known variously as Wyatt Town, Mitchell's Bluff, and, finally, Wyatt: it would become the primary port from which the cotton planters settling in the Cession would ship their crops down the Tallahatchie, the Yazoo, and the Mississippi to New Orleans. The Love brothers saw to it that the site went to one of their own — their brother Slone, who later sold it to speculators for a premium price.[6]

The Love connection was also centrally involved in the development of Holly Springs, the village that quickly outstripped its rivals and actually became the most important town in the Cession. Holly Springs got its start later than Wyatt. In fact, not until well into the year 1835 did the first building, a crude tavern, rise on the town site. But within a few months, settlers were flocking to the high and well-watered hamlet, and the value of the site became clear to many, including the Loves. In this instance, several family members reaped profits. The land on which the town stood was part of the allotment of Delilah Love and her husband, John B. Moore, a white man. The Moores advantageously disposed of their valuable holding to a speculating partnership headed by a west Tennessee trader, W.S. Randolph; among the 19 men involved with Randolph in the platting, advertising, and selling of the town lots were Henry Love and three other members of the connection.[7]

In January 1836, the United States government offered the first public lands of the Chickasaw Cession for sale, and the trickle of immigrants to north Mississippi became a

5 Charles J. Kappler (comp. and ed.) *Indian Affairs: Laws and Treaties* (Washington, D.C .• 1904), II, 356-64, 418-25. See also Mary Elizabeth Young, *Redskins, Ruffleshirts, and Rednecks: Indian Allotments in Alabama and Mississippi, 1830-1860* (Norman, 1961), 41-46, 114-20.

6 Franklin L. Riley, "Extinct Towns and Villages of Mississippi," *Publications of the Mississippi Historical Society*. V (1902), 348-50; John Cooper Hathorn, "A Period Study of Lafayette County from 1836 to 1860 with Emphasis on Population Groups" (M.A. thesis, University of Mississippi, 1938) 13, 31.

7 Reuben Davis. *Recollections of Mississippi and Mississippians* (1889; reprinted Jackson. 1972). 86; *Holly Springs Gazette*, November 4, 1842; Deed Book N, 692-94 and Book 118, 296, Marshall County Chancery Clerk's Office.

flood. During these flush times, the Love family continued to prove their business sense and their adaptability. Out of Henry Love's large allotment of six sections (a section is a unit of 640 acres), he sold the two sections of developed land on which he had been living near Martyn Station for high prices; and he moved to his other holdings — a block of 2,560 acres located six miles south of Holly Springs along Spring Creek. This tract the early white settlers referred to as the Indian Reserve. There, according to a contemporary, Henry Love erected a "well-built, pointed log house of six rooms," near a large Indian mound surmounted by an aged apple tree. The Reserve became the focal point for the most influential members of the Love family. John B. Moore sold all of his wife's allotted land, which included not only the site of Holly Springs but also that of Martyn Station; and with his profits he bought comparable acreage adjoining the Reserve. In late 1836, Benjamin Love, the richest member of the family, purchased a section of the Reserve from his brother, and began moving his slaves, stock, and equipment from his lands in the southern reaches of the cession to the Spring Creek place. From these plantations the Moores and Loves played a prominent part in the early history of what had now become Marshall County, Mississippi. Soon, in fact, the citizenry were referring to Henry Love as Colonel Love.[8]

Upon the opening of the cession lands, Marshall County experienced an almost unprecedentedly rapid growth in population. By the spring of 1836, it was occupied by almost four thousand settlers, and a year later the population stood at 13,498. The county seat, Holly Springs, was now a town of 1,544 - a miniature cotton capital with churches and schools, blocks of business houses, and streets lined with residences. All of this development took place before the government removed the Chickasaws to the West. Negotiations with the Choctaw tribe for the purchase of part of the vast Choctaw grant in Indian Territory, much of it potential cotton acreage along the Red River, were not concluded until January 1837. By official count in 1836, the Chickasaw Nation numbered 4,914 tribesman and 1,156 slaves. During the course of 1837, the Chickasaw agent oversaw the removal of most of the nation to Indian Territory. [9]

Remaining behind in Mississippi, however, were some of the prominent mixed-bloods, including the most influential members of the Love family. The rich Red River Valley lands on which they had determined to settle were still subject to continued raids

8 *Marhsall County Republican*, September 15, 1838; Jackson *Mississippian*, May 27, 1836; Sectional Indexes, Township 4, Range 3 and Township 4, Range 2, Marshall County Chancery Clerk's Office; Mrs. M.C. Taylor, "Some War Incidents and Other Things That Occurred on This Side of the River," c. 1900 typescript, 1-4, Marshall County Historical Society; Marshall County Tax List for 1838, Mississippi Department of Archives and History.

9 Jackson *Mississippian*, May 12 and July 7, 1837: *Woodville Republican*, May 6, 1837; Gibson, *The Chickasaws*, 163-73.

by roaming Kiowas and Commanches. The Loves were waiting until the United States extended its military authority in that part of Indian Territory before they relocated their planting operations to the West. They were also holding their Mississippi land for an expected increase in value. [10]

In the meantime they figured prominently in economic and cultural life in Mississippi. Along with neighboring planters, the Loves were appointed to committees .supervising the laying out of roads. They sent their children to the schools that had been established in Holly Springs shortly after the cession lands were opened to settlement. Henry Love's older sons, who had studied at the Choctaw Academy in Kentucky, finished their schooling at the Holly Springs male academy, which by the end of 1837 was housed in a two-story brick building. Some of the family were also active in the religious life of the town. In 1839, Benjamin Love liquidated his holdings in the southern part of the cession and settled on the Reserve, and his wife Charlotte joined the Holly Springs Presbyterian Church, along with two of her slaves. She became the most conspicuous of the several mixed-blood members of the small congregation, sweeping up to the little frame church on a sabbath, accompanied by her two servants, in the finest carriage in the county. [11]

Charlotte Love's carriage was an accurate index of the wealth of these mixed-blood aristocrats. In 1840, her husband Banjamin Love owned sixty-six slaves, and he had built a substantial two-story clapboard house on the Reserve. His brother-in-law John B. Moore lived in a similar structure nearby. When Moore died in 1839, he left forty-four slaves to be divided among his wife Delilah Love and his seven children — along with bequests of money, furniture, and jewelry. [12]

The Love family's involvement in the dominant culture then surrounding them is also reflected in the family marriages during this period. The four Moore daughters of marriageable age furnish good examples. They continued the family pattern of advantageous unions. The oldest, who married shortly after the Pontotoc cession treaty, chose a husband from the Colbert dynasty. The younger three, who came of age after the cession had been

---

10 Gibson, *The Chickasaws*, 188, 174.

11 Board of Police Minutes, I, 35, 72, 203, 254, Marshall County Chancery Clerk's Office; *Biographical and Historical Memoirs of Mississippi* (Chicago; 1891), II. 313-14; Carolyn Thomas Foreman, "The Choctaw Academy," *Chronicles of Oklahoma*, IX (1932), 410 and X (1933), 82-83; Netty Fant Thompson. Chalmers Institute worksheet, Notes for a History of Holly Springs, Mississippi Archives; Minutes of the Session, Holly Springs Presbyterian Church, 1836-1855; 7-13; Marshall County Tax List for 1839, Mississippi Department of Archives and History.

12 Interview with Charles N. Dean of Holly Springs about the Love-Pegues house, December 31, 1982; 1840 Census of Marshall County, Miss., Southern Division, 1; Ben Gray Lumpkin and Martha Neville Lumpkin, *The Lumpkin Family of Virginia, Georgia, and Mississippi* (Clarksville, Tenn., 1979), 55; Chancery Docket No. 14, Marshall County Chancery Clerk's Office.

opened to settlement, all married white men of some importance. One married a director of a Holly Springs bank; another, the son of a substantial farmer; and the third, the brother of the county probate judge. [13]

The marriage, however, that provided the most opulent social occasion during the Love tenure in Mississippi and that most dramatically reflected on the family's social position there was a union of two branches of the dynasty. On August 5, 1841, Henry Love's oldest son married his first cousin Narcissa, daughter of Benjamin and Charlotte Love. The extensive family connections and a group of other citizens gathered at the spacious plantation home of Benjamin Love, where the ceremony was held in a chamber decorated with fine French scenic wallpaper, probably procured in New Orleans and representing "a forest with Indians on ponies and on foot, with tomahawks, bows and arrows, and wild animals in trees and woods." The presiding minister, the Reverend Daniel Baker, conferred distinction on the ceremony. Then serving the local Presbyterian congregation, Baker had but lately arrived from Washington, where he had been a favorite preacher of both Andrew Jackson and John Quincy Adams. [14]

This wedding scene in the summer of 1841 marked a culminating point for the family, the end of one era and the beginning of transition into another. Conditions were changing both in Mississippi and in Indian Territory. Booming northern Mississippi had survived the Panic of 1837, buoyed by high cotton prices. But the cotton market hit bottom in the spring of 1840, and Flush Times came to an end. Whereas the value of the Loves' Mississippi holdings had been rising, now they were falling. Three months after the wedding, Benjamin Love sold his Reserve plantation to Malachi Pegues, a wealthy South Carolina planter. At the time Love knew that the United States government was laying plans to construct and fully garrison a fort on the Washita River in Indian Territory that would offer protection to the Chickasaw settlements in the Washita and Red River valleys. Love had chosen tracts for the family there in the summer of 1840, and he had already transported part of his slave force to the territory. But he remained in Mississippi while the older members of the connection disposed of the rest of the family holdings. Finally in the spring of 1844, Benjamin and Henry Love led a sizeable party of relatives, friends, and their slaves to Indian Territory. Included were nearly all the white families with whom the connection

13 William Baskerville Hamilton, "Holly Springs, Mississippi, to the Year 1878" (M.A. thesis, University of Mississippi, 1931), 5; John Bartlett Meserve, "Governor William Leander Byrd," *Chronicles of Oklahoma*, XII (1935), 434; O'Beirne, *Leaders and Leading Men of Indian Territory*, 272-73

14 Holly Springs *Southern Banner*, August 13, 1841; Mrs. M. C. Taylor, "Some War Incidents and Other Things," 2; William M. Baker, The Life and Labors of the Rev. Daniel Baker, D.D. (Philadelphia, 1858), 101-108, 227.

had intermarried. Now only a handful of tribal members were left east of the Mississippi. [15]

In the state of Mississippi in a time of great social and economic change, the Loves had proved their mettle, their adaptability, and their financial shrewdness. What they had learned on the rapidly developing frontier of north Mississippi cotton lands would serve them well in the West. The migration to the undeveloped lands in Indian Territory, however, again tested the Loves' powers of adjustment. Quickly they displayed their characteristic energy and flexibility. By the time that Henry and Benjamin had settled on their large plantations between the mouth of the Washita and Island Bayou in the Red River region, their brother Slone Love, who had preceded them, was already operating a cotton gin on his lands. The dynasty was now reunited and the family set to work building a new cotton empire. [16]

As the Loves increased their wealth during the 1840s, they also retained their political influence. The brothers Benjamin, Slone, and Isaac Love all served terms on the powerful seven-member Chickasaw Commission. The leader of the family during its early years in the territory, Benjamin Love, was also one of the region's richest and most influential men until his untimely death in 1849. Returning from a Biloxi village, where he had gone to recover a stolen horse, he was murdered five miles from his home by a renegade Shawnee. "He left a vacancy in the nation that cannot be filled," the Chickasaw agent wrote to the Commissioner of Indian Affairs; "he was the most talented man in the Nation; he understood and knew how business ought to be done."[17]

By the time of Benjamin Love's death, he had firmly established the position of his family in the new country. The younger generation now had merely to carry on. They did. It was not in the Love make-up to squander their advantages. Among the most prosperous and the most prominent of the rising generation were the children of Benjamin's brother Henry. Charlotte Love Tyson Coffee, Henry's daughter, survived her two white husbands to rule the fortunes of a great sweep of land along the Red River from the finest residence for many miles. Her younger sister Elizabeth Love (1833-1914) also occupied a high po-

---

15 William K. Scarborough, "Heartland of the Cotton Kingdom," in Richard A. McLemore (ed.) *A History of Mississippi* (Jackson, 1973), I. 315; Sectional Index of Township 4, Range 2, Marshall County Chancery Clerk's Office; Gibson. *The Chickasaws*, 190, 17 4; Grant Foreman, *Indian Removal*, 225-26; Muriel H. Wright. "Notes on Events Leading to the Chickasaw Treaties of Franklin and Pontotoc, 1830 and 1832." *Chronicles of Oklahoma*, XXXIV (1956-57). 470.

16 Grant Foreman, *The Five Civilized Tribes* (Norman, 1934). 107; Muriel H. Wright, "Early Navigation and Commerce Along the Arkansas and Red Rivers in Oklahoma," *Chronicles of Oklahoma*, VIII (1930), 82.

17 Muriel H. Wright and Peter J. Hudson, "Brief Outline of the Choctaw and Chickasaw Nations in the Indian Territory, 1820 to 1860," *Chronicles of Oklahoma*. VI I (1929). 402; Grant Foreman, *The Five Civilized Tribes*. 107, 177.

sition in the territory, and Elizabeth's husband, Holmes Colbert, was not only a wealthy man but one of some distinction. A graduate of Union College in Schenectady, New York, Colbert returned to Indian Territory in time to play an important role in the 1855 treaty between the Chickasaws and Choctaws that established for the first time since removal an autonomous Chickasaw Nation. The next year he was centrally involved in the Chickasaw government. He was signator of both the treaty committing his people to the Confederate cause and the postwar peace treaty with the United States. His death in 1872 occurred not in the territory but in Washington, where he was representing the interests of the tribe. His wife Elizabeth Love survived him many years, the revered widow of a Chickasaw statesman.[18]

Given the prominence of Henry Love's daughters, it was still his son Overton Love — of his whole generation — who met most successfully his family's dynastic goals. In the 1850s, he left his father's original tract on the Washita to settle in what came to be known as Love's Valley on the Red River. He continued to prosper even after the freeing of his large slave force at the end of the Civil War, and by the end of the century he controlled over eight thousand acres of bottom land. For decades he wielded great influence in Chickasaw affairs. Though he filled at various times the positions of National Councilman, District Judge, and Delegate to Washington, he was an even more powerful force directing the affairs of the Nation behind the scenes, often through relatives he had helped put in office. From the 1870s to the end of the century, Love was one of a handful of men who shaped Chickasaw policy. [19]

As the nineteenth century drew to a close, the power and influence of the still tightly-knit, though greatly extended, Love family were felt throughout Indian Territory. Three generations now figured conspicuously in economic, cultural, and political life. Of the many members of the Love dynasty, however, two stand out during these twilight years of the Chickasaw republic — Governors Benjamin Franklin Overton (who held the office 1874-1878 and 1880-1884) and William Leander Byrd (who served 1888-1892). According to their own lights, these two great-grandsons of Thomas Love the Tory and his Chickasaw wife fought forcefully and often ruthlessly to preserve the integrity of the

---

18 Wright. '"Jessie Elizabeth Randolph Moore of the Chickasaw Nation," *Chronicles of Oklahoma*, 34 (1956-57). 392-93; Wright, '"Historic Places on the Old State Line from Fort Smith to Red River," *Chronicles of Oklahoma*, XI (1933). 802-803; George H. Shirk, "A Wapanuck Legend," *Chronicles of Oklahoma*, 33 (1955-56). 110-11; Gibson, *The Chickasaws*, 232, 243; O'Beirne, *Leaders and Leading Men of Indian Territory*, 296-97.

19 Jessie R. Moore, "Thomas Mayberry Randolph, 1873-1943," *Chronicles of Oklahoma*, XXII (1944), 221; J. Y. Bryce, '"Judge Overton Love." *Chronicles of Oklahoma*, IV (1926). 288-91. Love County was named in honor of Overton Love by the delegate from his district to the Constitutional Convention for the new state of Oklahoma in 1907.

Chickasaw Nation. [20]

Overton's almost fanatical devotion to the matter of Chickasaw identity is explained in part by his early history: the abandonment of the family by his white father, the subsequent death of his mixed-blood mother, and the child's rearing by his great-uncles Isaac and Robert Love, two old men with long memories of tribal history. Before Benjamin Overton (1836-1884) was out of his twenties, he had served in both houses of the Chickasaw legislature and represented the Nation in Washington. In 1874, as the gubernatorial candidate of the Pullback Party, composed primarily of full-bloods and non-progressives, Overton boldly challenged the incumbent governor, whose supporters included many of the prosperous mixed-bloods, the class to which Overton himself belonged. The Pullbacks won the election, and Overton's chauvinism and force kept him in control of the governorship until his death ten years later; in 1878, prohibited by law from seeking a third consecutive term, he ruthlessly put his brother-in-law in office. Overton's political philosophy crystallized in 1876 during the Sioux War, when in his second inaugural address he called for a uniting of all the Indian tribes as the only way to preserve the rights and the identity of the American Indian. Always mindful of the increasing encroachment of the whites upon all phases of Indian life, he fought for the rest of his life all forces that he felt threatened the integrity of his tribe. [21]

Overton's death in 1884 left a gap in the leadership of the Chickasaw conservative party that was filled within four years by his cousin William L. Byrd (1844-1915), the grandson of Delilah Love Moore. After having served as a youth in the Confederate army, Byrd had followed his older cousin into the Chickasaw legislature. Subsequently he was Draftsman of the House, member of the committee of three men elected in 1877 to re-

---

20 The patriarch of the family was then Robert Love, one of the youngest sons of Thomas Love the Tory. Long active in Chickasaw government, Robert Love had been a member of the 1856 Constitutional Convention and a signator of the post-Civil War peace treaty with the United States. The owner of two hundred slaves before the war, he was still a man of wealth and influence at the end of the century. Among his many nephews prominent in the nation was Robert Love Boyd, who served eleven years on the Chickasaw Cabinet and ran for governor in 1886. In addition to Robert Love's two grand-nephews who served as governors of the Chickasaw republic, numerous others in the third generation of descent from Thomas the Tory played important roles in Indian Territory. Among these were Governor Byrd's brother Benjamin F. Byrd (1849-1915), Chickasaw National Treasurer for fifteen years, and the governor's first cousin Mary Bourland Phillips. daughter of a county judge, sister of a cabinet member, and wife of one of the richest men in the territory. See Arrell M. Gibson, *The History of Oklahoma*, (Norman, 1984), 52; Wright and Hudson, "Brief Outline of the Choctaw and Chickasaw Nations." 411; Gibson, *The Chickasaws*, 243; H.B. Cushman, *History of the Choctaw, Chickasaw and Natchez Indians* (1899; reprinted New York, 1972). 431; E.T. Winston, *History of Pontotoc County, Oklahoma* (Ada, Okla., 1976), 437-39; O'Beirne. *Leaders and Leading Men of Indian Territory*, 276, 272-73.

21 John Bartlett Meserve, "Governor Benjamin Franklin Overton and Governor Benjamin Crooks Burney," *Chronicles of Oklahoma*, XVI (1938), 221-33; O'Beirne, *Leaders and Leading Men of Indian Territory*, vii.

vise the Chickasaw laws, School Superintendent, Delegate to Washington, and National Agent. In 1886, he first ran for governor, being defeated by William M. Guy in a bitter contest that laid the groundwork for a party war that lasted for the rest of the century. Two years later, Byrd again ran on the National or Full-blood ticket against Guy; and after quarrels in the legislature over the election results and a narrowly averted shooting war between the parties, Byrd was declared the victor. The next year Byrd guided through the legislature a bill, authored by Lem Reynolds and Byrd's cousin Overton Love, disenfranchising the whites who had become citizens of the Nation by marrying Chickasaws. Thereafter, due to his altered constituency, Byrd easily won another term. Certainly it was all irony that Byrd, whose claim to Chickasaw citizenship lay back four generations and rested on one great-grandmother, the Chickasaw wife of Thomas Love the Tory, should be the leader who disenfranchised the white men who had married into the tribe. His enemies, in fact, were quick to point out that fact, some even suggesting maliciously that he had no Chickasaw blood, that he had been a white child adopted in infancy. But Byrd, like Benjamin Overton before him, had an intense awareness that historical forces were moving to deprive the Indian of his domain and the vestiges of his culture. This disenfranchisement measure, Byrd felt, was necessary to halt one of those forces, the tide of white immigration now engulfing the Nation. Byrd, of course, lived to see his own impotence in the face of history as he watched the United States government's increasing encroachment upon the five Indian nations of Indian Territory, the dissolution of their governments, and their assimilation into the state of Oklahoma in 1907. [22]

The reactionary stance of both Overton and Byrd brought them many enemies, who charged often that the governors were acting out of self-interest. Certainly, like their forebears these men were always mindful of their own welfare, but both were clearly also guided by concern for the interests of the tribe. Although for several generations members of their line had married whites and assimilated freely what they found attractive in the world of the white man, they had consistently rejected the chance to merge themselves with the dominant culture. For men like Overton and Byrd with only a small portion of Chickasaw blood running in their veins, as for most other members of this remarkable dynasty, it was still the Chickasaw part that conferred identity. More than a hundred years after Thomas Love took a Chickasaw wife, they still felt their most fundamental tie with the house of *In-cun-no-mar*.

---

22 Meserve, "Governor William Leander Byrd," *Chronicles of Oklahoma*, XII (1934), 432-43; O'Beirne, *Leaders and Leading Men of Indian Territory*, 256-57, 226-30, viii-ix; Gibson, *The Chickasaws*, 266-67.

Holly Springs' 1838 courthouse
A. Simplot, Harper's Weekly, January 10, 1863

Flush Times in Holly Springs

Hubert H. McAlexander

Published in the *Journal of Mississippi History* (February 1986, pp. 1-18)

During the 1830s, in the midst of one of the great business booms in United States history, the Choctaw and Chickasaw cessions opened millions of acres of potential Mississippi cotton lands to white settlement. The Indian purchases more than doubled the settled area of the state, and Mississippi's population increased 175 percent over the decade. This era that the contemporary writer Joseph Glover Baldwin called "The Flush Times" marked dramatically the history of the entire upper half of the state, but nowhere were the Flush Times more strongly felt than in the county of Marshall and the town of Holly Springs. Only a year after its formation Marshall, hailed as the "Empire County," boasted the largest white population in the state; and its county seat was already becoming a miniature cotton capital. The physical and cultural development of Holly Springs during the period indeed provides the state's most vivid reflection of the spirit and texture of the era.[1]

Holly Springs was totally a product of the economic boom. In October of 1832, when the Chickasaws signed the Treaty of Pontotoc ceding their tribal lands in north Mississippi, the site where the town would rise (Section Six, Township Four, Range Two, West of the Base Meridian) had attracted no attention. Judging from contemporary maps and field notes, not even a minor Indian trail passed anywhere nearby. By the spring of 1834, some squatters were living on section six; and two land-lookers evaluating the Chickasaw lands for speculating companies noted four cabins and a few fields scattered over the 640 acres. The men also remarked upon a great benefit of the tract, the "excellent Springs of cold water." Section six possessed an additional advantage: lying on high ground, it was healthful — an important consideration in a region conducive to various miasmic fevers. But these factors had still failed to attract a real settlement by the fall of the year. On September 17, 1834, when the United States government placed a post office in this part of the Cession, it was at Martyn Station, six miles southwest of section six on Pigeon Roost Creek near the crossing of several Chickasaw trails. Founded in 1826 by Presbyterian missionaries, the station was the center of a prosperous mixed-blood Indian community dominated by the

---

1 John Edmond Gonzales, "Flush Times, Depression, War, and Compromise," in Richard Aubrey Mc-Lemore (ed.) *A History of Mississippi* (2 vols; Hattiesburg. 1973), I, 284-86. 288-89: Joseph Glover Baldwin, *The Flush Times of Mississippi and Alabama* (New York, 1863); Jackson (MS) *Mississippian*, May 12, 1837; A.M. Clayton, Centennial Address on the History of Marshall County (Washington, D.C., 1880), 5.

Love family, a powerful force in the Chickasaw Nation.[2]

During the ensuing year, however, the site on section six became a center of activity. In the early months of 1835, a trader from west Tennessee named Whitmel Sephas Randolph, who had been operating an outpost a mile to the south for over a year, moved to the northern edge of section six near one group of springs. By this time hundreds of men were coming into the Cession, men connected with speculating companies based close by in Tennessee or Alabama or as far away as New York and Boston, and others mostly from surrounding frontiers looking for their own land to farm. A number traveling through the Cession stopped at Randolph's post and found good camping. Soon a tavern was built to accommodate the travelers, the first structure to rise on the actual town site. Described by a pioneer as "two roughhewn log rooms, with a passage between and a board shelter to eat under," it perched on the bluffs above a spring-filled basin bordered by holly trees, two hundred yards south of Randolph's post. By late summer established Tennessee merchants — Niles and Elder of Murfreesboro and Alexander McEwen of Fayetteville — had moved their businesses into the Cession and located near the tavern, and a real settlement was growing up at the holly springs.[3]

Word had now spread from the capital in Jackson regarding not only the boundaries of the counties that the legislature intended to cut from the Chickasaw purchase, but also the policy for placing county seats, in all but those counties bordering the Mississippi, "at the geographical centre, or the most convenient point within five miles thereof." The holly springs site lay only two miles east of the center of Marshall County. The trader W.S. Randolph may not have been the first to see the increasing value of section six, but he was the first to act. By fall he had bargained to purchase the section from John B. Moore, a white man who had married into the powerful Love family of Chickasaws. Reserving an undivided half-interest for himself, Randolph formed a partnership with nineteen other men — a group that included mixed-blood Chickasaw tribesmen, prominent speculators,

---

2 Map of Township 4, Range 2, West, of the Chickasaw Cession, September 4, 1834, Chancery Clerk's Office, Marshall County Courthouse; "Sketch of the Chickasaw Cession by Erasmus P. McDowell — to Samuel McCorkle, 1835, Nov.," in possession of Thomas C. Stewart, on loan to the Marshall County Library; Notes Taken by D.S. Greer in the Chickasaw Nation, 12. McCorkle Papers, Marshall County Historical Society; Samuel McCorkle's Day Book, April 21, 1834, in possession of Hugh H. Rather. Holly Springs; Broox Sledge to author, May 19, 1984; Dawson A. Phelps, "The Chickasaw Mission," *Journal of Mississippi History*, XIII (1951), 230.

3 Map of Township 4, September 4, 1834; Annette Nash Robnett, "Papers from a Family History of the Milam, Woods, d'Estille, Randolph and Related Families," 1971 typescript in possession of Mrs. Sam White, Holly Springs; *Holly Springs Gazette*, November 4, 1842; Catesby W. Edmondson to John Edmondson, November 24, 1835, John Edmondson Family Papers, Emory University; *Holly Springs Gazette*, August 4, 1841.

and people with political influence — to develop and sell the holly springs site.[4]

On October 9, 1835, the most important newspaper in Mississippi carried the first notice advertising "The Town of Holly Springs: FOR SALE." After remarking on the town's healthful situation in the midst of rich cotton lands and extolling the town's future as a probable county seat, an educational center, a refuge during the "sickly season," and a "considerable place of business," the notice concluded: "The site of the Holly Springs embraces more advantages and offers more inducements for the location of a town than any other place now known in the Chickasaw Nation." When this advertisement appeared, Randolph and his partners had yet to gain a clear title to the land, and they set the sale for a year in the future. No plat of a town had even been drawn, and the partnership merely promised that the task would be accomplished soon. But if they proclaimed a town that was a town fundamentally by proclamation, their faith in its future was quickly rewarded. One important sign came two months later: on December 7, 1835, the United States government moved its post office from Martyn Station to Holly Springs. By the first of the year, a crude village had taken shape — just in time for one of the most dramatic openings of a frontier in American history.[5]

Economic and geographical factors combined to make the Chickasaw lands an unusual frontier. The price of cotton was at its highest level in decades, and the Chickasaw Cession, comprising over six million acres, was the last great block of virgin land in the southeastern states. Many Americans saw the possibilities for quick profit in this potential cotton empire, but the great body of settlers were already poised and waiting nearby. The Chickasaw domain in north Mississippi was no remote wilderness; on three sides settlements surrounded it. To the south lay the Choctaw Cession, acquired by the United States in 1830 and sold off in 1833. To the north and east, settlers had occupied the adjoining Tennessee and Alabama lands for as long as two decades. Here were experienced frontiersmen, well aware of the rewards to be garnered in a new country, and waiting only for the government to put the land up for sale.[6]

In January of 1836, the United States offered the first tracts of Chickasaw lands, and the floodgates were opened. Settlers poured into north Mississippi. By a contemporary estimate, no more than twenty white men had ever lived within the bounds of Marshall

4 Laws of the State of Mississippi; Passed at a Regular Biennial Session of the Legislature (Jackson, 1836), 48; Harry Warren, "Some Chickasaw Chiefs and Prominent Men," *Publications of the Mississippi Historical Society*, VII (1904), 560-61; Deed Book N, 692-94. This and all other deeds cited are in the Marshall County Chancery Clerk's Office.

5 Jackson *Mississippian*, October 9, 1835; Broox Sledge to author, May 19, 1984.

6 Mary Elizabeth Young. *Redskins, Ruffleshirts, and Rednecks* (Norman, Okla., 1961), 115-16.

County before the Treaty of Pontotoc. In the spring of 1836, the county had a population of 3,100 "free" and 800 "colored." Perhaps a tenth of those were living in Holly Springs.[7]

On April 19, the recently-elected governing body of Marshall County met at Samuel McAlexander's tavern overlooking the springs to begin the process of choosing the location of the county seat. Certainly the selection was a foregone conclusion, but influential men owning other sites were at least given a hearing. Six days later, to the surprise of few, the tract on section six was chosen, "upon condition that the owners of said section make to said Board of Police, a warranty title in fee simple for Fifty acres of said Section, to be selected by said Board and also convey … to be used as a Commons the ground now enclosed around the Holly Springs and the Springs known as Randolph's Springs."[8]

The county board immediately changed the name of the settlement to Paris (a concession to a dominant group of pioneers from Paris, Tennessee, which the other townsmen had successfully protested within six weeks) and set the sale of lots for mid-June. The May 14, 1836, issue of the *Nashville Republican* carried an announcement of the sale, which opened with this statement:

> It rarely happens that a place is offered to the notice of the public possessing more present and certain advantages, and having higher claims to expect future prosperity and importance. Situated in the midst of the most fertile and delightful part of the Chickasaw Cession; a country which has excited the admiration of all by whom it has been visited, on a dry and elevated spot, surrounded by springs of the purest water, and pointed out by all who have seen it as the certain abode of health. The town … will offer many inducements as a place of business, or as a residence, where the comforts of life may be readily obtained, and good society may be found.

A reaction to the puffery of the advertisement and to the spirit of self-congratulation so in evidence was registered in the same newspaper soon afterward by the notice announcing the sale of lots in nearby Oxford, Mississippi. "Eulogy and exaggeration have become so common on occasions of this nature," the Oxford fathers wrote, "that but little attention is paid to it by the well informed; we shall say nothing therefore about the advantages that are here united to make this place a desirable asylum, believing that those wishing to purchase will view the premises and judge for themselves." Settlers, however, clearly found the "eulogy" of the holly springs site not undeserved. When the sale opened on June 16, Holly Springs (its original name now restored) teemed with buyers. Lots sold

---

7 *Marshall County Republican*, September 15, 1838; Jackson *Mississippian*, May 27, 1836.

8 Board of Police Minutes, 1, 3-5, Chancery Clerk's Office.

fast, at good prices.[9]

According to a contemporary report, the village was composed still of "only a few log cabins in the woods." These, for the most part, huddled on the bluffs above the deep basin filled with hollies where springs fed a pool, described by a pioneer as thirty feet wide and deep enough to "swim a horse." But spreading southward were acres almost of table land, where the proprietors had centered their plat for the town. A hundred yards south of the holly springs, they had staked out a large square lined with lots for business houses, facing a spacious park where the seat of government would be located. Radiating outward from this square were small lots for residences, which gave over to increasingly larger plots as one traveled away from the center of town. All the major streets were laid out as broad thoroughfares. [10]

Central to the plan was that hub and focus of county and town, the courthouse. It was to set the tone of the town growing around it, and perhaps nothing is a better gauge of the rapid development during the Flush Times than the contrast between the first two courthouses in Holly Springs. On July 6, 1836, when the Board of Police met for the first time in the "temporary courthouse" — a rough log building near the springs, raised at a cost of $150 — they had already laid plans for the permanent structure on the square. The design they chose was a brick building, forty-two by fifty-four feet, to rise two stories from a foundation of native rock (faced with a layer of cut stone "of a quality usual in Nashville, Louisville, or Cincinnati") to a domed octagonal cupola containing the town clock. Both the front south facade and the north facade were surmounted by pediments supported by Doric pilasters, and the double mahogany entrance doors were crowned with fanlights. In the interior, which drew upon both Tuscan and Ionic orders, a turning stair led to the large paneled second-floor courtroom. The Board soon concluded that this structure was not large enough, and they expanded the plan by adding two-story wings to the east and west, surrounded on three sides by colonnaded galleries. The added cost of more than doubling the size of the building forced the Board to build it of wood rather than brick, but they still permitted the county the extravagance of a copper roof. Because of delays in securing many of the materials, two years passed before the building was completed. [11]

---

9 Board of Police Minutes, I. 7; *Nashville Republican*, May 14 and July 26, 1836; John M. Mickle, "Spring Street Was the First 'Main Street' of Holly Springs," *Holly Springs South Reporter*, November 20, 1930, 1.

10 Nash K. Burger, "An Overlooked Source for Mississippi Local History: *The Spirit of Missions*, 1836-1854," *Journal of Mississippi History*, VIII (1945), 173; James H. Malone, *The Chickasaw Nation* (Louisville, 1922), 55.

11 Board of Police Minutes, I , 22, 203; Deed Book C. 170-75. A sketch of the 1838 courthouse appeared in *Harper's Weekly*, January 10, 1863, p. 29.

In the meantime, a town grew up worthy of the elegant building at its heart. The first notice advertising the site of the town had proclaimed its future as an educational center, and in January of 1836; five months before the lots were sold, a meeting was held to discuss the founding of a female academy. The gathering elected trustees, who employed a "Tutoress" for a school of three classes and oversaw the raising of "a modest but comfortable structure of hewn logs, with clapboard roof, overhung by friendly oaks," on a lot at the western edge of the village fronting the Hernando Road. Hardly had the building been finished when the trustees determined to add a music room.[12]

Interestingly enough, concern over the need for a male academy did not manifest itself until late summer, but that meeting was marked by a great deal more fanfare. A Presbyterian minister from Tennessee so stirred the assemblage gathered on August 24 as to "the necessity of immediate and energetic action on the subject" that the gathering chose a committee to draft resolutions on the spot. After a brief adjournment the men returned with proposals for "commencing an institution with reference to its becoming a College," and they suggested petitioning the legislature not only to grant an act of incorporation, but also to aid the institution financially. Trustees were elected, and a motion passed to publish the proceedings in seven newspapers covering the states of Mississippi, Tennessee, and Alabama. When the Reverend Dr. Hardin later determined to remain in Maury County rather than undertake the college in Holly Springs, the original impetus was lost. The Trustees, however, established a classical school for males, and, despite the failure to realize the original conception, still a grand dream had been born.[13]

At the time of these modest beginnings of educational endeavor, another civilizing force was making itself felt in a rough-and-tumble frontier existence — that of religion. When the Mississippi Conference of the Methodist Church met in Vicksburg in December of 1835, it created the Chickasaw District with three missionary circuits to serve settlers in the new purchase. A year later the name was changed to the Holly Springs District, a reflection of the dominance of the new town in the region. The first church in the village, however, was founded not by Methodists, but by Presbyterians. In the spring of 1836, a group of Presbyterians purchased a lot one block south of the square and put up a pole and mud cabin, where merchant James Elder and lawyer Robert H. Patillo began holding a sabbath school. In December, the Reverend Daniel L. Gray answered the "call" of twenty Holly Springs Presbyterians and organized the church, one of the first in the Chickasaw Cession. That winter the small congregation secured the services of the Reverend Samuel

12 Minutes of the Trustees of the Holly Springs Female Institute, 1-3, in the papers of the late Charles N. Dean, Holly Springs; Edward Mayes, History of Education in Mississippi (Washington, D.C., 1899}, 46.

13 Memphis *Enquirer*, September 1, 1836; *Biographical and Historical Memoirs of Mississippi* (2 vols; Chicago, 1891), II, 313.

Hurd, a well-educated man of considerable cultivation.[14]

In the year 1837, three other Protestant denominations established churches in the town. The Hardins from Kentucky, members of Randolph's partnership, were active in organizing the body variously known as the Christian, Campbellite, Campbellite Baptist, or Reform Baptist church - to whom the Board of Police conveyed a lot in March. The Baptist Church was given a lot by James Greer, patriarch of a prominent speculating family, and in September the Methodists purchased a lot on Hernando Road next to the female academy. [15]

Churches and schools, then, were already in operation and the walls of the courthouse already in place before the Chickasaws had been removed to the West. The first group, about five hundred strong, did not leave for Indian Territory until June of 1837, and the major migration effort occupied the following summer and autumn months, when the Chickasaw agent collected four thousand people in emigrant camps and moved them toward Memphis. The long column of humanity, the train of government wagons, the multitude of horses, dogs, and cats made a remarkable sight. The Indians, according to one observer, "were all most comfortably clad — the men in complete Indian dress with showy shawls tied in turban fashion round their heads — dashing about on their horses, like Arabs, many of them presenting the finest countenances & figures that I ever saw. The women also very decently clothed like white women, in calico gowns … & how beautifully they managed their horses, how proud & calm & erect, they sat at full gallop." The train passed through Holly Springs and encamped on the Coldwater River to the north. In November the party of emigrants crossed the river at Memphis, and a chapter in the history of north Mississippi had closed.[16]

The Marshall County Chickasaws left a county that in the spring of 1837 held the largest white population in the state. In just a year it had grown from under four thousand people to 13,498, of whom 8,274 were white and 5,224 were slaves. Holly Springs (incorporated as a town on May 12) had a population of 1,544. It had outstripped all the inland west Tennessee towns that so many of its citizens had once called home, for the

---

14 Gene Ramsey Miller, *A History of North Mississippi Methodism,* 1820-1900 (Nashville, 1966), 31, 33; Deed Book A, 96; Olga Reed Pruitt, *It Happened Here* (Holly Springs, 1950), 14-15; Minutes of the Session, Holly Springs Presbyterian Church, 1836-1855, 1-2; Clayton, *Centennial Address,* 11.

15 Deed Book D, 13-14, and M. 627; Greer and Hardin, Henderson genealogical papers, in possession of Judge Henry Woods, Little Rock; John M. Mickle, "History of the Five Churches of Holly Springs Dates Back to 1836," *Holly Springs South Reporter,* December 10, 1931, p. 10; Deed Book D, 372-73.

16 Arrell M. Gibson, *The Chickasaws* (Norman, Okla., 1971), 163-72; John E . Parsons (ed.), "Letters on the Chickasaw Removal of 1837," *New York Historical Society Quarterly,* 37 (1953), 280-81; John M. Mickle. "McEwen Home Linked to Holly Springs History," *Holly Springs South Reporter,* December 10, 1931, p. 12.

only time in its history it was almost the size of Memphis, and it was the third largest town in Mississippi, ranked behind Natchez and Vicksburg and slightly ahead of Columbus.[17]

By the time that the state census was taken, however, the great tide of emigration had been checked. The Panic of 1837, created in part by Andrew Jackson's Specie Circular and the resulting failure of many banks, ended America's business boom. With credit harder to come by, the Chickasaw lands of north Mississippi no longer exerted quite the magnetic attraction they once had. But Holly Springs, though it no longer grew so rapidly, was just entering a time of significant development. The state of Mississippi responded to the financial crisis and the failure of so many banks by creating still another state institution, the Union Bank, in 1838. Holly Springs citizens had reacted similarly a year earlier. In the fall of 1837, McEwen, King and Company opened its doors, the first bank in north Mississippi. Shortly afterward, one of the most active of the speculating brotherhood in the Chickasaw Cession, Samuel McCorkle, founded the Holly Springs Real Estate Banking Company on the town square. Though these unchartered institutions lacked specie on hand and relied instead on the assets of their stockholders and on highly speculative land transactions, both issued promissory notes freely. Reckoning would come not far in the future, but in the meantime the banks extended the feeling of prosperity in the town. A more conservative chartered institution, the Northern Bank of Mississippi, also joined the Holly Springs banking community in 1838.[18]

With confidence restored by the prospect of easy credit once again, Dr. W.P. King of McEwen, King and Company revived the question of a college. Over $20,000 was subscribed, and a two-story brick building stood ready by the end of 1837. In January of the next year with considerable advertisement, the Literary Institution at Holly Springs opened its preparatory department under the charge of the Reverend Consider Parish, a Presbyterian minister. Nor was the town to neglect its young ladies. Having secured appropriations from the Board of Police and pledges from citizens, the trustees of the female academy in June of 1838 laid the cornerstone of a "fine edifice of the Tuscan order," two stories upon a raised basement, large enough to accommodate 140 pupils and to board 60.[19]

---

17 *Jackson Mississippian*, May 12 and July 7, 1837; *Woodville Republican*, May 6, 1837; Samuel Cole Williams, *The Biography of West Tennessee* (Johnson City, Tenn., 1930), 134, 137, 151; Gerald M. Capers, Jr., *The Biography of a River Town* (Chapel Hill, 1939), 47, 73, 79.

18 William K. Scarborough, "Heartland of the Cotton Kingdom," in McLemore (ed.) *A History of Mississippi*, I, 315; Gonzales, "Flush Times, Depression. War, and Compromise," 292-93; Holly Springs *Gazette*, August 4, 1841; James H. Stone, "The Economic Development of Holly Springs During the 1840s," *Journal of Mississippi History*, 32 (1970), 343-44.

19 *Biographical and Historical Memoirs*, II, 313-14; Jackson *Mississippian*, December 15, 1837; Mayes,

The hammers were also ringing out in the commercial sector of the town. The first hostelry of any pretension, the Holly Springs Hotel, had been built across spring hollow from Samuel McAlexander's tavern; but it was only a log structure with three rooms below and two above. Ben Williamson's Marshall Inn had a similar beginning on a lot near the hollow, but in 1838 the Inn moved to a two-story frame building on the north side of the square. The public had high praise for the table Williamson kept — one citizen commending in print " he bounteous board on [a] previous evening, consisting in part of Cheese, old, new and Pine Apple, Preserved Peaches, Oranges and Grapes, richly spiced transparent Citron, gallons of Strawberries covered with Loaf Sugar and Ice." The finest establishment of all, however, was the Union House, built by Caruthers, Cain, and Finley on the east side of the square, a large clapboard structure with a two-story double gallery across the front. [20]

In the fall of 1838, the Democratic newspaper commented on this year of building. Numerous structures were still going up in the "outer portions" of the town, but the most dramatic activity centered in the square and its environs. On ground that two years earlier had been covered with mud and stumps stood the recently completed courthouse. On the south and west sides of the square were rising blocks of two-story brick buildings, and the editor claimed that some of them vied in "superior workmanship and ornament" with "the fashionable stores of New York and Boston." The residential sections were still comprised primarily of pioneer log dog-trot dwellings, but a number had been covered with clapboard siding, their central passages filled in with double doors and their interiors plastered and refined. Scattered also amid the great forest trees were a few Greek Revival frame cottages, the most impressive being the residences of Samuel McCorkle and Alexander McEwen built in 1837. [21]

The town now had twenty dry goods stores, two drug stores, a "watch and jewelry store," tailoring establishments, bakeries, produce and grocery houses, as well as several barrooms. Hatchell and Norfleet, cabinetmakers, who had set up their shop in the town's earliest days, were doing a flourishing business. In the fall of 1838, a Whig newspaper,

---

History of Education in Mississippi, 47-49.

20 Board of Police Minutes, I, *passim*; Deed Books D, 295, E, 464, and H, 513; "Old Dumm and Bishop Tavern To Be Razed." *Holly Springs South Reporter*, 1925 clipping in Kate Freeman Clark Manuscript Collection. Marshall County Historical Society; *Southern Banner*, June 2. 1839; Burger, "An Overlooked Source for Mississippi Local History," 173; Interview with Mrs. L.A. Smith, February 6, 1983.

21 *Marshall County Republican*, November 3. 1838; John M. Mickle, "Old Mickle Home A Log Cabin Long Ago," *Holly Springs South Reporter*, December 15, 1932, p. 12; Bills for McCorkle residence, in possession of Hugh H. Rather, Holly Springs; Leslie Frank Crocker, "The Greek Revival Architecture of Holly Springs, Mississippi. 1837-1867" (M.A. thesis, University of Missouri, 1967), 59.

the *Southern Banner*, brought competition to E. Percy Howe's Democratic organ begun in 1837 and called first the *Mississippi Mirror* and later the *Marshall County Republican*. The town was well supplied with doctors, and it had become an El Dorado for the legal profession. Due to the speculating mania of the previous two years, the docket for the March term of Circuit Court in 1838 contained over 1,200 cases. Word of the volume of litigation spread rapidly, and for a time the town held over forty resident lawyers.[22]

These men, many of them intelligent and cultivated, added tone to a place known from the beginning for its "good society." Always ready for oratory, the lawyers were active in organizing the popular public dinners tendered to visiting notables, affairs marked by countless speeches and toasts. The arrival of General Sam Houston provided the occasion for one of the most memorable of these events — a dinner at the Union House, after which the great hero addressed a huge crowd at the courthouse. The legal profession also swelled the ranks of the debating society, the Philogastic, and the Thespians, who in January of 1839 offered their first production before an audience of three hundred.[23]

Despite the benefits of the influx of lawyers, the crowded docket was a clear sign of trouble ahead. In the early months of 1839, the columns of both newspapers were filled with announcements of forced sales due to judgments in favor of creditors. By this time the McEwen and the McCorkle banks, both in deep trouble, were struggling to redeem their promissory notes and burn them. The female academy, now chartered, and known as the Holly Springs Female Institute, was feeling the effects of the times. Even after refusing to pay the contractor's full bill for the brick work, the trustees still lacked sufficient funds to complete the structure as planned. The Institute moved into its new quarters in June of 1839, but for several years the young ladies had their schooling in a rather grand but partially unfinished building. On the other side of town, the college also found itself in straitened circumstances. Many of the subscribers had never made good their pledges. Still, the Literary Institution opened its collegiate department in January of 1839, and shortly the legislature granted it a charter as the University of Holly Springs — the first appearance in the state of an institution styled a university. By spring, however, the trustees admitted that the school was in an "embarrassed state" (among other matters, the faculty had not been paid), and the trustees gladly transferred it to the Mississippi Conference of the Methodist Church. The Methodists retained four of the faculty of six, all with the

---

22 *Besancon's Annual Register of the State of Mississippi for the Year 1838* (Natchez, 1838), 172-73; *Marshall County Republican*, November 3, 1838; Board of Police Minutes, I, 99, 317; Clayton, Centennial Address, 12, 18; *Memphis Avalanche*, March 2, 1879; *Marshall County Republican*, August 11 and November 24, 1838.

23 William Baskerville Hamilton, "Holly Springs, Mississippi in the Year 1878" (M.A. thesis, University of Mississippi, 1931), 14-15, 10; *Marshall County Republican*, January 19, 1839.

degree of master of arts, and announced their intention of establishing "a Medical and Law department, in addition to the preparatory department and college proper." They also informed the public that new brick dormitories were open for the students. The University, however, never succeeded; and within three years, after several attempts at revival, it closed its doors for good.[24]

Despite these ominous signs, the town continued to attract those drawn to centers of some refinement and no little wealth. Portrait painters, teachers of music, and dancing masters appeared at various intervals. In June of 1839, the town received its first visit from a professional theatrical company, the Chapman and Hamilton troupe, who had a successful run. Fall brought another active racing season at the Holly Springs Race Course — lately expanded, its accommodations greatly improved, and renamed the North Mississippi Jockey Club. [25]

The pace of the town's development had slowed, but some important buildings were still going up. In April, the Episcopal missionary the Reverend Colly A. Foster had organized Christ Church and installed Judge Alexander Mosby Clayton as senior warden. Eighteen months later, the Episcopalians moved into their own building, the most charming of the little white-painted churches of Holly Springs. The year 1840 also saw the completion of the town's first imposing residence. At the southern edge of Holly Springs on a lot looking up the road to Memphis, the town's wealthiest merchant, William F. Mason, erected his two-story brick house, only one room deep, but with an imposing facade dominated by triple Greek windows.[26]

Some citizens, then, still had money for pleasure, ornament, and comfort. But in the spring of 1840, the cotton market collapsed; and, in the words of the chronicler of the era Joseph Glover Baldwin, "the frolic was ended." Flush Times — even in Holly Springs — were definitely over. Prosperity would come again. By 1849, in fact, with cotton prices again high, Marshall County would be riding another wave as the largest cotton producer in the state. But lying immediately ahead were the lean years of the early forties. By January of 1841, one Holly Springs columnist was speaking of "these iron times." The newspapers

---

24 Stone, "Economic Development of Holly Springs During the 1840s," 344-46; Minutes of the Trustees of the Holly Springs Female Institute, 20, 22, 38; *Biographical and Historical Memoirs*, II, 314; *Holly Springs Gazette*, January 3, 1845; *Southern Banner*, June 15, 1839.

25 Hamilton, "Holly Springs," 11, 13, 22; *Southern Banner*, June 22, 1839; Laura D.S. Harrell, "Jockey Clubs and Race Tracks in Antebellum Mississippi, 1795-1861," *Journal of Mississippi History*, 28 (1966), 311-12.

26 Christ Church Records, II, 3, 12; Mrs. N.D. Deupree, "Some Historic Homes in Mississippi," *Publications of the Mississippi Historical Society*, VII, (1903), 345; Deed Book G, 327-28, and K, 179-80; Interview with James G. Arrington on the construction of the Mason house, July 22, 1963.

were filled with warnings from merchants demanding payment of long-overdue accounts, with notices of legal proceedings brought against creditors, and with advertisements for the resulting forced sales of property. Among the bankrupt were a number of the town's wealthiest and most prominent citizens - members of Randolph's partnership, trustees of the academies, political leaders, planters with the largest holdings in land and slaves. Many left for Texas. The hammers were no longer ringing out in Holly Springs. The development of the town had come to a standstill. [27]

The Whig editor Thomas Falconer tried always to strike the optimistic note, proclaiming again and again that the times were improving, But finally, in the fall of 1842, just a few months before he was forced to declare bankruptcy himself, Falconer wrote an editorial that must have mirrored the feelings of his fellow townsmen well. In the midst of this severe depression, he looked not ahead, but back over the short seven-year history of Holly Springs, amazed now at the town's unprecedented development during the Flush Times. Falconer marveled at the "spirit of extravagance and enterprise of 1836, '37, and '38," when this miniature cotton capital "arose out of the silence of the woods."[28]

27 Baldwin, *The Flush Times of Alabama and Mississippi*, 90; Scarborough, "Heartland of the Cotton Kingdom," 321-22; *Conservative and Holly Springs Banner*, January 15 and September 10, 1841, and January 19, 1842.

28 *Conservative and Holly Springs Banner*, January 22, 1841; *Holly Springs Gazette*, November 11, 1841, March 28, 1843, November 4, 1842.

Tishomingo and Itawamba on the Alabama Line

Hubert H. McAlexander

East of the original boundary of Marshall County, the soil type changes, and the lands beyond that line never became big cotton producers. Among the 10 counties originally created from the Chickasaw Cession — Tishomingo, Tippah, Marshall, Desoto, Tunica, Panola, Lafayette, Pontotoc, Itawamba, and Chickasaw — the two eastern ones were dominated by foothills of the Appalachian Mountains. Those counties, Tishomingo and Itawamba, both carrying dramatic Chickasaw names, lay along the hilly Alabama border.[1]

Tishomingo had been translated as "warrior chief," and the county was named for Chief Tishomingo (1734-c.1830). Beginning in Appalachian foothills, the county contains Mt. Woodall, the highest point in Mississippi, at 806 feet., According to Robert Lowry and William H. McCardle, *A History of Mississippi* (1891), Tishomingo embraced more territory than any county in the state, nearly 1,000 square miles. The county seat, first named Cincinnati, then hurriedly renamed Jacinto for Sam Houston's decisive victory against Mexico, was placed near the center point, on the road to Ripley. For years the courthouse was the original log building, replaced in 1859 by a handsome brick federal structure that has now been restored (see "Old Jacinto Courthouse" website). In 1870, the most productive lands were placed in the new counties of Alcorn and Prentiss.[2]

Itawamba was named for Ita-Wam-Ba, or Levi Colbert, the chief counselor of the Chickasaw Nation. He was the son of James Colbert, the original Scottish-descended settler among the tribe. Itawamba, or Levi Colbert, disapproved of the Treaty of Pontotoc and was traveling to Washington, D.C., to protest it when he died in the winter of 1832 (Lowry and McCardle, pp. 493-494). The county historical society describes pioneer life as "primitive and harsh" ("A Concise History of Itawamba County" at the Itawamba County website). In 1866, much of the richest land was taken for Lee County. According to a 1975 study, what is called in Mississippi the prairie "stretches westward from mid-Alabama and then curves northward in a broad scimitar coming to a final point north of Tupelo," the county seat of Lee.[3]

---

1 See map on p. 29 of Mary Elizabeth Young, *Redskins, Ruffleshirts, and Rednecks* (Norman: University of Oklahoma Press, 1961)

2 Lowry and McCardle, 585-587.

3 Lowry and McCardle, 493-494. See Vaugh N. Grisham, Jr., "Tupelo, Mississippi from Settlement to Industrial Community," Ph.D. dissertation, University of North Carolina, 1975.

Statue of Col. William C. Falkner in Ripley Cemetery

Tippah County and Colonel Falkner

Jack D. Elliott, Jr.

> For the essence of life is presentness, and only in a mythical sense does its mystery appear in
> the time-forms of past and future. They are the way, so to speak, in which life reveals itself to the
> folk... For it is, always is, however much we may say it was. Thus speaks the myth, which is only
> the garment of the mystery.
>
> —Thomas Mann, *Joseph and His Brothers*

In the cemetery in Ripley, Mississippi, stands an approximately 25-foot-high monument, the tallest in the cemetery, dedicated to the memory of Col. William C. Falkner. It is within sight of the railroad, which he had constructed linking Ripley to the outside world. On top of a granite base stands the marble sculpture of the man, reaffirming his prominence in the history of Ripley and also in the literature generated by his great-grandson and name-sake, William C. Faulkner. In *Sartoris* (1929), the first novel set in mythical Yoknapatawpha County, Mississippi, the younger Faulkner described another monument, this one dedicated to Col. John Sartoris and located beside the railroad in the cemetery in Jefferson, county seat of Yoknapatawpha County, a monument that clearly found its prototype in Colonel Falkner's monument:

> He stood on a stone pedestal, in his frock coat and bareheaded, one leg slightly advanced and
> one hand resting lightly on the stone pylon beside him. His head was lifted a little in that gesture of
> haughty pride which repeated itself generation after generation with a fateful fidelity, his back to the
> world and his carven eyes gazing out across the valley where his railroad ran, and the blue changeless
> hills beyond, and beyond that, the ramparts of infinity itself.[1]

The younger Faulkner knew the monument well. Many times he pondered it, a material object that recalled the Confederate colonel, the author, and the railroad builder. Symbols acquire their power through complex associations that are open-ended. The monument's associations spread with a myriad of roots backward into time then forward to the culminating image. Through a brief history of Falkner and Ripley, objective history emerges only to take on a legendary component and in the interplay of the two—history and legend—the Yoknapatawpha narrative subsumed them both.

W.C. Falkner was born in Knox County, Tennessee, in 1825, the son of William Falk-

---

1 William Faulkner, *Sartoris* (NY: Random House, originally published by Harcourt, Brace and Company, 1929), page 375.

ner,[2] a farmer, and his wife, Caroline Word Falkner, both natives of North Carolina. By 1840 the family had moved to rural Saline Township, Ste. Genevieve County, Missouri, and about 1841 young Bill[3] departed Missouri and arrived in Pontotoc, Mississippi. His arrival was prepared by the 1832 Treaty of Pontotoc Creek that opened the Chickasaw Cession lands in north Mississippi for sale and settlement and thereby served as a magnet, attracting members of his mother's family, the Words. By about 1821 his great-uncle William Word and family had settled on the east bank of the Tombigbee River opposite what would become the 1832 Cession lands, an area that had just been organized as Monroe County.[4] Drawing on 1832 treaty and the subsequent surveys, William's son, Thomas Adams Word (who bore the same name as Falkner's grandfather), began working in March 1834 as a deputy surveyor out of the Pontotoc Land Office laying out the interior section lines of township after township.[5] By mid-1835, as land sales were beginning, Falkner's uncle, Col. T.J. "Jeff" Word, an attorney and former North Carolina legislator, settled at Pontotoc[6], and toward the end of the year, Jeff's sister and brother-in-law, Mr. and Mrs.

2 His name was William Falkner and not Joseph or William Joseph Falkner as some secondary sources have asserted. Every primary source lists his name as simply William, and it was not until the appearance of the error-filled biographical sketch of W.C. Falkner in *Biographical and Historical Memoirs of Mississippi*, vol. 1 (Chicago: Goodspeed Publishers, 1891), page 713, that the name Joseph was introduced from out of the blue. Subsequently Donald Duclos, a recognized authority on Falkner, who was not familiar with the primary sources in this regard used Joseph from the Goodspeed biography thereby giving credibility to an otherwise incredible source. Donald Philip Duclos, *Son of Sorrow: The Life, Works and Influence of Colonel William C. Falkner 1825-1889* (San Francisco: International Scholars Publications, 1998), page 16. This work originally appeared as a Ph.D. dissertation in 1961, hence its influence is far more pervasive than the 1998 publication date would suggest.

3 The use of the nickname "Bill" comes from a letter by his uncle. Letter, James Word to T.J. Word, Iuka MS, July 27, 1872, Box 1, folder 14, T.J. Word collection, East Texas Research Center, Stephen F. Austin University.

4 Helen Mattox Crawford and Mary Flo Word, "Capt. William Word: The Jailer," in The Monroe County Book Committee (eds.), *A History of Monroe County, Mississippi* (Dallas TX: Curtis Media Corporation, 1988), pp. 933-934.

5 The beginning date for his survey work is March 28, 1834, when he signed a contract to survey the interior section lines for a township in the Chickasaw Cession lands. See notes on the plat of Township 14, Range 5 East of the Chickasaw Meridian on the Bureau of Land Management website. T.A. Word subsequently had regular contracts for surveying through the end of 1837, and on September 22, he was paid for having completed his last contract for surveying over 73 miles. By this time most of the surveys of the Chickasaw Cession lands had been completed, which would explain why his work on the Chickasaw Cession came to an end. Letter, Thomas H. Blake, Commissioner G.L.O., to Walter Forward, Secretary of the Treasury, January 6, 1843, RG 49 Entry 13, volume 2, pages 253-258.

6 Word was in Pontotoc by July 1835 when he was involved in establishing a Sunday school. E.T. Winston, *The Story of Pontotoc* (Pontotoc: Pontotoc Progress Print, 1931), page 117. The following month he was listed among the trustees for the newly established "Pontatoc Academy." See advertisement for "Pontatoc Academy," *The Mississippian*, newspaper, Jackson MS, August 28, 1835. The advertisement continued to appear for months after its initial appearance.

J.W. "Wes" Thompson arrived.[7] In November 1836, both Jeff and Wes were admitted to the bar of Pontotoc County.[8] Soon after other family members arrived in northeast Mississippi including Jeff's sister Elizabeth and her husband/cousin, Charles Word Humphreys, and Jeff's two brothers, James and Cuthbert Word.[9] After Falkner had been in Ripley for several years, his mother and two of his siblings also settled there during the 1850s. [10]

In order to provide more effective local government for the Chickasaw Cession lands, the Mississippi Legislature passed legislation on February 9, 1836, establishing a group of new counties that covered most of the area. One located on the northern part of the area was named Tippah after one of its largest streams, the Tippah River. Five days later another bill was passed that appointed men to serve as commissioners to organize the first elections for the new counties. One of three commissioners appointed for Tippah County was T.J. Word, who had established himself as a person of distinction and reliability.

On or shortly before March 23, 1836, the commissioners certified official returns from the election to select members of the Tippah County Board of Police.[11] This was the main legislative and executive body in county government and equivalent to today's board of supervisors. With this election, the rudiments of the county government were established, while the process to fill out the government and locate and establish a county seat began. A month later, on April 25, 1836, a second election was held to select the remaining officials. [12]

In the meantime, the Board began considering proposals for a centrally located county seat. When one was chosen they purchased the land and engaged a surveyor to lay out the streets, blocks, and lots. On June 15, the Board advertised: "Valuable Lots…in the Town of Ripley will be offered for sale at public auction on the 1st Monday and days following in September next." Praising the prospects of the surrounding land for agricultural

---

7 Obituary for J.W. Thompson, *Memphis Daily Appeal,* newspaper, Memphis TN, July 4, 1873, reprinted from *The Ripley Advertiser.*

8 Winston, *The Story of Pontotoc,* page 115.

9 James Word, "Genealogy of the Word Family written by James Word, December 23, 1882," typescript in Ripley Public Library.

10 U.S. Census, Tippah County MS, 1860

11 Official Returns for Tippah County dated March 23, 1836 in Mississippi Department of Archives and History.

12 Captain J.E. Rogers, "History of Tippah County," in Tippah County Historical and Genealogical Society, *Heritage of Tippah County, Mississippi,* (Humboldt TN: Rose Publishing Company, reprint edition, 1999), page 148. This essay originally appeared in *The Ripley Broadaxe,* newspaper, Ripley, MS, August 21, 1878.

and mechanical development, the advertisement went on to note that the town "is laid out with a spacious, handsome public square, [while] elegant business lots surround the same."[13] Thus by June 15, the site for the county seat had been selected and named with a survey in the works and with the first sale of lots projected for September 5. The name chosen — Ripley — was probably taken from General Eleazear Wheelock Ripley (1782-1839), a hero of the War of 1812 and congressman from Louisiana at the time the town was established.

A temporary courthouse was constructed of logs off the northeast corner of the square, while a two-story brick building was later built in the center of the square. To provide needed services for the surrounding area, business houses were constructed and businesses opened. Among the business owners was Wes Thompson, who moved about the first of January 1837 from Pontotoc to Ripley, where he opened his law office and was remembered as the first lawyer in town.[14] On May 9, 1837, the town was chartered through an act of the Mississippi Legislature.[15] That same year, a branch of the ill-fated Mississippi Union Bank, for which Jeff Word served as attorney,[16] was established in Ripley.[17]

The formation of counties and towns was replicated simultaneously throughout the Chickasaw Cession and elsewhere at other times: Tippah and Ripley, Chickasaw and Houston, Lafayette and Oxford, Tishomingo and Jacinto, and Faulkner's fictional Yoknapatawpha and Jefferson, named after battles, generals, politicians, and Indian-named creeks. The same pattern that provided the geographical backdrop for both Colonel Falkner and Colonel Sartoris was described years later by Falkner's great-grandson:

> ...a Square, the courthouse in its grove the center; quadrangular around it, the stores, two-sto-

---

13 "Valuable Lots for Sale in the Town of Ripley," advertisement, *Columbus Democrat*, newspaper, Columbus MS, August 6, 1836.

14 Obituary for J.W. Thompson, *Memphis Daily Appeal*, July 4, 1873. The reference to Thompson as the first lawyer in Ripley comes from the anonymous "Ripley Pioneers," an article which appeared in 1895 in either the *Ripley Advertiser*, newspaper, Ripley MS, or *The Southern Sentinel*, newspaper, Ripley MS. According to Andrew Brown, author of *History of Tippah County, Mississippi: The First Century* (Tippah County Historical and Genealogical Society, Ripley, MS, 1998, pages 21, 24) the anonymous writer was actually Brown's cousin, Mary Etter Murry, daughter of Dr. J.Y. Murry and great-aunt of William Faulkner. He was probably correct.

15 "An Act to Incorporate the Town of Ripley, in the County of Tippah" *Laws of Mississippi*, 1837, pages 120-121.

16 See correspondence pertaining to the Mississippi Union Bank in box 1, folder 11, T.J. Word collection, East Texas Research Center, Stephen F. Austin University.

17 "An Act Supplementary to an Act to Incorporate the Subscribers to the Mississippi Union Bank," *Laws of Mississippi*, 1837, page 42.

rey, the offices of the lawyers and doctors and dentists, the lodge-rooms and auditoriums, above them; school and church and tavern and bank and jail each in its ordered place; the four broad diverging avenues straight as plumb-lines in the four directions, becoming the network of roads and by-roads until the whole county would be covered with it.[18]

While the circumstances behind Falkner's relocation to Mississippi are unclear, he presumably came seeking family support to advance his prospects in life. By the time of his arrival in Pontotoc, his uncle Jeff Word had served as a U.S. congressman from Mississippi (1838-1839), while also maintaining a lucrative law practice and serving in numerous civic roles. In late 1842, Word moved to Ripley[19], bringing with him young Falkner, who then found himself associated with another prominent kinsman, his uncle Wes Thompson, who by 1842 was serving as district attorney and would later serve as legislator and circuit judge. A Ripley newspaper later recalled that Falkner had arrived in town "a poor penniless boy," something of an exaggeration designed no doubt to emphasize his Horatio Alger-like achievements.[20] He may well have been penniless upon arrival in Mississippi, but he was not without the resources that family connections provided. With his attorney uncles as his primary connections, it is not surprising that he too became an attorney.

However, his career was far more diverse than merely maintaining a law practice. Furthermore, it was often tainted with controversy. He first came into the public eye when he published the confessions of a mass killer and hawked it at the man's hanging. When a company was raised in 1846 to help with the Mexican War effort, he enlisted and was elected first lieutenant, the second-highest office. Later, he killed two men in what were ruled justifiable homicides, published two small books, and edited a newspaper, *Uncle Sam* (1855-1856), associated with the short-lived Know Nothing party. He even ran for the legislature under the banner of that party against the democratic candidate, who happened to be Falkner's uncle, Wes Thompson. Thompson won. In 1858, Falkner was elected brigadier general of the Mississippi Militia.

With the outbreak of the Civil War, Falkner was elected colonel and commanding

---

18 Faulkner, *Requiem for a Nun*, page 39

19 Evidence of Jeff's move to Ripley comes from several lines of evidence: Deeds identifying Pontotoc County as his place of residence appear consistently through July 15, 1842, the last date that places him as resident in Pontotoc County. See Pontotoc County Deed Book 4, page 325. After July 15 correspondence begins placing him in Ripley: On September 8, a John Davis sent a letter to Word addressed at Ripley. Letter, John Davis, agent, Macon, MS, to Thos. J. Word, Ripley, Tippah Co., MS, September 8, 1842, in Box 1, folder 8, T.J. Word collection, East Texas Research Center, Stephen F. Austin University. On November 10, Davis wrote another letter addressed to Word in Pontotoc, with "Pontotoc" crossed out and replaced with "Ripley." In the letter Davis notes: "I understood you had moved to Ripley." Letter, John Davis, agent, Macon, MS, to Thos. J. Word, Ripley, MS, November 10, 1842, in Box 1, folder 7, T.J. Word collection.

20 *Southern Sentinel*, October 2, 1884.

officer of the Second Mississippi Infantry, which was shipped eastward to Virginia, where it participated in the Battle of First Manassas on July 21, 1861. The battle resulted in the rout of Union troops. The story was later told that as Falkner led his regiment in a charge against a Union position, General Joe Johnston, watching from a distance, pointed at Falkner and informed troops newly arrived on the field, "Men, follow yonder knight of the black plume, and history will not forget you."[21]

The following year, when new elections were held, Falkner was narrowly defeated and replaced as colonel by John M. Stone, who would years later serve as governor of Mississippi. Because he had only enlisted for a year, and that year being up, Falkner departed and returned to Mississippi, where he organized a company of cavalry known as the First Mississippi Partisan Rangers. The Rangers were authorized to serve as independent mounted irregulars attacking the enemy and destroying communications whenever the situation permitted, activities that were recalled in Faulkner's 1938 novel *The Unvanquished*.[22]

After the war, Falkner returned to civilian life, the practice of law, and a new endeavor, railroad building. Ripley was in need of a railroad. Transportation in Mississippi and surrounding states was revolutionized during the 1850s by the construction of trunk lines that connected major port cities to their hinterlands. As railroads were constructed, new towns were born and older towns that were fortunate enough to find themselves on a railroad were greatly augmented. However, Ripley was not one of these. Having been bypassed by trunk lines within miles to the east, west, and north, the town attempted to build a spur line to link it to a trunk line, and thereby to the outside world. Efforts to build such a line were initiated in 1857, 1858, and 1859, and all failed, apparently due to a lack of resources — not surprising, given Ripley's small size and the consequent shortage of capital.

In the aftermath of the war, Falkner, with his eloquence, flamboyance, and business savvy, finally produced results. In mid-1869 he became the spokesman for a spur line to connect Ripley with the Memphis & Charleston trunk line to the north.[23] After a fitful start, ground-breaking ceremonies were held on March 1, 1872[24], while soon after, a bill passed the Mississippi Legislature, transforming the little spur line into a major trunk line,

21 "The White Rose of Memphis," *Memphis Daily Appeal*, April 10, 1881, page 2.

22 Andrew Brown, "The First Mississippi Partisan Rangers, C.S.A.," *Civil War History*, vol. 1, no. 4, 1955, 371-399.

23 *The Weekly Clarion*, newspaper, Jackson, MS, August 26, 1869; "Important Enterprise The Ripley Railway Company," *Memphis Daily Appeal*, October 31, 1869, page 4.

24 "Ripley/Opening of the Narrow-Gauge Railroad," *Memphis Daily Appeal*, August 30, 1872.

Ship Island, Ripley, & Kentucky Railroad.[25] Most locals would have been satisfied with merely having their spur line constructed; few would have contemplated turning it into a trunk line connecting the Mississippi River to the Gulf of Mexico. Such an unbounded act of imagination and optimism was almost certainly the brainchild of Falkner.

In late August the railroad was completed to Ripley. The stockholders were so elated at Falkner's success that they named a locomotive "W.C. Falkner" and named the first station north of Ripley "Falkner," an accolade never offered to any other.[26] A festive day of celebration held in honor of the occasion was heralded as "one of the most memorable days in the history of Tippah county."[27] The *Memphis Daily Appeal* was effusive over the achievement, declaring that Falkner would "ever be deemed a great public benefactor, because he has shown how the greatest possible good may be done with the narrowest possible resources."[28]

Efforts to continue the railroad to the south subsequently stalled until 1886, when construction was resumed towards Pontotoc. In the meantime, Falkner delved again into writing. In 1881 he produced his bestseller, *The White Rose of Memphis*, and the following year published the less well-received *The Little Brick Church*. In 1883, he and his daughter Effie took the grand tour of Europe, an activity virtually unknown in north Mississippi and followed it with a lengthy travelogue, *Rapid Ramblings in Europe* (1884).

Beginning in late 1884, he renovated his home, transforming it into an extravagant Italianate mansion[29] called "Warwick Place,"[30] presumably after Warwick Castle, England, which he had visited while on his European tour. Towering over all the buildings in Ripley

---

25 "An Act to authorize the Ripley Railroad Company to change the name of said Company," *Laws of Mississippi*, 1872, pages 317-318. "An Act to amend an Act entitled 'an Act to incorporate the Ripley Railroad Company'," *Laws of Mississippi*, 1872, page 318.

26 Ripley Railroad Company journal, typed transcript, April 22, 1872, pages 8-14, in the Blotner papers, Louis Daniel Brodsky Collection of William Faulkner Materials, Special Collections and Archives, Southeast Missouri State University.

27 "Ripley: Opening of the Narrow-Gauge Railroad," *Memphis Daily Appeal*, August 30, 1872, page 4; "The Ripley Narrow Gauge Railroad," *New Orleans Republican*, newspaper, New Orleans LA, September 8, 1872, page 2.

28 *Memphis Daily Appeal*, August 27, 1872, page 2.

29 *Southern Sentinel*, November 13 & 20, 1884; *Ripley Advertiser*, November 15, 1884, January 31, 1885.

30 For references to "Warwick Place" see: *Southern Sentinel*, June 29, 1893; August 31, 1893; May 19, 1898. Because these references all postdate Falkner's death, it's possible that his daughter Effie provided the name. She resided in the house during the 1890s and also accompanied her father on his European trip. For the visit to Warwick see W.C. Falkner, *Rapid Ramblings in Europe* (Philadelphia: J.B. Lippincott & Co., 1884), 71-75.

and with a stuffed alligator standing erect in the front hall,[31] Warwick Place lent an air of the exotic and marvelous to the small town.

Although Falkner's character was such that he had a large following, his volatility also generated enemies. On the evening of November 5, 1889, he was shot on the west side of the Ripley square by former business associate, R.J. Thurmond, and died the following day in the home of his daughter and son-in-law, Dr. and Mrs. N.G. Carter. His funeral was held at the Presbyterian Church, and he was buried in the Ripley Cemetery within sight of the railroad that he had constructed. A newspaper recorded the effect upon the people attending the funeral: "Strong men wept as they looked upon the face of their friend for the last time.… Never in the history of Ripley has such a throng of sorrowing people gathered together to honor the dead. All felt that a friend was gone forever. Dry eyes were few. And so passes away the noblest man that ever honored Tippah county with his citizenship."[32] A writer for a Jackson newspaper reflected upon the extent to which Falkner's image had grown: "The tragic death of Col. Falkner has brought him before the eyes of the public to such an extent that his life and its achievement loom up before them as the colossal work of an enterprising, industrious, brave man. His business enterprises were gigantic; in that sense he was a Napoleon."[33]

Thurmond was brought to trial February 1891, on charges of manslaughter. While the fact was known that Thurmond had walked out of his office and shot Falkner, the defense brought evidence to the effect that Falkner had made threats to kill Thurmond and was seeking a "difficulty" on the day of the shooting. They further claimed that as Thurmond walked out of his office, Falkner had attempted to draw a gun, forcing the former to shoot. However, evidence was conflicting regarding whether Falkner was actually armed. Despite such ambiguities, Thurmond was acquitted.[34]

Within months of his death, the contract for a monument was awarded to C.J. Rogers of Grand Junction, Tennessee, and Rogers sub-contracted to a firm in Aberdeen, Scotland, to construct the granite base and a firm in Carrara, Italy, to carve the marble sculpture, with the resulting monument erected in the summer of 1891.[35]

---

31 Thomas S. Hines, *William Faulkner and the Tangible Past: The Architecture of Yoknapatawpha*, (Berkeley: University of California Press, 1996), pages 97-99.

32 From a photostatic copy of an unidentified newspaper clipping in the Ripley Public Library.

33 *The New Mississippian*, newspaper, Jackson, MS, November 20, 1889.

34 "Thurman [sic] Not Guilty," *The Bolivar Bulletin*, February 27, 1891, page 2, reprinted from the *Memphis Appeal Avalanche*. See also "Circuit Court," *Southern Sentinel*, February 26, 1891.

35 *Southern Sentinel*, July 10,1890; "C.J. Rogers, of Grand Junction, Secures the Contract over Memphis Builders for the Erection of a Handsome Monument," *The Bolivar Bulletin*, newspaper, Bolivar, TN,

Falkner's great-grandson and namesake William C. Falkner (who later added a "u" to Falkner) was born eight years after the colonel's death. During Faulkner's formative years, stories abounded about the exploits of the colonel. When William lived in Ripley as a child, the landscape had hardly changed: the colonel's house stood as did the home of his daughter Willie Falkner Carter, where he had died. Young William was a favorite of his great-aunt Willie and visited her home regularly where he would have seen the memorial stained-glass window with colonel's portrait inset where one might otherwise find the image of a saint or even Jesus Christ himself. The sunlight filtering through the stained glass gave an aura of otherworldliness to the room.[36]

Faulkner was greatly influenced by the legend of his great-grandfather. His brother Jack thought that he had either consciously or unconsciously modeled his life after the colonel's. As a child, he was asked what he wanted to become and he responded that he wanted to become a writer like his great-grandfather.[37] Reflecting upon the legend and the landscape, he remarked: "People at Ripley talk of him as if he were still alive, up in the hills some place, and might come in at any time. It's a strange thing; there are lots of people who knew him well, and yet no two of them remember him alike or describe him the same way…. There's nothing left in the old place, the house is gone and the plantation boundaries, nothing left of his work but a statue. But he rode through the country like a living force."[38]

The first lines of the first Yoknapatawpha novel, *Sartoris*, suggest the power of story to overcome time and space through the image of Col. John Sartoris, whose presence is brought back to life as his son, banker Bayard Sartoris, talks with Falls, an old and impoverished friend: "As usual, old man Falls had brought John Sartoris into the room with him…fetching, like an odor, like the clean dusty smell of his faded overalls, the spirit of the dead man into that room where the dead man's son sat and where the two of them, pauper and banker, would sit for a half an hour in the company of him who had passed

January 9, 1891, page 3; "Artistic Workmanship," *Bolivar Bulletin*, June 26, 1891, page 2.

36 William's brother, John recalled that William was a favorite of Willie's and that he would often visit her not only in Ripley, but later in Meridian where she and her husband moved in 1901. John Faulkner, *My Brother Bill: An Affectionate Reminiscence* (NY: Trident Press, 1963), 24. Joseph Blotner (ed.), *Selected Letters of William Faulkner* (NY: Random House, 1977), 20. Regarding the stained-glass window see Tippah County Deed Book 16, pages 442-444 where Willie upon selling the house reserved the right to remove the window. The window is now on exhibit in the Tippah County Historical Museum.

37 Murry C. Falkner, *The Falkners of Mississippi: A Memoir* (Baton Rouge: Louisiana State University, 1967), 6.

38 Robert Cantwell, "The Faulkners: Recollections of a Gifted Family," originally published 1938, reprinted in M. Thomas Inge (ed.), *Conversations with William Faulkner*, Jackson: University Press of Mississippi, 1999, page 35.

beyond death and then returned." [39]

It appears that Faulkner had come to realize that reality is not merely the sum total of historical events, because these events are in many ways conscious constructs derived from various sources. Historical events are construed as objective, yet are embedded in the conscious mind as if through the veil of legend and myth, all surrounded by a penumbra of the mystery that is native to human existence.

39 Faulkner, *Sartoris*, page 1.

Daguerreotype of "Groveland" taken soon after it was built
Courtesy of Edward G. Parham

THE CESSION'S FIRST GREAT HOUSE, GROVELAND

HUBERT H. MCALEXANDER

George Hubbard Wyatt, now a somewhat mysterious figure, must have built Groveland during the "Flush Times" of the 1830s. Born in Amelia County, Va., in 1805, he was married there in 1827 to Amanda Melvina Fitzallen Holcombe. In early 1828, in a party with her parents, they settled in La Grange, Fayette County, Tennessee, on the line with Chickasaw lands in northern Mississippi. George H. Wyatt appears in 1830 records as builder of the early section of the Hunt-Phelan mansion on Beale Street in Memphis. He must have been establishing himself and making his fortune. Likely he built Groveland in Fayette County within the next five years. His early children are all listed as born there. In 1838, a three-man commission determined that the state line be moved a couple of miles to the north. From that point, Groveland was in Marshall County, Mississippi, in the Chickasaw Cession.[1]

Wyatt appears in the 1840 Marshall County census as the owner of 99 slaves. On the plantation were two schools with roughly 30 students enrolled in each. On October 10, 1834, the *Randolph Recorder* of Tipton County lists him as a trustee of the Female Seminary at La Grange, and in June 1840, the *Conservative* and *Holly Springs Banner* announce that the Tippancanoe Clubs of Holly Springs and La Grange met at the "residence of Major Wyatt" (June 26, 1840). By this time, he must have been feeling the effects of the depression following all the speculation of the "Flush Times." Three years later, he sold the house and plantation to Richard Hill Parham of Va., for $25,000.[2]

Afterwards, George H. Wyatt moved to Louisiana, where his last child was born and where his wife died. Opening a new chapter, he took a group of 13 from Memphis to the gold fields of California in 1849. He appeared prominently in California for more than ten years. In 1859, the Washoe strike resulted in the discovery of the Comstock Lode. On October 10, 1861, George H. Wyatt registered in a Stockton hotel using a Washoe address. He then disappeared from history.[3]

Now let us return to 1843, when Richard Hill Parham bought the 2,115 acre plantation. The move from Virginia to Mississippi, made in carriages and wagons drawn by oxen, took two months to the day. On the first of March 1843, "a cold, blustery, wintry night,"

---

1 The George H. Wyatt information is taken from entries on Ancestry.com. Goodspeed's *Memoirs of Mississippi* (Chicago: Goodspeed Publishing Co., 1891), I: 98.

2 Helen Parham, *"Groveland," The History of Benton County, Mississippi* (Rochester, N.Y.: Book One, 2009), 557.

3 All information is taken from entries on Ancestry.com.

the party — consisting of "the family, the manager of the plantation and 125 slaves"—reached Groveland. They found "the house locked and were forced to camp in the grove that night while someone was dispatched in search of the keys."[4]

The mansion, set on a four-foot red-brick foundation, was painted white with green blinds. It was two stories, with front and back stairways and a colonnade across two sides. Those two colonnades were centered by fanlights over sets of double doors. The accompanying picture, while an excellent one that shows the hill-top setting and the outbuildings, is not the one I saw hanging in Miss Maude Parham's Holly Springs hall in the early 1950s. That view showed the fanlights in more detail.

To the left of the main entrance was the parlor with a square piano, "hair furniture brought from Virginia," and a "handsome mantle of Italian marble." The library was filled by "three large bookcases extending almost to the ceiling," a secretary, chairs, and tables. Behind the dining room were a large back hall and a bedroom. We will quote Miss Helen Parham on the whole scene:

> At the rear of the house was the two-room kitchen…the dairy, the store house, where the groceries which were hauled from Memphis, more than 50 miles, in wagons, were stored; the smoke house, where the meat was cured and packed; the ice house, where ice which was cut from creeks and ponds in winter was packed for summer use; the carriage [house] and several large barns for hay and corn and stables to shelter the many horses and mules necessary for such a large plantation. To the north was the overseer's house, the servants' quarters and the slaves' quarters; and with only the 125 slaves brought from Virginia, and housing accommodations for all these, "Groveland" must have presented the picture of a veritable little village on the slope of a beautiful hill.[5]

That "beautiful hill" was "situated on the north and south Stage Line road from Holly Springs to La Grange, less than two miles from Davis Mills, now Michigan City, five miles from the historic little town of La Grange, Tennessee, five miles from Lamar, Mississippi, about thirty miles from Holly Springs, Mississippi, and fifty miles from Memphis."

Miss Helen made the next comment from memories of the Civil War. When Sherman's Army passed on the road to La Grange in front of the mansion, "it required two days and one night.…" That night, the Parham family and some friends stood on the south porch of Groveland and watched the burning of the Mason house a half-mile south, while Major Mason was in the army away in the midst of the conflict.

In 1919, Groveland burned to the ground.[6]

---

4 Parham, 558.

5 Parham, 559.

6 Parham, 560.

The Founding of Oxford

Anne Percy

Settlers were already in the area when Lafayette County was established by the Mississippi legislature. A February 9, 1836, legislative act set boundaries and created Lafayette County and 12 other original counties from the Chickasaw Cession.[1] Many of these counties were given Chickasaw names, but Lafayette County was named for the Marquis de Lafayette, the young French aristocrat who had fought with the continental army during the American Revolution.

A February 14 act of the legislature appointed county commissioners to organize each county, and there were four commissioners for Lafayette County. This act called for an election for members of each county Board of Police, later known at the Board of Supervisors. County seats were to be located within a radius of five miles of each county's geographical center.[2]

The date of the election of the first Lafayette County Board of Police is unknown, but the first entry in the minutes of the Board of Police recorded that on March 21, 1836, the five board members appeared at the home of John P. Jones, one of the county's commissioners, and were sworn in by him. On April 2, Lafayette County elected its first officials, among them Sheriff Charles G. Butler.[3] Sheriff Butler would be a great-grandfather of Oxford's most famous citizen, William Cuthbert Faulkner.

Three of those who bought Chickasaw land in 1836 were John Chisholm, John D. Martin, and John J. Craig, and they bought some land jointly. On June 13, 1836, these men bought section 21, Township 8, Range 3 West in Lafayette County, for eight hundred dollars from a female Chickasaw named HoKa. HoKa signed the agreement with her mark, and George and James Colbert signed, certifying that HoKa was "capable to take care of her own affairs this 13th day of June, 1836." Indian Agent Benjamin Reynolds also signed the agreement.[4]

On June 22, 1836, soon after their purchase, John D. Martin and John J. Craig of Mississippi and John Chisholm of Alabama conveyed fifty acres in Section 21, part of the section purchased from HoKa, to the county Board of Police. No sum was mentioned in

---

1 1836 *Laws of Mississippi*, 9-14.

2 *Ibid.*, 46-49.

3 Lafayette County Board of Police Book, 1, 1-2.

4 Lafayette County Deed Book A, 125.

this deed. The boundaries of the fifty acres were measured in poles and began at "a certain Hickory Tree near Craig's store house." The agreement stated, "It is to be understood that the land is not yet surveyed, which will account for the singularity of the calls, the same is to be surveyed as soon as is convenient, and Regular formal deed made by the said John Chisholm, John D. Martin, and John Craig," The agreement was signed by the three men and witnessed by W.E. Buckner and Jesse Lowe.[5]

This was recorded in the Board of Police minutes that same day, when the board located the county seat for Lafayette County on the fifty acres donated to the board by Chisholm, Martin, and Craig. At the same time the Board of Police established and declared that the county seat be known as "the Town of Oxford."[6]

Chisholm, Martin, and Craig executed a formal deed on July 17, conveying fifty acres to the Board of Police. This land was conveyed for the sum of one hundred dollars as "a place on which to locate the seat of Justice." The Board of Police were to extend "the three main streets passing through said contemplated town as far as may be necessary to command the best view of the town." The area was described as "one certain tract or parcel of land Lying and being in said county, being a part of Sections 21 and 28, Township 8, Range 3 West in the Chickasaw Cession." The boundaries were measured in poles and were to begin at "a stake 22 feet southwest from the southwest corner of John J. Craig's Dwelling house." The agreement was signed by the three men and witnessed by Richard M. Craig and Thomas D. Isom.[7] The three men had shifted the location of the fifty acres, now part of Sections 21 and 28.

The men had not yet purchased Section 28. On December 8, 1836, Chisholm, Martin, and Craig purchased Section 28, Township 8, Range 3 West in Lafayette County, from a male Chickasaw, E an nah yea, for eight hundred dollars. E an nah yea signed with his mark, and Ishtahotapa and Benjamin Love signed, certifying the agreement. Indian Agent Reynolds also signed. The formal July 17 deed of the three men to the Board of Police was recorded by the probate clerk on February 6, 1837.[8]

The legislative act incorporating Oxford on May 11, 1837, stated that the town boundaries encompassed "all of the south half of section twenty-none and the north half of section twenty-eight, in township 8, range three west of the basis meridian."[9] A map

---

5 *Ibid.*, 136-137.

6 Lafayette County Board of Police Book, 1, 6.

7 Lafayette County Deed Book Am 161-162.

8 *Ibid.*, 126.

9 1837 *Laws of Mississippi*, 133.

of Oxford in Lafayette County's Chancery Building states that Oxford was built on land bought from HoKa and E an nah yea, Chickasaw Indians. Charles Lynch, a Whig, was governor of Mississippi and Martin Van Buren, a Democrat, was president of the United States when Oxford was incorporated.

Local legend has it that a group of citizens, including Thomas Dudley Isom, had gathered and approved his [Isom's] suggestion that the town be named Oxford, in the hopes that a university would be established there, as had been the case in Oxford, England.

The conveying of fifty acres to the Board of Police for one hundred dollars by Craig, Martin, and Chisholm, was commendable, but it was also shrewd, as their surrounding acres became more valuable. They paid HoKa and E an nah yea no more than the minimum price set by the federal government for Chickasaw land. From 1976 until 1996 a rustic movie house and café named the HOKA operated in a hollow just off Oxford's Square, proprietor Ron Shapiro having named it for the Chickasaw woman Hoka.

John J. Craig's grave marker south of Oxford states that he was born in Williamson County, Tennessee, and immigrated to Lafayette County in 1834. He built a trading post in the Indian territory that was to become Oxford, and he persuaded his wife's younger brother Thomas Dudley Isom to come from Maury County, Tennessee, to work for a while in the store.[10]

---

10 *Biographical and Historical Memoirs of Mississippi*, Vol. I (Chicago: Goodspeed Publishing Company, 1891), 1006. This states that Thomas Dudley Isom was the second child of James and Mary Gayle Isom. The Buckner-Craig-Isom cemetery markers show that Sarah G. Isom Craig and Robert Isom were the other children of James and Mary Gayle Isom.

In my youth, ruins of Col. Volney Peel's mansion "Hickory Park"
still stood a few miles north of the site of Wyatt. (HHM)
Photography by Chesley Thorne Smith

The Ghostly History of
Wyatt on the Tallahatchie

Hubert H. McAlexander

The site of Wyatt is roughly a mile south of Marshall County on the Tallahatchie River. Though it is in Lafayette County, it is counted in Marshall in the 1840 census. In a sense it is in the middle of nowhere, but that was obviously not always the case.

The earliest treatment of the place—Franklin L. Riley, "Extinct Towns and Villages of Mississippi," *Publications of the Mississippi Historical Society* (1902), volume 5, 5:348-350 — has a mythic quality. It begins:

> Wyatt—Another product of the flush times was situated in Lafayette county, about thirteen miles from the present town of Oxford, on what was once thought to be the head of navigation of the Tallahatchie river. The place was settled about the time of the Chickasaw cession and flourished before Oxford had been named or Holly Springs thought of.

A modern reader needs to be reminded that the Chickasaw Cession was created by the Treaty of Pontotoc Creek in 1832 and that the towns of Oxford and Holly Springs were begun in 1835 (see McAlexander essay, "Flush Times in Holly Springs"). So the span of years is not great. Riley quotes Dr. Thomas D. Isom of Oxford (1816-1902) as saying that in the fall of 1835, he saw the streets of Wyatt "as much crowded by trade wagons as is now the Front Row of Memphis in cotton season."[1]

The earliest settlers thought Wyatt would "eclipse" other towns of the Cession and rival Memphis. A man named Brooks established a gin factory, and the machine manufactured was widely used throughout north Mississippi. "At the time of its greatest prosperity," Franklin L. Riley writes, the town contained 14 "merchantile houses" and "a large and pretentious hotel." A bridge across the Tallahatchie was built, and a "'urnpike across the river swamp."[2] Aiken dates the plat 1840, and in the 1840s five steamboats were making the trip from Wyatt to New Orleans, shipping between 10,000 and 25,000 bales of cotton.[3]

---

1 In this essay, I depended upon the research of Will Lewis and Richie Burnette of Oxford. Riley, 348-350.

2 The plat of Wyatt appears on page 72 of Charles S. Aiken, William Faulkner and the Southern Landscape (Athens GA:2009).

3 James H. Stone, "The Economic Development of Holly Springs During the 1840s," *Journal of Mis-*

The bluff, on which the town had its beginnings, was first called Redman's Bluff. The 1833 Chickasaw Cession map in the Marshall County Chancery Clerk's office shows the bluff as owned by Slone Love. He was member of the powerful mixed blood family in north Mississippi (See McAlexander, "The Saga of a Mixed-Blood Chickasaw Dynasty"). Probably later that year, Volney Peel and Wyatt Mitchell agreed to buy it from Love, and the name was soon changed to Mitchell's Bluff (Riley, 349).

Mitchell's Bluff quickly became Wyatt. Franklin Riley names these as the prominent citizens of the town:

> Thomas H. Allen, later of Memphis and New Orleans, and A[ngus] Gillis, his partner in business, Andrew Murdock, Major [James] Alston, Dr. Robert O. Carter, and Dr. Edward McMucken. Dr. Robert Watt, a Scotch gentleman of education and refinement, a graduate of Edinburgh, who had studied under the celebrated Dr. Gregory, bought a plantation near Wyatt and established his office in the town. He was perhaps at that time the best physician in North Mississippi. He died in 1843. Col. Volney Peel, of Marshall county, a polished and cultured gentleman of wealth, was inspired with the belief that Wyatt would grow into a city. He made large investments in town lots and erected several houses in that place, thereby losing a large part of his fortune.[4]

A surveyor like his father, Peel was a leading figure in the mapping of the Chickasaw Cession and made a great deal of money by speculating. His beautiful Georgian brick house, "Hickory Park," was built in 1840.[5]

Riley comments that Wyatt was profoundly affected by the financial crash of 1837, and that "in a few years its glory had departed." Allen and Gillis founded one of the many banks established during the early days of the Chickasaw Cession. It flooded the area with its "shin plaster" issue. The expression "as good as A. Gillis's bill" was for a time a mark of soundness and stability, but later, a bogus claim. Like the majority of these institutions, the Allen-Gillis bank failed.

Another of the "flush times" figures, Samuel Ramsey McAlexander, had the rough log tavern on the site of Holly Springs.[6] After his bankruptcy in Marshall County, he ran the hotel at Wyatt. On June 15, 1839, he placed this notice in the *Marshall County Republican*:

sissippi History (1970), 32: 351-352.

4 Riley, 349.

5 See McAlexander, *A Southern Tapestry: Marshall County, Mississippi*; 1835-2000 (Downing Co., 2000) pp. 21-22.

6 See *Southern Tapestry*, 11-13, 26

The Subscriber has taken charge of the WYATT HOTEL (the principal Tavern in the Town of Wyatt) on the immediate stage road leading from Holly Springs to Oxford and Coffeeville—where he respectfully solicits a share of public patronage. His house will be in good repair, and is provided with comfortable private rooms for families. His TABLE shall be equal to any in the country, and supplied with the best the market will afford. His STABLES shall be supplied with the best of provender and well attended. He will commence business on the first of July next, and flatters himself, from his experience in business, that he can render general satisfaction.

The cotton market hit bottom in the summer of 1840, and the frolic of flush times was over. In the spring of 1842, the "elegant Frame Tavern" was offered for sale.[7]

The 1850s opening of the Mississippi Central Railroad, just a few miles to the east, spelled the end of Wyatt. By 1902, only a few bricks were left. But Dr. Calvin Brown, the son of a University of Mississippi professor, was fascinated with the site, particularly because of its relevance to William Faulkner's work. In his 1996 book on Faulkner, he comments that "[a]fter the railroad put an end to navigation on the Tallahatchie, Wyatt disappeared." Then he closes with this experience:

I may have driven the last car across Wyatt Bridge about 1936. The bridge was still intact, but to reach it from Oxford I had to patch gaping holes in a couple of bridges across sloughs in the river bottom with odd rotten planks and logs. By that time the main street of Wyatt was a gully forty feet deep, though old wells, traces of houses and odd bits of broken china still marked the site. Last time I was there (1972), there was hardly a sign of human habitation.[8]

I went there a little later, and there was none.

7 *Holly Springs Guard,* June 19, 1842.

8 Calvin Brown. *A Glossary of Faulkner's South* (New Haven: Yale University Press, 1996), 237.

The Hudsonville Presbyterian Church

Rev. Milton Winter and Wilson Golden

This is a story of a band of mostly Presbyterian settlers of Scots-Irish descent who, beginning in 1836, converged in the gentle wilderness of northeast Marshall County. Powerful historical forces attracted these families from across the Appalachian Mountain region — from the mid-Atlantic British colonies of Pennsylvania, Delaware and Maryland, southward through western Virginia, the Carolinas and Georgia, then westward to the region then known as the American "West." They emigrated from places bearing such mythical names as Fair Forest, Sparta and Iredell along the Appalachian chain to the newly-created states of Tennessee and Alabama, and finally to the Chickasaw area that would became Marshall County, Mississippi, situated just south of the Tennessee border and east of the Mississippi River.

Prominent among the Presbyterians who originally settled Hudsonville some nine miles north of Holly Springs were families who, like so many of the Scots-Irish pioneers who migrated westward, brought their minister with them. He was the Rev. Daniel Lewis Gray, the founder of the Hudsonville Presbyterian Church (1837), as well as two other Marshall County congregations located in Holly Springs (1836) and Waterford (1838).

Born April 24, 1803, in the Abbeville District of South Carolina, Gray was the fourth child and second son of John and Hannah Allen Gray, one of a family of eleven children. He was brought up on his father's farm and, after receiving preparatory training at Union Academy, completed his formal education at Miami University in Ohio. Gray's uncommon energy and deep moral conviction became manifest early in his South Carolina ministry. "I thought," he wrote, "that my appropriate work was that of an evangelist, and I soon determined to remove to the West, which, to some extent, was in a formative state."[1]

In 1831, Gray, his wife and a group of kinfolk and allied settlers, eventually 15 families in all, set out from Fair Forest, South Carolina — first to Tennessee, then Arkansas — before finally settling in northwest Mississippi. Gray's first service as a missionary came in the Western District of Tennessee, where he "preach[ed] as God gave me opportunity":

> During the year I organized one church, and was permitted in the good providence of God
> to witness the outpourings of His Spirit at a camp meeting, when many were added to the Lord.
> In this settlement I suffered much, being exposed in the woods under a cloth tent for three weeks,

---

1 This and all quotes following by Rev. Gray are taken from Robert Milton Winter, *Shadow of a Mighty Rock* (Franklin, TN: Providence House Publishers, 1997) (*Winter Shadow*). The Reverend Winter has written in detail in that study about the Hudsonville church.

when everything was frozen up.

In the fall of 1832, Gray and his small colony moved on to White River, Jackson County, in northeast Arkansas:

> Here, too, I was exposed to all the difficulties and privations incident to a new country. Without houses, or food, or roads, or mills, exposed to freezing weather, I made my settlement among 'Christianized paganism' — hunters, and stock growers and refugees from justice, many of whom had never heard the voice of a minister…. I traveled extensively and was instant in season and out of season. No one who has not been a pioneer, who has not rode [sic] all day through cane, and mud, and water, and lain down on the ground, with his saddle for a pillow, and preached to a company of native population under some shady tree, with their guns in their hands and hats on their heads, can realize for a moment the labors to be done and the sufferings to be endured by the first ministers in a new country.

After living in Arkansas for three years, Gray, his wife, Mary, and three children in tow, headed back east just over 100 miles to settle and engage in farming in the Hudsonville area of the newly-organized Marshall County, Mississippi:

> Thither I removed my family in 1836, and was amongst the first Presbyterian ministers to enter this goodly land. Here I labored much and spent most of seven years as a missionary in hunting up scattered sheep and organizing churches. During this time I was engaged in many glorious revivals, and my own church near Hudsonville, Miss., was blessed with the gracious outpourings of the Spirit of God.

The church Gray established was located on a Chickasaw travel artery known as the "wet weather trail" running from Memphis via Collierville, Mt. Pleasant, Hudsonville, Old Salem, and thence down the Appalachian ridges to Indian towns near the present city of Tupelo and "Pontetok," capital of the Chickasaw territory. A survey conducted by the Bureau of Land Management dated September 3, 1834, shows a "Memphis to Cotton Gin Port Road" that passes approximately a mile and three quarters northeast of what was to become the town of Hudsonville and terminating at a point on the east side of the Tombigbee River a few miles from present day Amory in Monroe County, Mississippi. The trail's name derived from the fact that it could be traveled year-around with no river crossing between old Pontetok and Memphis. Since the Indians were not bridge builders nor did they operate ferries, for several years following the Indian removal the road was extensively used by pioneer settlers during the rainy seasons when streams could not be forded.[2]

---

2 *Ibid.*, 122, and map in Paul Calame Collection.

The town of Hudsonville that grew up around the little Presbyterian Church was named in honor of Virginian John C. Hudson, who early on bought large tracts of land and offered lots for sale around the Grand Junction — Holly Springs stage coach line and mail route relay station which ran through the area. A post office was established April 21, 1836, followed shortly by a tavern and livery stable. There the Hudsonville Presbyterian Church was organized February 5, 1837, under the authority of the Presbytery of Western District, Synod of Memphis. At its founding, the congregation included twenty-four charter members: 16 whites and eight African American slaves, as recorded in the original session book:

> The State of Mississippi. Marshall County. Be it remembered that on the first Sabbath, being the fifth day of February, in the year of Our Lord 1837, the Rev. Daniel L. Gray, a minister of the Gospel of the Presbyterian Church of the United States of America proceeded to organize a Church composed of the following members, denominated the Hudsonville Presbyterian Church, viz: John H. Anderson, Mrs. LeAnn [Lee Ann] R. Anderson, Alexander B. Lane, Mrs. Thomas, William B. Means, Mrs. Rachel Means, Ebenezer Kilpatrick, Mrs. Rebecca Means, Mrs. Mahon, Hannah Means, Mrs. Harmon, Jane Means, Mrs. Mary Lane, Mrs. Sarah Boyd, Henry H. Means, and Mrs. Mary Gray.

Slave charter members were Abraham, Grandison, Hannah, Betsy and Sampson (owned by William B. Means); Peggy (owned by Rev. Gray); and Judy and Scipio (owned by Mrs. Sarah Boyd). At least 36 other African American "servants" are listed in church records during the period 1837-51.[3]

In October 1837, the Hudsonville church was received by the Presbytery of Tombeckbee (a variant spelling of Tombigbee), then part of the Synod of Alabama, at the presbytery's meeting in Starkville, Mississippi. Presbytery minutes reflected that "Rev. D. L. Gray reported that he had organized a Presbyterian Church in Marshall County, Miss., called Hudsonville, consisting of 24 members; another at Holly Springs consisting of 27 members; and one at Oxford consisting of 39 members. On motion [voted] that we receive these churches under our care."

The site of Rev. Gray's original log cabin church and cemetery with a few scattered headstones, less than a mile distant from the town tavern, is all that now marks this once bustling pioneer community. The church and cemetery were located on a slight plateau about one-half mile south of the later 1846 church, just east of the Atway Store at the intersection of modern South Slayden, Kimbrough Chapel, and Duck Pond Roads. The original church is believed to have burned in 1845, its foundation stones visible until

---

3 *Winter Shadow*, 122, 125, 558.

recent times. Although no longer maintained, a cemetery still exists at the site. The graves of Mary W. Gray, wife of the Rev. Gray, and Sarah Means Boyd, Gray's mother-in-law, are here, and stones bearing the names Means, Jones, Mahon, Boyd, Ervin, Erwin, Isom, Rogers, Threadkill, and White remain today.

Several of the Hudsonville pioneers bore the surname Means, long prominent in South Carolina history. Besides a governor of the state (John H. Means, 1850-52), family member Gen. Hugh Means, a ruling elder at the Fair Forest church, had distinguished himself in the Revolution at the pivotal Battle of Cowpens and later commanded a regiment during the War of 1812. Among the Mississippi-bound 1831 party were General Means's second wife and widow, Mrs. Hannah Means [d. 1838], who accompanied their son William B. and wife, Rachel, from Fair Forest to Hudsonville.[4] The roll of charter members of the church included William and Rachel and five other members of the Means family, with two Meanses among the first elders and deacons in the church and at least three of the church's earliest infant baptisms. Means family matriarch Sarah, mother of Rev. Gray's wife Mary, lies at rest near her daughter at the old Atway cemetery. Land for the 1846 church and graveyard was donated by William B. and Sophia Means.

Another close connection among the church's founding families occurred between the Means family and the Andersons of Sparta, Tennessee. In 1845, Hugh Harvey Means of Union County, South Carolina, married Sarah Ann Roberts of Sparta (White County), Tennessee, an Anderson descendant. Sarah's father, John Wayne Roberts, was named after Revolutionary War hero General "Mad" Anthony Wayne, a relative by marriage and fellow native of Chester County, Pennsylvania. In 1824, Roberts moved from Chester County to Sparta, Tennessee, where he met and married Mary Gibbons Anderson the following year. Hugh's father, James Means (1767-1847), one of the original pioneers of Fair Forest, traced his Pennsylvania ancestry back to Antrim, Ireland.[5]

Not surprisingly, the legal profession was well-represented among the early settlers. John Harmon Anderson, a brother of Mary Gibbons Anderson Roberts, was an attorney in Sparta and partner with Alexander Bullard Lane in the firm Lane and Anderson. A generation before Lane formed his Sparta law partnership with Anderson, his father, Turner Lane (1762-1840), was a youthful Revolutionary War patriot and veteran who relocated from his native Virginia to the newly-formed White County, Tennessee, finally settling in Sparta around 1806. There, Lane quickly became a political leader, serving as one of the seven original White County commissioners and by 1816 postmaster of the county courthouse. He also served as the register of deeds for Sparta and surveyed the town's original boundaries.

---

4 *Ibid.*, 45.

5 *Winter Shadow*, 120-21, and Ancestry.com and sources cited therein.

In 1828, Turner Lane's son Alexander married Mary "Polly" Gist and later led a Sparta group of original Hudsonville settlers that included John Harmon and Lee Ann R. Anderson, Mary Anderson Campbell and husband, Dr. Anthony W. Campbell, Reuben Anderson, and Matthias Anderson. Alexander, like his pioneer Sparta father, promptly became a leading citizen of Hudsonville and Marshall County. The leadership of these families in the community becomes evident in the church's earliest session minutes: "Alexander B. Lane was elected, ordained, and installed as the first ruling elder. Additional elders, elected November 25, 1837, were William B. Means and John H. Anderson." Lane was the session's first clerk, succeeded in 1842 by John H. Anderson. After helping found the Hudsonville church, just four years later, Lane and his family moved to Holly Springs, where in 1842 he was elected to the session of the Holly Springs Church. He served until his death on June 30, 1844. In an 1876 oration observing the centennial of the American Declaration of Independence, Mississippi Supreme Court Justice A. M. Clayton spoke of Lane as "profoundly versed in legal learning, a skillful advocate of singular modesty, of unblemished integrity, without guile, a sincere friend, a devout Christian [with] an enviable standing among his peers." His wife, Polly, survived him by 60 years, living until age 97 in 1904.[6]

Another founder of the Hudsonville church was Capt. Ebenezer Kilpatrick. His Scottish grandfather, Joseph William Kilpatrick (1700-1757), began a stair step west North Carolina trek from Orange County (Chapel Hill) through Rutherford County, where a son, Joseph William, Jr., was born in 1738, to Iredell County, in the Statesville area, Captain Kilpatrick's 1781 birthplace. He settled in Marshall County after living in various Tennessee communities following service as a War of 1812 commander in the Tennessee militia. In 1811, Kilpatrick married his first wife, the widow Polina Branch Fore (1785-1852), in Maury County, Tennessee. All but one of their ten children were born in middle and west Tennessee over the period 1812-1829.[7]

Kilpatrick—like the Andersons, Meanses and Lanes—quickly became a Hudsonville community leader and church founder, with close family connections with the other settlers. His son Elihu (1822-1875) in 1854 married Sarah Roberts Means's sister Mary Jane Roberts (1834-1878). Another son, Joseph, practiced law and became editor of *The Holly Springs Guard* in 1843, later marrying Carolyn V. Clark, daughter of General William Clark, treasurer of the state of Mississippi. Following the 1852 death of wife Polina, Ebenezer remarried in 1858 at age 78, sired another child by his 33-year-old wife, and died in October 1861 at the outset of the Civil War.

After eighty eventful years, Ebenezer Kilpatrick was laid to rest in the peaceful church-

---

6 Genealogical collection on Sparta family assembled by Mary Jane Calame Chotard and Ancestry.com.

7 Kilpatrick genealogical collection assembled by Wilson Golden and Ancestry.com.

yard of the Hudsonville Presbyterian Church he helped found 24 years earlier. A visitor to the fenced in Kilpatrick family plot might imagine the patriarch Kilpatrick lying beneath his large broken stone tablet, envisioning a map of Scotland where Kilpatrick ancestral lands were once described as situated "in wood and plain, in meadows and pastures, in pools and mills, in fishings…held…freely, quietly, fully and honourably." In that fabled Scotland of William Wallace, Robert the Bruce, Robert Burns, and Sir Walter Scott, one encounters the Kilpatrick bloodlines over the centuries in Scotland's west — Campbeltown, Argyll, Ayrshire, Ardrossan, Dunbartonshire, and Renfrewshire — eastward to Lanarkshire, Midlothian, and other points near the North Sea. Kilpatrick's Scottish roots ran deep — ancestor Patrick Kilpatrick had been a nobleman in the early 15th century during the reign of England's Henry IV, and Ebenezer's grandfather, Joseph William Kilpatrick, had wed Mary Hunter in 1720 near the hotly-disputed Scots-English border at Glencairn, Dumfrieshire.[8]

Captain Kilpatrick's daughter Elizabeth (1818-1887) married first Joseph Mahon, who is buried at the old cemetery and, following Mahon's death, John McFayden. Her son Joseph Richard Mahon (1838-1914) married Amanda Kirby in 1859. Richard was a member of the Marshall County board of supervisors for 16 years, 12 as board president. Sons and grandsons of Richard and Amanda Mahon followed in their father's footsteps as lawyers, legislators, and judges. Son Hugh Kirby Mahon, Sr., elected a deacon of the Presbyterian Church before age 21, was a founder of the Mississippi State Bar and served multiple terms in the state senate and house of representatives. He also served as a circuit judge. Amanda and Richard's earthly remains are interred at the Hudsonville graveyard along with other close relatives, including a daughter, Annette Morgan, who returned home to assist in her mother's last illness, only to contract a fatal illness herself.

In subsequent years, the Andersons, Lanes, and Robertses all moved to Holly Springs, followed by a group of Mahons somewhat later. These families attached themselves to the stalwart core of the Holly Springs Presbyterian Church. Sons of the founding families attended the classical school established in the town in 1837. Chalmers Institute, as it came to be known after a few years as the University of Holly Springs, lasted until 1879. William Albert Anderson, son of Elder John H. Anderson, was headmaster during the school's final decade.

The Hudsonville Presbyterian Church, after years of declining membership and a brief

---

8 Ancestry.com.

revival in the 1890-1917 period, was omitted from the local presbytery's roll but not dissolved. Pastors from the Holly Springs and other nearby Presbyterian churches conducted periodic services over the following 70 years. Finally, by action of the St. Andrew Presbytery in March 1989, the Hudsonville church was designated a chapel of the nearby Lamar church. In 2014, the church building was sold and dismantled, with its still active 1846 graveyard and the old Atway cemetery the sole remnants of its storied legacy stretching nearly 140 years to those pioneer days of 1836.[9]

9 *Winter Shadow*, 425-33; interview October 2015 by Wilson Golden with Rev. Don L. Wilson, Hudsonville pastor 1965-89. According to Rev. Wilson, the Lamar church session allowed the church building to be moved because it had become structurally "too feeble." Instead, the building was dismantled and at last report is in storage in Holly Springs.

An Ohio Schoolmaster in the Cession

Dr. Seymour David Carpenter

From Genealogical Notes of the Carpenter Family Including the Autobiography and Personal Reminiscences of Dr. Seymour D. Carpenter, Lieutenant Colonel, in the War for the Union, with Genealogical and Biographical Appendix. (Springfield, Ill., Illinois State Journal Co., Printers, 1907.) Edited by Edwin Sawyer Walker, A.M., pp. 87, 92, 94-100

The School-Master, Abroad

After three years — pleasant ones — I finished the course of studies mapped out, and concluded that I must do something. It was very customary in those days for young men after finishing school, to engage as teachers of country schools for a year or two, before entering into active life. The majority of the leading professional men of Lancaster began their careers as school masters. I was entirely willing to follow the beaten track, but was not willing to seek a situation near home. I had inherited the roving disposition of "Old Heinrich," which has stuck to me all though life. I had heard a great deal about the "South" from old men who had made trips to New Orleans by flat-boats, and returned home on horseback by way of Nashville and Louisville. There was a romance about the "Southern Chivalry" very attractive to all the young men. I insisted upon going to the southern country, where I had heard School Masters were in demand, and where wages were high.

Life in Southland.

Memphis in 1846 contained from 12,000 to 15,000 inhabitants, and was the great cotton-mart for West Tennessee and North Mississippi, where, during the busy season, hundreds of teams daily thronged the streets. When I landed several steamers were lying at the wharf, and there seemed to be acres of cotton-bales lining the bank. Not being accustomed to seeing colored people, it seemed to me that pretty much the whole population was black. Hundreds of them were rolling the bales upon the steamers, and there for the first time, I saw the whip used on grown men. The slave-drivers poured a continual stream of oaths, very often combined with the last.

The young man takes lodging in a Memphis hotel. Then he rides into the countryside where he meets an intelligent planter.

Learning why, and for what purpose I was in the country, he said there was a woeful deficiency of educational facilities; that the plantations were large, containing two or three thousand acres each, and the houses were necessarily long distances apart, too far, as a rule, for small children to attend a common school; that they had no tenant farmers, who might want a school for their children. The poor whites, such as I had met at the cross roads, were all illiterate and wanted no schools. Even if they did, he would not have his children associate with such people. That in his own case his wife had taught his daughters until they were old enough to be sent away to school, and that now the daughters were teaching the younger children, until such time as they were advanced enough to be sent away in turn. He did not doubt, however, that by a little looking about, I could find some place where two or three planters could unite together, and have a common teacher for their children. That he was acquainted with the teacher of a school in Holly Springs, the county seat, to whom he would give me a letter, and through him I might find what I wanted. I left my new friend in the morning with many thanks; I had tact enough to perceive that I would offend him by tendering payment, and struck out for Holly Springs, fifteen miles away. When about five miles from the town, at an intersecting road, I was joined by a middle aged gentleman, with an amiable countenance, well dressed, and splendidly mounted. He at once engaged me in conversation, and when I had told who I was, and what I was in search of, he at once said I was the very person he was looking for; that he lived about five miles away, and was going to Holly Springs in search of some one who could teach his sons, and the children of two adjacent planters. I, for once, realized that "the Lord takes care of his own," and mentally considered myself one of the elect. He said that his name was Clopton, "Major John H. Clopton," that he had seven sons, the eldest eighteen and others younger. That his neighbor, Colonel Clayton, had eight children, and that another neighbor, Judge McAlexander, had as many more; that there was an empty house near a church, and about equal distance from each of their homes, which would do for a "School-House," and all that was wanting was a teacher. Then the Major began to look me over and ventured the remark that I seemed pretty young for a teacher. I assumed as old an air as possible, and said I was nearly twenty, and had spent many years in acquiring an education. "Very well," he said; "we will go to Holly Springs and I will have the teacher there examine you. If he says you are competent, I will take you home with me, and you shall have a fair trial." When we arrived n town, I found that the examiner was the same teacher to whom I had the letter of introduction. The examination, which was of a very perfunctory character, was had at once, and I was given a written paper, certifying that I was competent to teach mathematics and the languages, after which the major and I rode back to his home, ten miles from the town. His house was a large double, hewed-log house, a story and a half high, with a twenty-foot space between the buildings, the whole under the same roof, with a shed rood extending back of each of the buildings, where the house was only one story. There were four large rooms below, and two above, and the wide hall, where the family sat most of the time. The building was whitewashed, and stood in a park of fine trees, about twenty acres in extent. Off to one side, about a hundred yards distant, were the negro cabins, about twenty in number; within fifty feet was the kitchen, a large cabin about twenty feet square. Back of the main building, about fifty yards distant, and the same distance from each other were hewed-log houses, one story high, and also negro quarters. This house was comfortably furnished, there being many old mahogany pieces, including a sideboard, and two four-post bedsteads, with canopies, which occupied one of the large front rooms, that served as a guest chamber, as well as a parlor. The bed-spreads and pillows in this show-room were profusely embellished with ruffles. There were no carpets or rugs. Several large mirrors adorned the walls. The Major's wife, a cultured, amiable, pretty woman, and as the mother of eight children, looked very young. The seven boys were all very sturdy chaps, while the youngest, a daughter, was a winning child of three years. In addition, there was the Major's father, a gentleman of the old school, about seventy years of age, and his daughter, just verging on old maidenhood, sprightly and air-ish. The Major's wife, and six younger children, occupied the main house. The old father and the daughter occupied one of the one-story houses, and the two older boys, myself and the overseer, the other. I mention these particulars as I spent the next seven months with that family very happily in that house. Both the Major and his wife treated me in a paternal manner, and I soon became hand and glove with the two older boys. There were about 100 slaves, of both sexes and sizes, who lived in the quarters, each family having a cabin, with a small vegetable garden attached.

The Major at once called upon the other two planters interested in the school. They set to work and had the old cabin near the church renovated and repaired, and in about a week I opened the school with sixteen pupils, five girls, the rest boys, ranging from eigh-teen down to six years. A few had to learn their letters; others studied arithmetic, geogra-phy and grammar. Our school hours were from 9 to 12 and from 1 to 4, with a fif-teen-minute recess forenoon and afternoon. None were far enough advanced to seriously tax my abilities, and very little discipline was required; in fact, I had an easy and pleasant time, with Saturday and Sunday entirely free. My compensation was $50 per month, with board and washing free, which to me seemed a large salary, being twice as much as I would have been paid in Ohio. We breakfasted at seven; a black boy brought us a generous lunch at noon, and we had supper at half-past six. During the week before the school began, I rode with the eldest sons to the store of a neighboring cross roads, where we met an old planter, who admired my horse, and asked if he was for sale. Not having any use for him, I said yes. He asked the price; I said $150. He said the price was too high, but that he had a gold watch worth $150, which he would trade for him, at the same time showing what I thought was a very fine timepiece, and as I had never owned a watch, and needed one for school duties, I thought I would trade, but asked $40 to boot, secretly resolving I would trade, boot or no boot. The gold chain attached particularly took my eye. He said $40 was too much, but he would split the difference and give me $20, and I accepted at once. He took the horse and I the watch and chain. I walked home in great glee, displaying the chain over my vest, to the best advantage, when I met the Major and boasted of my great bargain. He looked at my new property, said the watch and chain was worth at the outside not more than $50 and I had got nothing for my saddle and bridle, which were worth at least $20. I felt very much as did Moses, in the Vicar of Wakefield, after his horse trade. The Major proposed to remonstrate the man, but I concluded to "grin and bear it." The Major was a devout Methodist and held religious services night and morning. He was not an educated man, and did not venture on extemporaneous prayers, but read from a book. Evening prayer was about 8 o'clock, and all the family assembled in the dining room; as the prayer was pretty long, the three younger boys invariably went to sleep during the service. While saying grace at table, the colored boy who kept off the flies with long peacock plumes, while not attending strictly to business, would occasionally give the Major a brush in the face. He would pause, open his eyes, and seize the delinquent by the ear, which sometimes I feared he would tear off, then closing his eyes again, he would conclude. On Saturdays we went hunting or fishing, or, if the weather was not propitious, we sat in the hall, where I read for the Major's edification from d'Aubigne's *History of the Reformation*, it being about the only book, aside from the Bible, in the house. Sunday was a great day; all, old and young, white and black, went to church. The ponderous carriage was brought out, which carried the old gentleman, Mrs. and Miss Clopton, and some of the smaller children. The Major and the rest of us went on horseback; the negroes walked in a procession, headed by one of the oldest, who carried a written pass, allowing them to go and return from church. The Church building was two miles away, and if the day was fair, there would be a large congregation, sometimes as many as fifteen or twenty carriages, for every planter of any standing had one. And the woods were full of horses and swarmed with the colored people. They were not allowed in the church, but back of the pulpit was always a large window which had only a shutter; in fact, none of the windows were glazed, and the colored people occupied rude benches on the outside of the building, where they could hear, but not see very much. Before and after the service there was much visiting among the old folks, and a great deal of flirting among the younger ones. Occasionally the Major would take guests home to dinner, or would himself dine with some of his friends. His house was the headquarters for the preachers, and on his porch I laid in a stock of theology, which has lasted all through my life. There were only two denominations in that part of the country — the Methodist and the Baptist, the former predominating. In the fall there was a Camp-Meeting held about six miles from our house, which lasted a week. School was dismissed; and all repaired to the camp-ground. There were no tents; wood buildings were built about the Square, constructed much as their houses, with a wide hall through the center, and a long kitchen extending in the rear. The Major, his wife and some of the children remained on the ground all the time, while the rest of us went home at night. He kept a four-horse team, hauling daily supplies to the camp-ground, and dined fifty or sixty people daily. It was one of the grand times of my life, for by that time I had made many acquaintances, the Southern young people being very sociable. The colored people held their services in a shed, about a hundred yards from the white people, and I never heard more moving music than their singing, especially at night, when, as they said, "The power got hold of them." I thus had a pretty good opportunity for studying slavery, as it existed on a cotton plantation, fifteen years before the war. I very easily fell into the habit of being waited on, and having servants at my beck and call all the time. In the early part of the season, while the cotton and corn was being cultivated, they did not seem to have a particularly hard time, and during that season very few of them were punished. The bell rang at daylight, they had their breakfast, and immediately went to the fields. If working near their cabins, they came in at noon for an hour, after which the worked till sundown, then came home and cooked their supper. Men, women and children old enough all worked in the fields. They used mules in cultivation exclusively. Each family had a garden where they raised their own vegetables; they were also allowed to raise chickens, and now and then one had a pig. They were allowed to sell their chickens, and in that way got money to buy Sunday clothes, and on Sunday most of them were fairly well dressed. Their hard time began when cotton picking commenced, which was late in September, and lasted until Christmas. The laborers on a cotton plantation could always cultivate more cotton than they could gather, and hence the great need of promptly securing the crop, which would go to waste unless picked in due season. As soon as the cotton bolls began to open, all hands, big and little, were taken to the fields. The hours of work were changed. At daylight the bell sounded and all went to work before having their breakfast; at 10 o'clock a team hauled out their food for the first meal, which consisted of corn bread, bacon and sweet potatoes or greens. They were allowed half an hour for the meal, then they set to work again and continued until it was so dark that they could not see a cotton boll. Each person had a sack suspended about the neck, into which the cotton was put. When the sack was filled it was emptied into an individual basket, which was duly numbered. The amount that each one was required to pick was determined by age and dexterity. There was great difference in the amounts, some having naturally much greater skill than others. The work, I presume, is something like type setting. When each individual amount was once determined, the person was expected to produce that much every night. The overseers blew a horn when the time came to stop, and the baskets were all collected. In the meantime four-horse wagons with wide racks had been brought from the barns. The roll was then called, each in turn bringing his basket, which was weighed and placed upon the wagon. Those persons whose weight fell short were ranged in a line, and as soon as the loading was completed, were subjected to the lash, without regard to sex or age. The amount of punishment was proportioned to his deficiency. The method was to make the sufferer lie on the ground, face downward, while the overseer stood a few yards away and wielded a whip with a short handle and a long leather lash. You could hear the sound of the blows a hundred yards away, and the shrieks of the victims for half a mile.

I was present upon one such occasion, but soon fled the scene, horrified and indignant, and with barely prudence enough to keep my mouth shut. The terrible impression there received made me thence forth a deadly enemy to the institution. The loaded wagons were driven to the Gin-House, where the contents of the baskets were spread out on a large platform, after which the ginned cotton, now cleaned, was carried to the press and baled. After this, the slaves went to their quarters and cooked their meal, not having had anything to eat since the meal at 10 o'clock in the forenoon. They were not able to get to bed until after 9 o'clock. Day by day, this work continued till the end of the picking season, which was about Christmas, at which time they were given a week's vacation, the time being filled during the holidays with great festivities. The Major was a Christian man, and as things went, was not considered a harsh master. He was, to his family and friends, a courteous and kind-hearted gentleman, and towards me, a father could not have been more kind; but down there in the South, the distinction between the whites and blacks was so radical as not to be measured by the same rule.

Georgians to Desoto, Panola, and Tunica

Hubert H. McAlexander

On January 27, 1835, Lemuel Banks wrote back to Georgia from Memphis, Tennessee. He told his wife, Louisa, that he had bought land in "the Nation" but that he did not expect to move for three or four years and that, if her father (James Minor Tait) should settle "in the upper part or near Horn Lake," they would be within fifteen or twenty miles of him (letter in possession of George Banks Ready of Hernando, Mississippi). Just a bit over a year later, as soon as the lands were opened to settlers, Lemuel Banks moved to Desoto County, Mississippi, in the Chickasaw Cession.

Three years later, his brother Henry sold his Georgia plantation and his "elegant" house in Lexington, Georgia, and set out to join his brother. The journey took a month. The family genealogy quotes "one who witnessed the picturesque scene":

> It was an imposing and interesting spectacle. First came 'my lady' [nee Judith Oliver] with three young children and maid in the family carriage; which was followed by numbers of 'white topped' canvassed-covered wagons bearing negro women and children, and the furniture and household stuff. After these came the men and boys driving the herd of cattle and droves of hogs. The slaves were all comfortably clad and well shod… Wherever night found them there they camped usually near a stream of water or a pioneer's cabin where the wife and children might lodge. The ruddy glow of the camp-fire against the blackness of the night, the moving figures of those feeding the tired animals, the sizzling of frying bacon, the bubbling and boiling of big coffee pots sending out rich aroma on the sweet night air, and the lusty pones of corn hoe cakes, these and many other details have been remembered for nearly seventy years.

Henry Banks settled near Hernando.[1] He died in 1846, leaving only two daughters who lived to adulthood and married. His brother Lemuel Banks followed him in 1854, leaving four sons. Within the decade his widow, Louisa Tait Banks, married Charles Meriwether, another of the Georgia emigrants.[2]

A map of the Broad River Settlement in Georgia shows a group of prominent landowners spread over three counties—Oglethorpe, Wilkes, and Elbert. Many emigrated to the Chickasaw Cession. They settled in Desoto (the county honoring Hernando Desoto, who discovered the Mississippi River either in that county or a bit further north, near

---

1 *The Genealogical Record of the Banks Family of Elbert County, Georgia*, 3rd edition, ed. by Sarah Banks Franklin (Danielsville, GA: Heritage Papers, 1972), 331.

2 James Edmonds Saunders. *Early Settlers of Alabama* (New Orleans: L. Graham and Sons, 1899), 447-448.

Memphis), Panola (south of Desoto and given as its name the Choctaw word for "cotton"), and Tunica (on the river and named for the Tunica tribe who inhabited the area in the late 1600s). Those involved in the migration to the Chickasaw Cession include the Banks, Tait, McGehee, Oliver, Meriwether, and Coxe families. Most were intermarried, either by that time or later. For that reason, this essay becomes a sea of names. The Coxes went to Marshall County. All the rest went to Desoto and Panola. Added to these are descendants of Shelton White of Elbert County, who came to Desoto and Tunica. With some few exceptions, the families were Methodists. They were or became quite rich.[3]

Besides a daughter who married a Banks, and, later, a Meriwether, James Minor Tait also had a son, Dr. George Gallatin Tait. He married Ann McGehee (1819-1854), daughter of Hugh McGehee and Sarah T. White, and settled in Panola County. After her death, he married the Vermont-born Mrs. Martha Jane Starks Boardman. Thus he married two great aunts of the active literary figure and McGehee descendant, Stark Young, drama critic, translator, essayist, and novelist.[4]

In 1860, these Georgia families were important planters in Desoto, Panola, and Tunica counties. In Desoto were found Abner McGehee, James Oliver Meriwether, V. H. Meriwether, Simeon Oliver (1825-1874), James Minor Tait, and Thomas William White. In Panola were W.C. Banks, Dr. George G. Tait (1813-1865), John Scott McGehee (1789-1870), and his sons, James Blanton McGehee (1826-1866) and Edward F. McGehee (1816-1879). In Tunica County was W. W. White. Stark Young memorializes all. But Young makes the McGehees the major symbol of the Southern tradition.[5]

The grand figure in the McGehee family was Hugh McGehee (1793-1855), Young's great-grandfather, who moved into the Cession in 1836. In *The Pavilion*, Young has this to say about this revered figure's attitude toward slavery:

> Like his brother and like many of his plantation class, my great-grandfather did not believe in slavery; the very idea of it was a torment to him, but the system was too strong for him. (26)

Keeping that statement in mind, read carefully the next selection and absorb it fully. It is taken from the book *Thirty Years a Slave*, published in 1897 in Milwaukee. It was written by Louis Hughes, a slave of Hugh McGehee's nephew (married to Hugh McGehee's granddaughter).

---

3 Saunders, 334 and passim. Keith A. Baca, *Native American Place Names in Mississippi* (Jackson: University Press of Mississippi, 2007), 78, 124.

4 Stark Young, *The Pavilion* (New York: Charles Scribner's Sons, 1951), 96. Jane N . and Ethel C. Woodall Grider, *McGehee Descendants*, 3rd ed. (Baltimore: Gateway Press, 1991), 286-290, 279-280, 171.

5 Joseph Karl Menn, *Large Slaveholders of the Deep South*, 1860 (Ann Arbor, Michigan: Xerox University Microfilms, 1974), II: 981-985.

Thirty Years a Slave

Louis Hughes

Introduction and commentary by
Hubert H. McAlexander

"I was born in Virginia in 1832, near Charlottesville, in the beautiful valley of the Rivanna River," Hughes begins his narrative. "My father was a white man and my mother a negress, the slave of one John Martin." But Hughes moves quickly to his experience, at age twelve, of being sold at the Richmond Slave market to a Mississippi planter.

The white man was Edmund McGehee (though Hughes designates him as Edward), soon called "Boss." He was of the family of the writer, theater critic, and Agrarian, Stark Young. In his two best known novels, Young used the McGehees as representatives of the Southern agrarian aristocracy. This excerpt resonates with several essays in this volume. *Thirty Years a Slave* was published by South Side Printing Company in Milwaukee in 1897. I was told of the book's existence by Sledge Taylor of Como, a McGehee descendant.

After a train ride to Atlanta, "Boss" takes his carriage and the slaves walk twenty miles a day, to arrive at the McGehee house at Pontotoc on Christmas Eve. The house Louis Hughes describes thusly:

The "great house" as the dwelling of the master was called, was two stories high, built of huge logs, chinked and daubed and whitewashed. It was divided, from front to rear, by a hall twenty-five and twelve feet wide, and on each side of the hall, in each story, was one large room with a large fireplace. There were but four rooms in all, yet these were so large that they were equal to at least six of our modern rooms. The kitchen was not attached to the main building, but was about thirty feet to the rear. This was the common mode of building in the south in those days. The two bedrooms upstairs were very plain in furnishings, but neat and comfortable, judged by the standard of the times. A wing was added to the main building for the dining room. In the rear of the kitchen was the milk or dairy house, and beyond this was the smoke house for curing the meat. In line with these buildings, and still further to the rear, was the overseer's house. Near the milk house was a large tree, and attached to the trunk was a lever; and here is where the churning was done, in which I had always to assist. This establishment will serve as a sample of many of those on the large plantations in the south. The main road from Pontotoc to Holly Springs, one of the great thoroughfares of the state and a stage route, passed near the house, and through the center of the farm. On each side of this road was a fence, and in the corners of both fences, extending for a mile, were planted peach trees, which bore excellent fruit in great profusion.

House Servant and Errand Boy

My first work in the morning was to dust the parlor and hall and arrange the dining room. It came awkward to me at first, but after the madam told me how, I soon learned to do it satisfactorily. Then I had to wait on the table, sweep the large yard every morning with a brush broom, and go for the mail once a week. I used to get very tired, for I was young and consequently not strong. Aside from these things which came regularly, I had to help the madam in warping the cloth. I dreaded this work, for I always got my ears boxed if I did not or could not do the work to suit her. She always made the warp herself and put it in, and I had to hand her the thread as she put it through the harness, I would get very tired at this work, and, like any child, wanted to be at play, but I could not remember that the madam ever gave me that privilege. Saddling the horse was at first troublesome to me, but Boss was constant in his efforts to teach me, and after many trials, I learned the task satisfactorily to the master and to bring the horse to the door when he wished to go out for business or pleasure. Riding horseback was common for both ladies and gentlemen, and sometimes I would have to saddle three or more horses when Boss, the madam, a friend or friends desired a ride. Bird hunting parties were common and were greatly enjoyed, by the young people especially. Boss always invited some of the young people of the neighborhood to these parties and they never failed to put in an appearance. Williams, Bradford, and Freeman were the sons of rich planters, and were always participants in this sport, and their young lady friends joined in it as on-lookers. The young men singing and whistling to the birds, I in the meantime setting the net. As soon as I got the net in order they would approach the birds slowly, driving them into it. There was great laughter and excitement if they were successful in catching a fine flock.

Cruel Treatment

I was but a lad, yet I can remember well the cruel treatment I received. Some weeks it seemed I was whipped for nothing, just to please my mistress' fancy. Once, when I was sent to town for the mail and started back, it was so dark and rainy my horse got away from me and I had to stay all night in town. The next morning when I got back home I had a severe whipping, because the master was expecting a letter containing money and was disappointed in not receiving it that night, as he was going to Panola to spend Christmas. However, the day came and all the family went except me. During the time they were gone the overseer whipped a man so terribly with the "bull whip" that I had to go for the doctor, and when Dr. Heningford, the regular family physician, came, he said it was awful—such cruel treatment, and he complained about it. It was common for a slave to get an "over-threshing," that is, to be whipped too much. The poor man was cut up so badly all over that the doctor made a bran poultice and wrapped his entire body in it. This was done to draw out the inflammation. It seems the slave had been sick, and had killed a little pig when he became well enough to go to work, as his appetite craved hearty food, and he needed it to give him strength for his tasks. For this one act, comparatively trivial, he was almost killed. The idea never seemed to occur to the slave holders that these slaves were getting no wages for their work and, therefore, had nothing with which to procure what, at times, was necessary for their health and strength—palatable and nourishing food. When the slaves took anything the masters called it stealing, yet they were stealing the slaves' time year after year.

About 1850, Edmund McGehee bought a plantation in Bolivar County on the Mississippi at the far southwest end of the Cession and moved his planting operation there. He settled his family in Memphis. There he built a fine two-story brick columned mansion named "Greenwood." The staff consisted of a cook, chambermaid, lady's maid, nurse, wet nurse, dairy maid, laundress, gardener, and coachman. An addition position was house boy and butler, one filled by Louis Hughes. He tried four times to run away, each time being caught and returned.

At end of the years of slavery, Hughes published "A Word for My Old Master."

In closing this account of my years of bondage, it is, perhaps, but justice to say of my old master that he was in some respects kinder and more humane than many other slaveholders. He fed well, and all had enough to wear, such as it was. It is true that the material was coarse, but it was suited to the season, and, therefore, comfortable, which could not truthfully be said of the clothing of the slaves of other planters. Not a few of these did not have sufficient clothes to keep them warm in winter; nor did they have sufficient nourishing and wholesome food. But while my master showed these virtues, similar to those which a prudent farmer would show in the care of his dumb brutes, he lacked in that humane feeling which should have kept him from buying and selling human beings and parting kindred—which should have made it impossible for him to have permitted the lashing, beating, and lacerating of his slaves, much more the hiring of an irresponsible brute, by the year, to perform this barbarous service for him. The McGees [sic] were charitable—as they interpreted the word—were always ready to contribute to the educational and missionary funds, while denying, under the severest penalties, all education to those most needing it, and all true missionary effort—the spiritual enlightenment for which they were famishing. Then our masters lacked that fervent charity, the love of Christ in the heart, which if they had possessed they could not have treated us as they did. They would have remembered the golden rule: "Do unto others as ye would that men should do to you." Possessing absolute power over the bodies and souls of their slaves, and grown rich from their unrequited toil, they became possessed by the demon of avarice and pride. And lost sight of the most vital of the Christly qualities.

He ends the volume with this paragraph:

I have endeavored, in the foregoing sketch, to give a clear and correct idea of the institution of human slavery, as I witnessed and experienced it—its brutality, its degrading influence upon both master and slave, and its utter incompatibility with industrial improvement and general educational progress. Nothing has been exaggerated or set down in malice, although the scars which I still bear upon my person, and in the wounds of spirit which will never wholly heal, there might be found a seeming excuse for such a course. Whatever of kindness was shown me during the years of my bondage, I still gratefully remember, whether it came from the white master or fellow slave; and for the recognition which has been so generously accorded me since the badge of servitude was removed, I am profoundly and devoutly thankful.

Closely identified with the Chickasaw Cession is Pontotoc County's "Lochinvar."
Historic Architecture in Mississippi by Mary Wallace Crocker

PART II:
HIGH COTTON

THE GORDONS OF "LOCHINVAR" IN PONTOTOC COUNTY

HUBERT H. McALEXANDER

Southerners like to think that the old social system was modeled on the English aristocracy. But it may be even better to trace your family back to Scotland, the lairds, the clans, the tartans. North Mississippi offers many examples, but it boasts one founding citizen who came directly from that bonny place and gave his home a bonny name.

Robert Gordon (1788-1867) was born in Minnegaff, Scotland, and emigrated to the United States in 1810, settling first in Nashville, Tennessee. During the 1820s, he moved to the frontier town Cotton Gin Port on the upper Tombigbee River, near the present-day town of Amory in Monroe County. The upper Tombigbee became the eastern border of Chickasaw territory, and Gordon established a store at Cotton Gin Port and began to make his fortune.[1]

When the Chickasaws ceded their land in 1832, Gordon and John Bell, son of the Rev. Robert Bell, the Cumberland Presbyterian missionary who had begun a mission and a school in the early 1820s near Cotton Gin Port, formed a speculating partnership. In 1835, Gordon founded the town of Aberdeen in Monroe County, though he never lived there. He chose instead Pontotoc, where the government had established the Chickasaw Land Office.[2]

According to a fulsome essay on the Gordon family, the Chickasaw nation was ruled by King Ish-taho-topa and Queen Puc-caun-la. During Gordon's years in Cotton Gin Port, he became the close friend of Chief Levi Colbert, also known as Itawamba. The Chickasaw lore continues. The section of land that he purchased is now about two miles

---

1 . Jack D. Elliott, Jr., Review of *Gordons of Lochinvar* in *Tombigbee Country Magazine*, April 2009. See also Jack D. Elliott, Jr., and Mary Ann Wells, *Cotton Gin Port: A Frontier Settlement on the Upper Tombigbee* (Jackson: Mississippi Historical Society, 2003).

2 Mary Elizabeth Young, *Redskins, Ruffleshirts, and Rednecks* (Norman: University of Oklahoma Press, 1961), 116-118. Elliott and Wells, *Cotton Gin Port*, 100-102, 68-69.

south of the town Pontotoc. He purchased it from Mollie Gunn, a Chickasaw married to a Tory from Virginia.[3]

Robert Gordon built a fine mansion there and named it Lochinvar for the hero of Sir Walter Scott's popular poem "Marmion" (1808). It was and is a fine house. The WPA-sponsored *Mississippi: A Guide to the Magnolia State* (New York: Hastings House, 1949), originally published in 1938, gives this description:

> Lochinvar is two-and-a-half stories in height and contains a broad central stair [spiral] and eight high-ceilinged rooms, each 22 feet square. A spiral stair leads to the third floor. At the rear, separate from the house, is a brick kitchen that contains the original brick Dutch oven. Timber used in the house is heart pine and the framework is of solid hand-hewn pine. The columns of the front portico are of the Roman Doric order and rise two stories in height in support of a classic pediment. (462)

When I visited the house about 1959, I was impressed with the fine millwork and period color scheme. Different levels of woodwork, in the door and window framing and in the cornices, were painted different colors. I recall particularly a striking mauve and brown treatment. Another interesting feature was that, in the bedrooms, small doors closed to make one window space a small and private dressing room.

Col. Robert Gordon, as he was styled, lived in regal ease in the house, though both he and later, his son, had their large plantations in Monroe County. The expert on the Gordons and librarian at Aberdeen library, the diminutive Miss Lucille Peacock, had Gordon's picture on the wall. According to Jack Elliott, she enjoyed pointing to the overweight colonel and wondering just what kind of horse could carry him.[4]

Gordon's partner John Bell was appointed, in May of 1833, the first surveyor general of the Chickasaw lands. But in February of 1838, after Bell's resignation, the appointment went to Patrick Henry Fontaine, loyal Democrat who had come down from Virginia. Then Bell rather mysteriously disappears from history. That is not the case for Gordon's son.[5]

Col. Robert Gordon was married twice, first to Joanna Hobson, and second to Mary Elizabeth Walton of Cotton Gin Port. He had living issue only by his second marriage, a son, James Gordon (1833-1912), an 1855 graduate of the University of Mississippi. At the outbreak of war in 1861, James organized a cavalry company, the Chickasaw Rangers,

---

3 Sketch of James Gordon in Goodspeed's *Biographical and Historical Memoirs of Mississippi* (Chicago: Goodspeed Publishing Co., 1891), 1:805-807.

4 Joseph Karl Menn, *Large Slaveholders of the Deep South, 1860* (Ann Arbor: Xerox University Microfilms, (1974), II:1,105. Elliott, Review of Gordons of Lochinvar.

5 See Elliott essay "The Pontotoc Land Office" at the beginning of this volume

and led them off as captain. His father, Col. Gordon, left Lochinvar to his son and moved to Okolona. James Gordon was elected to the Mississippi legislature in 1858, 1866, and 1878, and to the state senate in 1904. Following the death of U. S. Senator McLaurin in 1909, he was appointed to fill the term of sixty days in 1909-1910. He had mortgaged Lochinvar three times before he lost it in 1893, and moved to Okolona.[6]

Soon after his college graduation, James Gordon had married Caroline Virginia Wiley, daughter of Yancy Wiley and Ann Eliza Thompson of "Cedar Hill Farm" in Lafayette County, proudly a niece of the Hon. Jacob Thompson of Oxford, briefly a member of James Buchanan's cabinet. The Gordons had a daughter, Annie, and after his wife's death in 1903, James Gordon married the next year Miss Ella Neilson of Oxford. There was no issue from this autumnal union. James Gordon was also a poet, who left a volume of verse, *The Old Plantation and Other Poems* (1909).[7]

Lochinvar was owned for most of the 20th century by members of the Fontaine family, another historic Pontotoc line. In 1966, the property was bought by a Pontotoc County native, Dr. Forrest Tutor, who has cherished and sustained the place over the decades. Jack Elliott best describes what happened and Dr. Tutor's mettle and care:

> On the night of Saturday, February 24, 2001, a storm system generated a tornado that swept from southwest to southeast across Pontotoc County leaving in its wake a swathe of destroyed homes, fallen trees, and dead people. Lochinvar was in the direct path and was left so devastated that most considered it to be unsalvageable. However, Dr. Tutor was undeterred and set out on a long campaign of rebuilding and restoration, eventually bringing Lochinvar back to its original condition.

That is not the end of the story, for in 2008 Dr. Tutor, then in his 80s, published *Gordons of Lochinvar*. Dr. Tutor proudly leads people thorough the great, historically important structure to this day. He is the true hero of Lochinvar.[8]

---

6 All biographical information is taken from Forrest T. Tutor, M. D., *Gordons of Lochinvar* (Lulu.com Publishing, 2008).

7 Notes by Jack D. Elliott, Jr., from *Gordons of Lochinvar*. Notes sent to HHM, December 30, 2016.

8 Mary Wallace Crocker, *Historic Architecture in Mississippi* (Jackson: University Press of Mississippi, 1973), 144. Elliott, review of *Gordons of Lochinvar*.

Shortly before the Civil War, Thomas E. B. Pegues built this mansion, after a design
by Calvert Vaux, on a hundred-acre plot on the north side of Oxford.
Mary Wallace Crocker *Historic Architecture in Mississippi* (University of Mississippi Press, 1973)

The Pegues Skein

Hubert H. McAlexander

The Pegues family was once a vast South Carolina skein covering northern Mississippi. I grew up with a fabulous sense of them. Again and again I heard, "No one was ever good enough to marry a Pegues, but another Pegues." And there was also an eccentric strain. "That's the Pegues in them," I was told. The source of all this was no doubt my close older friend Charles Nunnally Dean, whose mother was kin to Robert Hicks Wall of Marshall County, who married Martha Pegues in the early 1830s.

The first to settle in this state was the South Carolinian Malachi Pegues (1780-1847), who was living near Sylvestria Methodist Church (roughly five miles northeast of Holly Springs) by its 1837 establishment. In just a few years, he and another trustee of the church, Nathaniel Jarrett, moved to fertile lands on Spring Creek, southeast of the county seat. This was the Reserve, owned originally by the powerful mixed-blood Love family. The U. S. Indian agent, A. W. Upshaw, called Col. Benjamin Love "the most powerful man in the [Chickasaw] nation." Educated in Washington City, Benjamin Love was the official interpreter during all the years of Cession negotiation and subsequent settlement.

Malachi Pegues purchased Love's land, on which stood his two-story house, after Colonel Love decided that it was time to join the other Chickasaws in the West. Malachi Pegues lived there for six years until his death, and two accounts mention an Indian motif on the walls of the house. In *My Father's House*, Mattie Pegues Wood writes of the walls "decorated with Indian paintings." In the 19th century, neighbor Jarrett's daughter commented on the wedding of a Miss Pegues in the mid 1840s held in a chamber with paintings of "Indians on ponies and on foot, with tomahawks, bows and arrows, and wild animals in trees and woods." This was a decoration added by Love when the house was built, she adds. I posit that the room was probably papered with the Zuber wallpaper depicting a Frenchman's version of the American Indians.

Malachi's wife, Charlotte Johnson, died on an 1837 trip to Tennessee. In 24 years of marriage, she and Malachi had 15 children. Malachi was described by a daughter-in-law as "a tall and fine looking, very handsome — in every sense of the word a gentleman- dignified, polite, and affable, and always genteel in his appearance — a man of fine sense and observation and a true Christian." He was a staunch Methodist. Pegues left a long, literate will naming all the children, but let's take them in birth order.

1. Oliver H. Pegues (1807-1875) married Ann Eliza Alston and was the first to settle in Marshall County, Mississippi. He died in Gregg County, Texas. Issue.

2. Alexander Hamilton Pegues (1808-1871) married in 1844 his first cousin Rebecca Anne Evans Pegues, daughter of Claudius Butler Pegues and Eliza Hodge Evans of "The Cedars," Dallas County, Alabama. An important planter and political figure in Lafayette County, Mississippi, Alexander Pegues will be discussed more fully below.

3. Martha Pegues (1810-1885) married, in 1832, Robert Hicks Wall, a wealthy planter of "Cloverland," near Sylvestria, Marshall County. Their lineage comes down to the present. Of the several children of the union, the great beauty was Charlotte, who in 1857 married Edward Cheatham, an important railroad official of Tennessee.

4, Henry Randolph Pegues (1811-1850), listed as a physician in the 1850 Lafayette County census, married Mary E. Coleman and had two children, Coleman and Joella. After Henry's death in California, Joella was reared in the Oxford home of her aunt Charlotte and uncle, T. E. B. Pegues. In 1862 Joella married Manes Shegog, son of the builder of the Faulkner house in Oxford. She lived to be 89.

5. Eliza Jane Pegues (1813-1843) married, in 1835, Dr. Thomas Ingram of Madison County, Tennessee. She died, and her daughter Charlotte Vernon Ingram (1839-1906) was reared in her grandfather's house in Marshall County. She married, in Oxford in 1866, Thomas Dwight Witherspoon, Presbyterian minister. They had several children and lived in Louisville, Kentucky.

6. Charlotte Johnson Pegues (1814-1883) married her first cousin Thomas Evans Bedegood Pegues (1812-1874), son of Christopher Butler Pegues of "The Cedars," Dallas County, Alabama. Thomas Pegues came to Lafayette County, Mississippi, about 1850 and settled on a plantation at Lafayette Springs. He built the grandest house in Oxford. See the discussion in greater detail below.

7. Malachi Murphey Pegues (1816-1872) never married and was a successful planter in Lafayette County.

8. Mary Johnson Pegues (1818-1877) married, in 1845, Phillip Jenkins, of prominent

stock near Chulahoma in Marshall County, the Pryor-Alexander connection. A elder in the Presbyterian church, he conducted a successful male school, Philadelphia Academy (Phillip Jenkins Letter Book, collection of Kenneth Rose of Holly Springs). Issue.

9. Harriett Strong Pegues (1820-1863) kept an important diary at the Love-Pegues plantation, now in the Marshall County Historical Museum in Holly Springs. She married, in 1850 as his second wife, James Lewis Phillips, successful Chulahoma planter, and had several children.

10 James Johnson Pegues (1821-1822).

11. Jane Johnson Pegues (1824-1880), the beauty of the family, married, in 1842, as his second wife, Col. William Blanton Lumpkin, graduate of the University of Georgia, and one of the great planters of Marshall County. During the Civil War he left unfinished a brick mansion with sandstone foundation named Morro Castle, four miles south of Holly Springs. Issue.

12. Ann Lucy Pegues (1825-1881) married, in 1848, William W. White (1811-1866) and settled in Tunica County, where, by 1860, White was a leading planter. Their first child, Col. Zachary Taylor White (1850-1915), lived on Linden Avenue in Memphis. He married, in 1905, his third wife and his cousin, Lottie Pegues, daughter of Nicholas Pegues and Mary Catherine Saunders, and had one child, Lottie Vernon White. (See p. 103 for more details.)

13. James Johnson Pegues (1827-1873) was presented in an 1858 Rebecca Pegues Pegues diary entry as "a source of trouble and anxiety to [his oldest brother] & all of the family. He has sown the wind and is reaping the whirlwind." See Pegues Diaries and Letters. He married Susan Blair, then Louisa Schiligs, and lived in Water Valley. Issue.

14. William Claudius Pegues (1830-1884) was a planter in Marshall County. He was a graduate of the Chalmers Institute of Holly Springs and earned a bachelor's degree from the University of Mississippi in 1851. He was a member of Winburn's Company and Company G, Fourth Mississippi Cavalry, Confederate States of America. he is buried in Oxford.

15. Marlborough Claudius Pegues (1831-1898)was a planter in Marshall County, a graduate of Chalmers Institute of Holly Springs. He earned a bachelor's degree from

the University of Mississippi and was the founder of the Rainbow Fraternity, which later became Delta Tau Delta. He was a member of the Ninth Mississippi Infantry, then Company K, Second Kentucky Cavalry under John Hunt Morgan, Confederate States of America. He was a Methodist minister at Snow Creek Church. He married Emily Rogers, and they had no children. An obituary notes that in late life he devoted himself to his ministry and his books.

In contrast to Malachi Pegues, who experienced heavy losses before he came to the Chickasaw Cession, was his wealthy younger brother. Christopher Butler Pegues (1789-1846) and his wife, Eliza Hodges Evans, left South Carolina unencumbered with debt and settled comfortably on a plantation called The Cedars in Dallas County, Alabama. They had 15 children, three of whom came to the Chicksaw Cession and were prominent in Lafayette County history.

Lafayette County Children of
Christopher Butler Pegues and Eliza Hodges Evans

Thomas Evans Bedegood Pegues (1812-1874), graduate of the University of South Carolina, married, in 1834, his first cousin, Charlotte Johnson Pegues (1814-1883), daughter of the Marshall County pioneer Malachi Pegues. Thomas Pegues came to Lafayette County about 1850 and settled on a plantation at Lafayette Springs. Then he returned to Cheraw, South Carolina, to manage land he had inherited from two aunts. In 1855, he was a founder of the University of the South at Sewanee, Tennessee.

A bit later he moved back to Mississippi, and he and his brother-in-law Alexander Hamilton Pegues bought 100 acres at the top of North Street in Oxford, planning to build town houses. Alexander never acted, but Thomas chose an Italianate design by noted architect Calvert Vaux and began building a mansion rumored to cost $14,000, the grandest house in Oxford. The house on its 100 acres obviously inspired *Absalom, Absalom*. In 1860, he followed Alexander Pegues as a member of the Board of Trustees, University of Mississippi. At the start of the war, he held 103 slaves, and by 1864 he was a captain in the Confederate army. A later owner gave the mansion, originally called Edgecomb, the name Ammadelle. Thomas E. B. Pegues and his wife had nine children. He died in Oxford in 1874.

Rebecca Anne Evans Pegues (1816-1889) married, in 1844, her first cousin, Alexander Hamilton Pegues (1808-1871), Malachi Pegues's most important son in the region. Sacrificing the collegiate training that seemed his assured future, Alexander took over the management of his father's business affairs upon the move to Mississippi and then settled in a plantation located on Woodson's Ridge, seven miles northeast of Oxford in Lafayette

County. He lived there as a bachelor, and Dr. Thomas Dudley Isom, another early settler, remembered his first sight of Sandy Pegues "with a gun on his shoulder and a pack of hounds at his heels" (quoted in *My Father's Family*, p. 151). Finally he married his cousin, Rebeeca Pegues. He represented his county in the Mississippi senate and was appointed in 1848 to the first Board of Trustees of the University of Mississippi. Reared a Methodist, he became an Episcopalian upon his marriage and a member of the first vestry of St. Peter's Episcopal Church in 1851. In 1860, he was the largest cotton planter in the county with 107 slaves. He died in 1871, and his close friend L. Q. C. Lamar delivered his eulogy.

Rebecca Pegues Pegues was a bluestocking, a great reader of history, fiction, and philosophy, and of the Bible, whose lessons she applied closely to the care of her slaves. She was an exceptional gardener, and she named her plantation Orange Hill, for the dramatic flowering of the Osage orange hedges that she planted.

In my mid-twentieth century youth, hedgerows of bois d'arc (Osage orange) trees were still found often in the landscape. One Marshall County plantation keeps its original name, Hedge Farm. The most dramatic hedgerow in the county was immediately outside Holly Springs on Peyton Road (the road was named for its destination, a port created in the 1830s on the Mississippi River in Tunica County). The border of trees on Peyton Road is no more — the old crooked trees cut down and the sand road bed long ago "improved." L. A. Smith III and I hiked over the old sand bed many times in youth. I have a painting that he did of the old road.

The second son and namesake of Rebecca and Alexander Pegues, A. H. Pegues (1857-1938), merchant of Columbus, married Elizabeth Hamlin Lumpkin (1870-1932). Their daughter Martha Maxwell Pegues Wood is the author of the family history, *My Father's Family*.

Mrs. Rebecca Pegues Pegues, a devout Episcopalian and supporter of St. Peter's Church in Oxford, provided for the steeple erected in 1893. She kept a diary that is an important historical reference. It is reproduced in Pegues' *Diaries and Letters*, a copy of which is available in the University of Mississippi archives. Note that both Pegues books are self-published typescripts.

Nicholass Bedegood Pegues (1821-1894), a graduate of the University of South Carolina, married in 1852 his cousin Mary Catherine Saunders (1833-1914). After his marriage, he settled a plantation near Lafayette Springs and became a prosperous planter. Over a long period, the Nicholas Pegues connection displayed another Pegues trait, family loyalty and support of family members having financial difficulty.

The Nicholas Pegueses had ten children, the youngest being Lottie Pegues (1874-1956), who married, as his third wife, her cousin Col. Zachary Taylor White (1850-1915) of Memphis and a wealthy planter of Tunica County, son of William W. White and Ann

Pegues. Col. White and Lottie Pegues had Lottie Vernon White, a popular student at Ole Miss and friend of William Faulkner. In 1923, he drew a much-reproduced sketch of the two of them dancing (though he was not a dancer), named "The Post Office Blues." She married Guy Turnbow, and had the present Guy Turnbow, who has graciously given us access to *My Father's Family* and the book of Pegues diaries and letters. In 1905, Nicholas Pegues' widow, Mary Saunders Pegues, bought a cottage on University Avenue in Oxford, now called The Magnolias, and still occupied by her Turnbow descendants.

No white person of the name now lives in northern Mississippi, but a number of black citizens remain. Pegueses played dramatic roles in the early decades of the Chickasaw Cession, and their blood continues to run in all classes and races of our region.

HILL COUNTY PLANTERS IN THE DELTA

HUBERT H. MCALEXANDER

The Chickasaw Cession covered only one Delta county — Tunica, although land in two more (Coahoma and Bolivar) was opened in the Cession act. Hill counrty planters went early to the mighty river in Tunica County, and made the Cession stretch from Commerce Landing on the Mississippi to Cotton Gin Port on the Tombigbee.

An early and wealthy and important, but now somewhat mysterious, figure is Ransom Hinton Byrne (1804-1864). Born in North Carolina, he married two daughters of the Virginians Joseph Tweedy Cocke and Sarah Wade Winston. Both weddings were in Madison County, Tennessee. Immediately after the Cession lands became available, Byrne settled at Commerce. According to the Robert Lowry and William H. McCardle's *History of Mississippi* (1891), Commerce was the first town in the county. At its founding, many believed that it would be "a place of large commercial importance," but in a short span it was claimed by the Mississippi. The original county seat, also on the river, was Peyton. An obscure reminder of this extinct town is a two-mile stretch of road southwest of Holly Springs (in my youth a sand road) named Peyton Road.[1]

Ransom H. Byrne was a well-known public figure in Tunica County, serving in the Mississippi House of Representatives 1844-52 and 1861. He and his family (his second wife and seven children) are found in the 1850 census of that county. He was also connected with Holly Springs. In 1845, he deeded to the town land for its cemetery. In 1853 for $10,000, he bought the grand brick house at the south end of Memphis Street in Holly Springs, built by William F. Mason about 1840 (Marshall County Deed Book S:460).[2]

Among the major planters in Tunica County in 1860 were Byrne and A. J. Polk, a Tennessean from a prominent family. Other big investors were Col. James Brown of Oxford and two of his sons-in-law, William Francis Avent and A. T. Shotwell. Carroll Leatherman's grandmother told her that, at the time of the Civil War, citizens of the important hill towns considered Tunica County "little more than a swamp" and still "real pioneer

---

1 Robert Lowry and William H.. McCardle, *History of Mississippi* (Jackson: R. H. Henry & Co., 1891), 588. Virginia Webb Cocke, *Cockes and Cousins*, Vol. II of *Descendants of Thomas Cocke* (c1639-1697) (Ann Arbor, Michigan: Edwards Brothers, Inc., 1974), 64; Carroll Seabrook Leatherman, *Goodbye Ole Miss* (Memphis: Toof Printing Co., 2003), 72.

2 Robert Milton Winter, ed., *Among Some Excellent Company* (Holly Springs, MS: Spring Hollow Publishers, 2003): 282. Throughout this essay, I have drawn on Joseph Karl Menn's dissertation, "Large Slaveholders of the Deep South, 1860" (Ann Arbor, Michigan: Xerox University Microfilms, 1974), copy in University of Georgia Library.

territory." But a great deal of money has been made there over the years.[3]

On January 4, 1859, Ransom Hinton Byrne of Tunica County sold the Holly Springs mansion at the south end of Memphis Street to Rugby, Blair and Company of New Orleans (X:235). The $5,000 increase in price of the property may be an indication that the two-story wing (two rooms and hall) and the six-column portico were added during Byrne's ownership. Renting the mansion at the time of Van Dorn's Raid, December 20, 1862, were Carrington Mason and his wife, Maria Boddie Mason, of Memphis. When Byrne's son Andrew joined the Confederate cavalry in 1863, he gave his home address as Commerce. Ransom H. Byrne died in Lowndes County in 1864. Thus end the important years of his presence in north Mississippi. In 1871, the Holly Springs brick mansion was purchased by Judge Orlando Davis and passed back into individual ownership (32:375).[4]

Directly below Tunica County, on the Mississippi, is Coahoma County. Though the land was given by the Choctaws earlier, it was added to the Chickasaw Cession and opened to settlement and sale in 1836. The name, which means "red panther" in both native American languages, conveys the wildness of the land. The river land was wild. In early hill country depositions, absent citizens were sometimes described as being away in the "Mississippi bottom." The term "Delta" was not used until much later.

The first Coahoma county seat was Port Royal at the eastern point of Horseshoe Bend on the river. It was followed by the village of Delta, likewise on the river, and then in 1850 by Friars Point, which held its position into the 1890s. The Lowry and McCardle history of 1891 lists among the earliest settlers Robert Friar of Louisiana and Aaron Shelby of Kentucky, both of whom represented the county in the legislature in the 1830s and 1840s. By the time of the Civil War, several north Mississippi planters had accumulated significant holdings in Coahoma County. And so the names Rozell, Fant, Lea, Brown, and the Honorable Jacob Thompson all figured in the early history.[5]

Let us first take the name Rozell. In 1850, Ann Eliza Fant, daughter of Col. John Berry Fant of Marshall County, married the Reverend Claiborn W. Rozell, Methodist minister, who died in 1856. In 1860, the Rozell Friars Point plantation was being run by B. L. Rozell (age 40), probably a brother of Reverend Rozell. But by 1870 Ann Fant Rozell and her children were living there with her brother Charles Henry Fant.

The youngest of eight children, Fant (1837-1910), had attended Chalmers Institute in Holly Springs; the University of Mississippi, 1855-56; and was graduated from Florence Wesleyan College in Alabama. There he married Lula Foster, daughter of leading Florence

---

3 Menn, II: 1,168-1,174. Leatherman, 79-80.

4 Ransom H. Byrne entries on Ancestry.com.

5 Linton Weeks, *Clarksdale and Coahoma County* (1982), 99-101.

citizens. During the war, he was a lieutenant in Forrest's Cavalry, and in 1867, he moved to his father's mound plantation near Friars Point. His wife dying in 1875 leaving four children, he married Addie Maynard, daughter of prominent pioneer Decatur Maynard, by whom he had one child. In 1891 Goodspeed's *Memoirs* described Charles Henry Fant, now a Coahoma leader and patriarch, as "tall, large-framed, rugged and hearty" (I:715).[6]

Wildwood Plantation, home of Dr. Willis Monroe Lea, was very near the land of Col. John Berry Fant west of Holly Springs. A native of Caswell County, North Carolina, Dr. Lea (1802-1878), was a a graduate of the University of North Carolina and the Medical College of Philadelphia. He settled in Marshall County in 1837 and devoted himself primarily to his profession until a fall from his horse in 1860 made that impossible. In the meantime, he had accumulated a large land holding, including a plantation in Coahoma County. His eldest son, Nathaniel Wilson Lea (1835-1911), educated like all Leas and Fants at Chalmers Institute in Holly Springs, was then sent to LaGrange College in Alabama and for three more years to the University of Virginia. After making a distinguished record as a Confederate captain, he set about reclaiming his father's neglected Coahoma plantation, and a year later, he married Emma Hopson, daughter of a prominent Kentucky family of Coahoma pioneers. He built a substantial plantation house in 1872.[7]

Colonel James Brown of Oxford owned land in Coahoma County as well as in Tunica. Profits from the Coahoma plantation might well have financed the building of the grand mansion of Colonel Harvey Walter and Fredonia Brown Walter on Chulahoma Road in Holly Springs. Certainly it supported the Walter family after Colonel Walter's death. (See the essays devoted to Colonel James Brown and to the building of Walter Place in this volume.)

The Honorable Jacob Thompson (1810-1885) was a prominent figure in Oxford and in the nation's capital. Born in Caswell County, North Carolina, and a graduate of the University of North Carolina, he was a Mississippi congressman throughout the 1840s. In 1856, he was appointed Secretary of the Interior by President James Buchanan.[8]

On the great river, below Coahoma is Bolivar County, the land granted earlier by the Choctaws, but also attached by legislation to the Chickasaw Cession (1836 Laws of Mississippi, 9). Named for Simon Bolivar, the great liberator of South America, it became among the richest cotton-growing regions in the world. Its potential was realized almost immediately.

Twenty-four years after the lands were first offered for sale, the 1860 slave census re-

---

6 George F. Maynard III, ed. *Memoirs and Letters of George Fleming Maynard* (2003).

7 Goodspeed's *Memoirs*, I: 1106-1107.

8 Goodspeed's *Memoirs*, II: 898-901.

veals that hill county planters were among a varied group heavily involved in the Bolivar lands. Among the large slave owners and land owners were Edmund McGehee (1812-1864), then of Memphis, formerly of Pontotoc County, and his cousin Miles Hill McGehee (1813-1865) of Panola County. They joined the Polks and President Jackson's kinsman Andrew Jackson Donelson, Tennessee investors. Included also were the Shelbys and Yergers of Coahoma and the Gaydens, Murfrees, Burruses, and Nebletts, who would become important citizens of the Delta. William Pickett, owner of Flodden Field Plantation in Yazoo County at the far end of this alluvial area, had sent his new son-in-law Samuel Dupuy Goza up to manage his interests.[9]

At the end of the Civil War, Capt. James Dinkins well describes the Delta landscape:

> At that time, the "Mississippi Delta" was known as the "Bottom," and was invariably referred to as such. The country was sparsely settled, and in many cases farm-houses were five and six miles apart… Less than ten per cent of the country had been cleared; therefore the timber and cane made it a wilderness. (264)

It would take decades more before this country was tamed and settled.[10]

---

9 Menn, II: 927-934. Hubert H. McAlexander, Richard Douglas McCrum, Dan Morse Woodliff, *Francis Fontaine the Builder* (Baltimore: Otter Bay Books, 2009), 69.

10 *Personal Recollections and Experiences in the Confederate Army, by an "Old Johnie,"* facsimile of 1897 edition (Dayton Ohio: Morningside Bookshop, 1975), 265.

Walter Place is the most impressive mansion in North Mississippi.
Collection of Chesley Thorne Smith, Holly Spring

Col. James Brown of
Oxford and Walter Place

Hubert H. McAlexander

One of the most important men in the development of the Chickasaw Cession was Col. James Brown of Oxford. But no full study exists of him. *Biographical and Historical Memoirs of Mississippi* (1891) presents the first sketch of his life, and this volume the second.

Born in Nashville in 1796 to Joseph Brown and Sarah Thomas, he settled in the 1820s in Madison County, Tennessee. His first wife, married about 1825, was Ann Williamson (1809-1832), who bore him four daughters, the middle ones twins, before her own death in childbirth. All the additional information about the Brown children comes from Ancestry.com. James Brown had a large extended family to care for his children; thus he was free to speculate during the opening of the Choctaw and Chickasaw lands in Mississippi. Goodspeed's *Memoirs* notes that he became a government surveyor, working both in the Chickasaw lands and on the border between Mississippi and Tennessee. At his death, he owned plantations in Lafayette, Panola, Tunica, Coahoma, and Bolivar counties.[1]

Redskins, Ruffleshirts, and Rednecks establishes Brown among those buying over 10,000 acres of Choctaw and Chickasaw allotments. He settled in Lafayette County when the Chickasaw lands opened, and became one of the important men in the state. By May of 1837, he owned 11 1/2 sections of land in Lafayette County alone. Two months before, on January 9, for $60,000 he had purchased from Lemuel Smith of Memphis 55 slaves (ages one to fifty-five), a horse and buggy, a family carriage, a stock of hogs, 16 mules, and five horses.[2]

In 1838, James Brown was among the incorporators of the Oxford Female Academy (Hathorn, p. 68). In 1840, he married again. The bride was Mary Ann Strong (1807-1890), by whom he had three more daughters. In 1841, he was one of the founders of the Cumberland Presbyterian Church in Oxford, of which he was long one of the main supporters. By Brown's first marriage, he was brother-in-law of its first minister, Reverend William S. Burney. The *Oxford Observer* of September 16, 1843, speaks of the church's

---

1 *Biographical and Historical Memoirs of Mississippi* (Chicago: Goodspeed Publishing Company, 1891), I:945-946.

2 Mary Elizabeth Young, *Redskins, Ruffleshirts and Rednecks* (Norman: University of Oklahoma Press, 1962), 169. John Cooper Hathorn, *Early Settlers of Lafayette County* (1980 reprint of 1938 M. A. Thesis, University of Mississippi), 7. Lafayette County Deed Book A:259, cited in Anne Percy, *Early History of Oxford, Mississippi* (2008), 14.

"very elegan [sic] brick edifice." It became the largest congregation in town. Built in 1854 the handsome brick structure is frequently pictured.[3]

Chairman of the meeting of the Democratic Party in June 1844, Brown was still leading the Lafayette County group in 1850 (Percy, pp. 22, 49). He served in the Mississippi House of Representatives in 1850 and in the state Senate in the three years after the war. In 1846, James Brown was appointed to the board of trustees of the University of Mississippi, serving on the executive committee until 1870.[4]

In the early 1850s, Brown was an influential backer of the Mississippi Central Railroad, that campaign led by his son-in-law Harvey W. Walter of Holly Springs. The two Lafayette County men appointed trustees were Alexander H. Pegues and Brown. Colonel Brown used his position as a University board member to make sure that the railroad was charted next to the university. Professor Hilgard designed the necessary engineering adjustment, called the Hilgard Cut (Percy, p. 54).[5]

Over the decades, Brown's standing as a landowner increased. In 1850, he owned more than 70 slaves in Lafayette County (Percy, p. 16). By 1860, Brown had a large holding in Coahoma County as well, and the colonel and two of his sons-in-law, W.F. Avant and A. T. Shotwell, held a huge acreage in Tunica County. His mansion sat at a corner of Depot Street (present-day Jackson Avenue and Martin Luther King Drive). We have no description of it, but it was surely one of the fine houses of Oxford. Grant stayed there in December 1862. Along with the Jacob Thompson residence, Brown's mansion is mentioned in all accounts of the August 1864 burning of Oxford. Colonel Brown died January 16, 1880, and is buried in the family plot, St. Peter's Cemetery, Oxford.[6]

CHILDREN OF COL. JAMES BROWN

1. Elizabeth Jane Brown (1828-1849) married William H. D. Wendell (a leader of the Whig Party in the county in the 1840s). She is buried in the Brown lot, St. Peter's Cemetery, Oxford.

---

3 Percy, 34. *Memoirs*, I:945. C. John Sabota, *A History of Lafayette County, Mississippi* (1976), 12.

4 Percy, 22, 49.

5 Percy, 54.

6 Percy, 16. Joseph Karl Menn, *Large Slaveholders of the Deep South*, 1974 microfilm (Xerox University Microfilms, Ann Arbor, Michigan), II:969, I:l69. Don Harrison Doyle, *Faulkner's County* (Chapel Hill: University of North Carolina, 2001), 204. Percy, 91.

2. Frances Sarah Brown (1830-1865), a Brown twin, was married on January 30, 1851 to William Francis Avant (1827-1881) by Reverend William S. Burney, pastor of the Cumberland Presbyterian Church. Today, these Avants or Avents are something of a puzzle. Part of the confusion is due to an unsigned piece in the *Oxford Eagle* of August 22, 1957, on the Avant-Stone house, the author identified by the Phil Stone biographer as the young writer Philip Alston Stone. Either young Phillip invented the Avant story presented in "Built by a Man Who Wanted to be a Southern Aristocrat," or this was a confused version told to him, which he, in turn, scrambled. He does clear up the fact that the Tamlin (whom he calls Tomlin) Avant family left no kin in the county, but he erroneously presents Tamlin as the builder, rather than his son William Francis.[7]

The Brown bridegroom was the only son of Tamlin Avant (1801-1875) and Sarah Elizabeth Dupree of Poplar Mount, Greensville County, Virginia. it is unclear whether or not Tamlin Avant ever lived in Mississippi, but in 1860 he owned 2,400 acres in Lafayette County. Before 1850, William Francis Avent settled in the county, where one W. W. [sic] Avent is listed with a significant land holding. In 1854, William Francis Avent married, and in 1856 and 1859, he bought the acreage, where he built the frame mansion later owned by the Stones, with windows to the floor, Italian marble mantles, colored glass in the sidelights, a long curved iron balcony, and brackets on the cornice. When the Civil War began, he was an important planter, having vast holdings in Lafayette County and Tunica County in the Mississippi Delta. He sponsored two local military companies, the Avant Southrons and the Avant Cadets, and he served as a captain under Forrest. After the war and the death of his wife, he was bankrupt like many Southerners. He returned to Virginia, where he died in 1881.[8]

The mansion was sold at a tax sale in 1868. Edward Mayes, author of several books, chancellor of the university, and son-in-law of L.Q.C. Lamar, bought it in 1875. He sold it to James Stone in 1892. (II:583). William Faulkner, when an aspiring writer, spent much time in the house with his friend and early mentor Phil Stone. He evidently used it as a model for the Sartoris house in his first novel.[9]

3. Martha Fredonia Brown (1830-1898), the other of the Brown twins, was married on December 24, 1849, by Reverend William S. Burney, to Harvey W. Walter of Holly Springs (1819 -1878). An important figure in the state, Harvey Walter was a Whig until

---

7 Susan Snell, *Phil Stone of Oxford* (Athens: University of Georgia Press, 1991), 341-342.

8 Hathorn, 114, 93. Lafayette Deed Books H:437, I:291.

9 Lafayette County Deed Book M:557, T:41, II:583. Thomas S Hines, *William Faulkner and the Tangible Past* (Berkeley: University of California Press, 1996), 58-59.

the Secession Convention, to which he was sent as one of the four delegates from Marshall County. His grand house, Walter Place, was financed with his father-in-law's funds (Marshall Co. DB 50:8-10), and after Colonel Walter's death, the family relied upon income from a plantation on the Coahoma-Tunica line probably inherited from Colonel Brown (Marshall County Will Book I:143-145, and obituary in *Holly Springs South*, June 23, 1898).

4. Ann Williamson Brown (1832-1916) was married on August 10, 1854, to Col. William Francis Dowd (1820-1878), one of the most distinguished lawyers in the state, a member of the firm Coopwood, Herbert, and Dowd of Aberdeen (Goodspeed's *Memoirs* I:659). In 1857, he was appointed to the board of trustees of the University of Mississippi. He was later colonel of the 24th Mississippi Infantry. One son was James Brown Dowd, a University alumnus who settled in Seattle in the late 19th century.

5. Julia Minerva Brown (1841-1898) first married, on July 12, 1859, Andrew Shotwell (1834-1880), and in 1886 married Col. Ira G. Holloway (1832-1902). In 1860, Shotwell had a large land holding in Tunica County. Julia Minerva is buried in the Brown plot, and Holloway's sketch in Goodspeed's *Memoirs* contains Colonel Brown.

6. Mary Porter Brown (1845-1869) buried in the Brown plot.

7. Sallie Polk Brown (1847-1853) buried in the Brown plot.

SLEDGES, McGEHEES, AND PANOLA COUNTY

HUBERT H. McALEXANDER

The Sledge name is now familiar throughout the northern reaches of Mississippi and in Memphis, Tennessee, the capital of this region. The family goes back to the early days of the Chickasaw Cession. Norfleet Ruffin Sledge came from Raleigh, North Carolina, to La Grange, Tennessee, in the early 1830s, and was married there to Catherine Jones, of the family of North Carolinian Fanning Jones, a planter of great wealth. There Sledge opened his own construction business. In 1838 he emigrated to Marshall County, Mississippi, just two years after the Cession was opened to settlers. According to the Sledge sketch in *The History of Panola County*, put out by the Panola Genealogical Society in 1987, he supposedly built the first courthouse in Holly Springs. Seven years later, he settled in Panola County, where he established the village of Sledgeville.[1]

In Holly Springs, he built the frame house on Salem given the 20th-century Pilgrimage name "Shadow Lawn," which he sold to Adrian N. Mayer. In Panola County, he immediately founded a large mercantile establishment and acquired significant acreage. By 1860, he was the second largest planter in the county. Three years after the end of the war, he moved to Como, three miles west, on the Mississippi Tennessee Railroad. When completed in 1858, the rail line ran from Memphis to Grenada, Mississippi, and opened up that part of the Cession. Previously, the main modes of transportation had been roads (many formerly Indian trails) and the Tallahatchie River. Two now extinct towns on the Tallahatchie, Belmont and Panola, yielded to two new towns on the railroad, Sardis and Batesville, both of which became seats of judicial districts, but neither of which produced the Shintoists of Como.[2]

Norfleet Sledge became known for lending money at 10 percent. From that practice and his other interests, he became the richest man in Panola County. Three of his sons were married in Como—William David (1837-1922), Norfleet Ruffin, Jr. (1839-1910), and Oliver Daniel (1840-1909). All served in the Confederate Army. Norfleet R., Jr., was a captain, and Oliver Daniel rode in Forrest's cavalry. William David and his first wife, Mary Thomas Brown, had five children, among them Kate Lee Sledge (who married Ernest Goodrich Taylor of Como) and Joel Thomas Sledge, grandfather of the actress Tallulah

---

1 "The Sledge Family," *History of Panola County* (Dallas, TX: Curtis Media Corp., 1987), 489. See also sketches of three Sledge sons in *Biographical and Historical Memoirs of Mississippi* (Chicago: Goodspeed Publishing Co., 1891), II:783-787.

2 *Memoirs*, II:78, I:251. Franklin L. Riley, "Extinct Towns and Villages of Mississippi," *Publications of the Mississippi Historical Society* (1902), 4: 362-363.

Bankhead. After William David Sledge's second marriage, in 1888 to Bessie Newman Cruse, he removed to Memphis. Stark Young makes the erroneous statement that Talullah Bankhead and William Faulker are both Sledge descendants and therefore cousins. He, of all people, should not have made such a Faulkner error.[3]

The second son, Norfleet Ruffin Sledge, Jr., a graduate of the University of Mississippi, married, first, his cousin Catherine Jones and, second, in 1882, Lucille Meriwether, daughter of James Oliver Meriwether. He had two children by each marriage. His brother Oliver Daniel Sledge married, first, Dora Jones and, second, Mattie Brahan, daughter of Col. John C. Brahan. Oliver D. Sledge also had two children by each marriage. In 1870, Colonel Sledge built his own house in Como, named "Twin Stairs." At the colonel's death in 1881, the sons formed "Sledge Brothers." They also were involved in Sledge and Norfleet, cotton commissioners in Memphis, and part of their extensive planting operation was southwest of Como at the Delta village of Sledge, since 1877 in Quitman County, and at Lula in Coahoma County.

So there are many descendants in Mississippi, in Memphis, and throughout the region. The family have long been supporters of the Episcopal Church, the most charming evidence being Holy Innocents, the Episcopal church in Como, built in 1872. Col. Norfleet Ruffin Sledge was the first warden, from 1871 to 1881, and the subscription list to erect the structure was in the hands of Norfleet R. Sledge, Jr. (See "The Panola Story" [1981], 21-24).

The village of Como, toward the northern border of Panola County, has long been known as a rich farming region. Before the Civil War, that area was dominated by the Taits and their relatives, the great McGehees (pronounced McGhee). In the 20th century, that family was centrally placed in a Southern mythology by descendant Stark Young, well-known New York literary figure.

In 1926, Young wrote his first novel, *Heaven Trees*. He goes back to the 1850s in Panola County. The George Gallatin Tait house becomes the plantation mansion mentioned in *Heaven Trees*. This house was torn down in 1892, but Young describes it in his memoir *The Pavilion* as "a fine place that had seven halls, and, on three sides, porches in the Palladian manner with columns" (96). The novel begins:

> It all seems romance now to me so far back in the fifties, like a gentle elegy of remembered things, never quite real almost, unless it be as music and light are real.

This mood of Vergilian sweetness and sorrow is sustained as the narrator recalls through

---

3 Goodspeed's *Memoirs*, II:786. Stark Young, *The Pavilion* (New York: Charles Scribner's Sons, 1951), 59.

a romantic haze life at this north Mississippi plantation during a golden age of graceful and sophisticated simplicity. The mood brings us to this purely platonic conclusion:

> She sat on, looking down the garden at the shining water of the pool. Over one side of the pool hung a spray of mimosa leaves. There was a spray of leaves above, and beneath was the water; each had its own perfection.

Among the characters in the novel is Stark Young's great-grandfather Hugh McGehee (1793-1855). Just out of Como, a brother, John Scott McGehee (1789-1870), had a plantation and great house, Hollywood. While both Tait House and Hollywood are no longer extant, they have been represented in books; those images are included in this volume.[4]

At Dr. George G. Tait's death in 1865, his property was inherited by his daughter, Mrs. Monroe Pointer, and the site was mapped and lots sold. The Sledges and other families moved to the village. Had the Sledges not intermarried with McGehee stock, woe to them.

---

4 Stark Young, *Heaven Trees* (New York: Charles Scribner's Sons, 1926), 1, 287. Hubert H. McAlexander, Jr., "Stark Young," *American Novelists, 1910-1945* (Detroit: GaleResearch,1981), *Dictionary of Literary Biography*, 9, Part 3:202. Jane N. Grider and Ethel C. Woodall Griner, ed., *McGehee Descendants*, Volume III (Baltimore: Gateway Press. 1919), 278-298. "Tait House" is on page 63 of Thomas S. Hines, *William Faulkner and The Tangible Past* (Berkeley: University of California Press, 1996), and "Hollywood" is pictured on page 278 of the Griner genealogy of the McGeehees.

"Hollywood," John Scott McGehee's plantation home near Como
Dr. J. Lucius McGehee IV

Jack McGehee and Hollywood House, Panola County

J. Lucius McGehee, IV

John Scott McGehee (1789-1870) came to north Mississippi from upper Georgia in 1836. The Creeks had been defeated by Gen. Andrew Jackson at Horseshoe Bend in 1814, and the Chickasaw and Choctaw Cessions were negotiated at the Treaties of Pontotoc and Dancing Rabbit Creek in the early 1830's. When Congress finally mandated the removal of the eastern tribes, there was a veritable land rush in 1836 as thousands of settlers moved to take up lands in Mississippi in order to grow cotton. J.S. McGehee, his younger brother, Hugh, and his eldest son, Miles bought land, sometimes directly from the Chickasaws to whom it had been assigned prior to sale, and sometimes from land speculators who had held the land only a month or two.

J.S. McGehee's original purchases amount to 7 and ½ sections of land (4800 ac.) in two places west and east of the present town of Como, Panola County, Mississippi for a total of $32,700, about $6.81 per acre. In subsequent years, he would come to own seven sections more.[1] Some of the names of the Chickasaw Indians (as given in the deeds) from whom the land was bought are Ulla-ta-cha, Ah-ba-na-tubby, and Oka-la-co-chubby. The 1840 census lists him as owning 42 slaves.[2] His home place was on the plantation east of present Como, on the road now labeled Hwy. 310. Jack and his brother, Hugh, moved their families, slaves and stock overland from Wilkes County, Georgia. Frank Smith says that Malinda Hill McGehee, J.S. McGehee's wife, rode the whole way on horseback, and that the family's gold was transported in a keg on the bed of its own wagon in the middle of the train.[3]

At first, the pioneers would have planted corn and lived in a dogtrot cabin made of logs on a farm which was just a clearing in the great forest. Each season new ground was made by girdling trees and grubbing out brush; work done by the slaves, of course. All along the new frontier, fires would light the night in the winter as log heaps were burned and the great Southern forest with its panthers and bears was inexorably destroyed. As soon as possible, cotton and more cotton was planted. As each new cotton crop was made and sent down the Tallahatchie to the Yazoo and thence to New Orleans, the Panola settlers

---

1 Panola County Courthouse, Sardis, Miss., Deed Books A and B

2 U.S. Census, 1840, Panola County, Miss.

3 Frank E. Smith, The Yazoo River. (Rivers of America Series), New York: Rinehart, 1954, p. 45

were able to establish more civilized and comfortable lives fairly quickly.

Proper houses such as we associate with the antebellum South began to appear in the 1840's. Downstairs were four big rooms separated by a central hall. Upstairs, the plan was the same. In front was the portico with white pillars. The kitchen, washhouse and slave cabins were in back. J.S. McGehee and his brother, Hugh, by avoiding debt, weathered the collapse of credit brought on by the President Jackson's Specie Circular of late 1836 which mandated payment for government land in gold or silver and not state bank-issued banknotes which the land office had previously accepted. Many of his neighbors could not meet their payments and moved on to the newly independent Texas Republic, sometimes taking their mortgaged slaves and stock with them to beat their creditors. (To this day, Texas state law is friendly to debtors!) Cotton prices held up well (in the 10-14 cent range) until a worldwide depression reduced demand for cotton in the English mills. The cotton price collapsed in late 1839 and stayed low throughout the 'hungry forties', not reaching ten cents again until 1850. Mississippi planters had to adapt by producing their own provisions, corn and salt pork, rather than obtaining these on credit from a commission merchant, many of whom had gone bust in the 1837 Panic. The also achieved more efficient cotton production, introducing mule-drawn steel plows and other improved equipment.[4]

The decade of the 1850's was the apogee for the antebellum plantation South. I've heard it said that Panola County in the 1850's was the richest county per capita in all the United States, though surely Adams County and Natchez must have been richer. With the return of flush times, a 500-lb bale of cotton might be worth as much as $100 gold, and a big operation like Jack McGehee's might produce a thousand bales in a season. While not in the absolute upper echelon of planters (those owning more than 250 slaves, perhaps about 350 planters in 1860), the McGehees were certainly on the next rung down. They exhibited most of the defining characteristics of their class. "Among these were large families; a relatively high infant mortality rate; an extraordinary degree of intermarriage, extending not infrequently to first-cousin unions; a cosmopolitan lifestyle and outlook; surprisingly close social, economic and cultural ties with the Northeast; an emphasis upon quality education for both males and females; a catholicity of intellectual interests; and— not least—a confident belief in God as the omnipotent regulator of human affairs."[5]

Jack and Malinda McGehee were stalwarts of the Methodist Church in their district. He and others of the neighborhood finished the Fredonia Methodist Church, a fine frame

---

4 John Hebron Moore, The Emergence of the Cotton Kingdom in the Old Southwest: Mississippi, 1770-1860. Baton Rouge: Louisiana State University Press, 1988. p. 18-36

5 William K. Scarborough, Masters of the Big House: Elite Slaveholders of the Mid-nineteenth Century South. Baton Rouge: Louisiana State University Press, 2003. p. 19 (Miles McGehee, of Bolivar County, Mississippi, owned several plantations, was immensely wealthy and likely did own in excess of 200 slaves.)

building with glass windows built just across the road from J.S. McGehee's home place in 1842. He also gave a few acres of land for another small church, McGehee's Chapel which is west of Como. A memoir of his life published in 1886 lays heavy stress on his and Malinda's good works on behalf of the Methodist Church. "He filled the office of steward in his church for long years. No pastor left the charge with salary unpaid; a deficit was always assumed by him."[6] In 1856, Francis Marion White's Mississippi and Tennessee Railroad came to Panola County, and the planters began to send their cotton to Memphis rather than down river. By 1860, at the age of 71, he reported to the census taker real estate valued at $89,600, and personal property worth $95,150, this last representing the value of his slaves.[7] He had 42 slaves on his place west of Como (which family tradition says was called Gregnon) and 55 at his home place, Hollywood.[8] His house had white pillars and a Greek pediment, was faced with brick, and stood in a grove of cedar trees.

Jack McGehee thoroughly fulfilled the role of family patriarch. He set up my great-great grandfather, James Blanton McGehee, as a cotton planter in 1852. He gave amply of his lands and property to his other sons and sons-in-law. He was known for his willingness to provide help to those in want. He enjoyed yearly sojourns at Bailey Springs near Florence, Alabama, a popular health resort and mineral springs. The Florence Gazette mentioned his arrival there in May for the 1859 season along with his son-in-law, Malcolm Gilchrist and their families.

The people of this section were not in favor of secession, for the most part. In the 1860 election, Panola County went for John C. Bell of the Constitutional Union Party. But, after Fort Sumter when Mr. Lincoln called for volunteers to put down the rebellion, north Mississippi firmly supported secession. Two of J.S. McGehee's sons, Miles McGehee and Edward Francis McGehee, signed the Ordinance of Secession taking Mississippi out of the Union.[9] Miles was appointed Quartermaster General of the 60-day volunteers called for by Gov. Pettus. Edward F. McGehee was elected Captain of the Como Avengers, the local company raised in the early months of the war. They were attached to the 25th Mississippi (later 2nd Confederate) Regiment, Col. John Donelson Martin commanding.

---

6 "John S. McGehee, Our Dead, No. 9", Memorial Sketches of Deceased Prominent Citizens, Sardis (Miss.) Southern Reporter, 1886

7 U.S. Census, 1860, Panola County, Miss., p. 80, lines 25-26.

8 www.freepages.genealogy.rootsweb.ancestry.com/~ajac/mspanola.htm (I am making the assumption that the property listed under "J. S. McGehee" is the home place, and that listed under "John McGee" is his place west of Como. This site is no longer accessible)

9 An Ordinance to Dissolve the Union Between the State of Mississippi and the Other States United With Her Under the Compact Entitled the Constitution of the United States of America (photocopy in author's possession).

E.F. McGehee became the Lt. Col. of the regiment. J.S. McGehee's youngest son, William T. McGehee, joined the Como Avengers but transferred to the cavalry and rode with Gen. Nathan B. Forrest. His grandson, McGehee Dandridge, was First Sergeant of the Como Avengers and was killed at Shiloh on the first day, April 6, 1862.[10]

The reckless and ill-advised War for Southern Independence brought nothing but ruin and sorrow to the McGehees of Panola County. J.S. McGehee's grandson, Mack Dandridge, was gone, buried in the Fredonia churchyard the day after his body had been brought from the battlefield to Memphis by way of Corinth on the cars of the Memphis and Charleston Railroad.[11] His well-beloved wife of 53 years, Malinda, died of "paralysis" (presumably a stoke) on April 15, 1864. His son-in-law, Dr. Charles Dandridge, accidentally shot himself in 1864, an event Louis Hughes describes. A coffin was made for Dr. Dandridge and lined with silk from the ladies' dresses and Mrs. Dandridge's opera cloak. The body proved too bloated to fit into the coffin, and "Old Master Jack" had the coffin put aside, saying, "it would do for him to be buried in."11 His son-in-law and nephew, Edmund, died on New Year's Day, 1864, trying to recoup his wrecked fortunes by means of a salt works project in Alabama. His eldest son, Miles, died Jan. 15, 1865, on the run after killing a Yankee officer who was leading a detachment to burn his plantation house in Bolivar County in retribution for a gun boat's being fired on from the river bank. His son, J. Blanton McGehee (my great-great grandfather) died Sept. 27, 1866 from a fever acquired on a visit to Memphis.

J.S. McGehee's plantations were in ruins, his servants were no longer his property, and the specter of starvation stalked the Southland. I think there is some clue to the effect on him of these searing experiences at the very end of life in a story told in the memorial sketch published in the Southern Reporter years later. "In one instance after the war he cared for a colored woman with small pox (for no one else would go near her); she lives yet to testify to this act of humanity and gratefully remembers him, never forgetting his birthday or the anniversary of his departure." The end finally came for him on March 2, 1870 at the age of 81. I cannot imagine that his death, when it came, was not welcomed

---

10 Panola County Genealogical and Historical Society, History of Panola County, Mississippi. Dallas: Curtis Media Corp., 1987 p. 9 (early history of Panola County), p. 54-90 ("The Civil War Years", John Nelson III), Memphis Daily Appeal, April 10, 1862 (report of the casualties of the Como Avengers by Lt. C.K. Carruthers, acting captain of the company)

11 Louis Hughes, Thirty Years a Slave. 1896. Montgomery: New South Books, 2002, p. 117 (Ironically, my best source for the lives of the McGehees during the War is Louis Hughes's probably ghost-written autobiography, first published in Milwaukee in the 1890's. Louis was a slave owned by J.S. McGehee's nephew and son-in-law, Edmund McGehee who, by the 1850's, lived a few miles outside of Memphis on the Memphis and Charleston Railroad in a very grand house. After the fall of Memphis, Louis was sent down to Jack McGehee's with some of Edmond's other servants, and got to know the Panola McGehees well. Louis is none too flattering in his description of Jack McGehee, or "Old Jack" as he calls him.)

with resignation.

His house, Hollywood, became the home of his daughter, Annie Dandridge, Mack Dandridge's mother and Dr. Dandridge's widow. Annie McGehee Dandridge (1818-1888)[12] was the owner of Hollywood House and the section of land on which it stood. The house and section 32 passed to John S. McGehee II through his mother, Sarah E. McGehee, Edmond's widow. Ownership of the land (not the house) was contested in Panola Co. Chancery Court in (William T.) McGehee v. (J.S.) McGehee in 1896. J.S. McGehee II prevailed on review by the Miss. Supreme Court[13] and sold the property to his brother, William E. McGehee of Memphis, who in turn sold it (1898) to his cousin Edward F. McGehee, Jr. The house burned down around the turn of the 20th century, but the beautiful grove of old cedars where it stood, now the property of Sledge Taylor of Como, is still producing pretty jonquils. The land passed to Ed. McGehee's sister, Pattie (Mrs. Phil) Pointer, and they sold it to Anne Fargason Ward in 1951. Sledge's grandfather bought the place in 1956.

12 Obituary, Ann McGehee Dandridge, 1888 (a clipping in the possession of the author, probably from the Sardis Southern Reporter)

13 McGehee vs. McGehee, in Cases Argued and Decided in the Supreme Court of Mississippi, Vol. 74, p. 386 (available on Google Books)

Old Salem, Long Ago, An Important Center

John M. Mickle

Originally published in Holly Springs *South Reporter*, September 4, 1930
Reprinted in Robert Milton Winter, Ed., *Amid Some Excellent Company*

Grouped around old St. Andrew's Church near Old Salem, in what is now Benton County but was then part of Marshall County, was one pf the best neighborhoods in North Mississippi in the days before the War of the Sixties.

The families who lived in it were mostly Whig in politics; Episcopalian in religion and many came from Virginia. The fame of the neighborhood spread afar and Jefferson Davis, who was later to be president of the Confederacy, visited it with a view of buying the plantation of Dr. Frank W. Dancy, who was moving to Memphis, and later to Holly Springs. Mr. Davis did not buy.

No pretentious houses were built in the neighborhood, the peak of prosperity out of which such things would come being arrested by the war. Judge A.M. Clayton's "Woodcote," and Mr. Govan's "Snowden" [or "Snowdoun"] nearer approached such types.

The homes were comfortable, however, and hospitality characteristic of the time was dispensed. The Hull, Clayton, and Thomas plantations are still possessed by their descendants, though none live on them.

Many of the plantations bore names, and were settled in 1836 or a little later. "The Lodge" was the first house built and lodged the other families of the Hulls until they could buy and built—hence its name. It was situated midway between Hudsonville and Lamar and was the western boundary of the neighborhood. Here lived Charles Thomas and his wife, Mrs. Elizabeth Hull Thomas.

Mr. Thomas was a courtly gentleman of the old school, a lawyer, and was active in public affairs of the state, though he did not aspire to office beyond some service in the state legislature.

His office was in Holly Springs and he drove to town, later using the railroad. He was associated with Judge J.W.C. Watson in the practice of law, and I think with Judge J.W. Clapp.

A mile from "The Lodge" was "Woodcote," the home of Judge A.M. Clayton, also a lawyer and a planter, a scholarly man who had accumulated a good library and papers of historical worth. Shortly after his death in 1890 the house was destroyed with all its contents by fire of unknown origin. The first house was burned during the war.

He possessed a large landed estate in Marshall County, and a plantation in Tunica

County on which Clayton is situated. He lived for a time in Holly Springs and practiced law and was senior warden of the young parish of Christ Church. He served several terms on the state supreme bench, retiring in 1850, serving the last term with Judges William M. Sharkey and C.P. Smith, who became chief justices.

"Greenwood" might be called the fountainhead of the Hull family in north Mississippi. Here came Mrs. [Elizabeth Herndon] Hull, a widow from Spotsylvania, Va., near Fredericksburg, and her sons and daughters and their families composed no small part of the neighborhood; and her descendants were to enrich the citizenship of Holly Springs and Memphis.

In Holly Springs lived her son John Hull, father of the late Brodie S. Hull, and her grandsons Brodie S., William, Edward H. and James M. Crump. In Memphis were Congressman Edward Hull Crump, Frank M. and Dabney H. Crump, John D. Martin, and also William Crump of Greenville, Miss. And D. Minor Mickle of Hong-Kong-Singapore, in the Far East.

"Greenwood" was destroyed by fire August 8, 1930.

Andrew Govan of "Snowden" owned a princely estate in Marshall and Tippah Countues, and a large acerage in Grenada County. He maintained an establishment in keeping with his estate.

His wife, Mary Pugh [Jones] Govan, was one of the loveliest old ladies I ever knew, beautiful in face and character to the end. Their descendants took high rank in Mississippi, Arkansas, and Tennessee, notably General Daniel Govan, who was a major general in the Confederate army, and filled a high place in public life in Arkansas, and Col. George M. Govan of McComb, Miss., who was secretary of state in Mississippi. The Govans have given a good account of themselves from Memphis to Helena.

Dr. Frank W. Dancy was a planter and the beloved physician of the neighborhood for a while, later going to Holly Springs where his son Henry S. Dancy was born. He was the most courtly gentleman I ever knew; his face bore a striking resemblance to that of George Washington.

Melchizedek Robinson was another planter in the neighborhood. Mrs. S.W. Mullins of Holly Springs is his granddaughter, and her father, James Robinson, was one of the most popular young men of the neighborhood. He entered railroading and was one of the first conductors of Mississippi Central Railroad, now the Illinois Central. Railroading was very hazardous then, but Robinson held a record for never killing a passenger or losing a piece of luggage.

Governor Joseph Matthews of this neighborhood was the only governor Marshall County has furnished Mississippi. He was a colorful statesman, and his ability was shown in landing the office in the face of a strong Whig opposition. His grandson, E.A.C. Davis, lives now in Memphis.

Dabney Minor and his wife, Jane Hull Minor, lived at Woodlawn, and their only child was the late Mrs. Belton Mickle.

Mr. Minor was not so much of a money maker, but he loved farming and Woodlawn plantation might be called a forerunner of the modern experiment station. He believed a farmer should live on his farm, and he practiced diversification, and even planted flax from which the household linen was spun. It is doubtful if anyone living ever saw a stalk of flax grow in Marshall County.

His house was comfortable, not pretentious, but the plantation, with its front yard, gardens, orchards, and fields was the most picturesque and beautiful of them all. Mr. Minor was the pillar of St. Andrew's Episcopal Church, and his home was practically the rectory for the minister when he filled his appointments.

WITHERS IN MARSHALL, DESOTO, AND TUNICA

HUBERT H. MCALEXANDER

Sterling Withers was an honorable settler in the Chickasaw Cession, as evidenced by this story told by an era chronicler. "Sterling Withers," said Dr. Thomas J. Malone upon seeing him on the town square, "Do you know that ten years ago you bought a tract of land from me, and you haven't got a scratch of the pen to show for it? Then come over to the courthouse and let me write you a deed" (Robert Milton Winter, ed., *Amid Some Excellent Company: Holly Springs, Mississippi through the Life and Words of John M. Mickle* [2003], p. 159).

On the southeastern corner of the Withers place long sat the Victoria gin. Victoria is a community that grew up when the Kansas City, Memphis & Birmingham Railroad was put through Marshall County in 1885. Just four miles east of Byhalia, this section was settled fifty years earlier by men who became important in the region — bearing the names Withers, White, and Raiford. When Sallie Goodman Davenport Withers wrote back to Virginia immediately after her marriage to the mature widower Sterling Withers, she reported that "the family stands as high as any in Marshall" (Susan Dauro Collection, "Dear Mama" from Sallie Withers, Feb. 12, 1849).

In the 1850 census, we find Spires Boling, the architect (who became well-known later), listed between Clark C. White and Sterling Withers. Sallie Goodman Davenport Withers wrote that the White house is "as fine a house [and] as well furnished as any you… see in this country." In the same letter, she quotes Sterling Withers as saying that the Withers house has six bedrooms, "three above and three below" for guests to choose among. Neither of these structures still stands. They were burned by federal troops during the Civil War. But the Robert Raiford residence on Hedge Farm does remain. Boling is perhaps responsible for all three. The Raiford house is a fine Greek Revival clapboard cottage of one story. Boling's being the builder would explain the refinement of detail.

Sterling Withers (1782-1862) was married twice, first in Virginia to Elizabeth Moyler, second in middle age to a widow, Mrs. Sallie Goodman Davenport. According to the letter cited earlier, in 1849 Sterling Withers had only three living children, all settled near him. In the course of the 19th century, Withers descendants made their mark in three counties of the Cession— Marshall (the home county), Desoto, and Tunica.

The oldest daughter, Mary, married in 1839 widower Clark C. White, son of Shelton White and Mildred Clark, a family prominent from Georgia to the Mississippi, and White became a name running through these north Mississippi families. The ceremony was performed by Reverend Joseph Travis, then president of the University of Holly Springs.

White was an important Marshall County planter, but after the burning of the mansion, the Whites moved to Buntyn Station outside Memphis, where they died toward the end of the century. They apparently had only two children who lived and had issue — Rosalie, who married John Donelson Martin of Memphis and had a son and namesake on the federal bench, and Shelton Withers White (1846-1930).

The oldest of the pioneer Sterling Withers' sons was Albert Quarles Withers (1819-1903). He married, in 1843, Matilda, the daughter of William Jones, a wealthy Georgia planter whose plantation was near Tallaloosa in Marshall. The esteemed Presbyterian divine, Daniel Baker, performed the ceremony. A.Q. Withers was a man of public affairs for many decades, being an inventor and serving in the state legislature. He ran a large plantation, Percalpa, near his father's land. During the Civil War, he raised his own cavalry company, of which he was captain. Federal troops burned the Withers houses, and the family moved to Holly Springs, where he was a merchant until the yellow fever epidemic of 1878, when he returned to his land at Victoria. A sketch in Goodspeed's *Biographical and Historical Memoirs of Mississippi* (1891) characterizes him as noted "for his hospitality [a trait long associated with the Withers family] and marked individuality" (2:1067).

A.Q. Withers had seven children, of whom only three concern us here. Lou Withers married Houston Cannon, a wealthy planter of Red Banks in Marshall, and had issue. Sterling Withers married Oliver Dockery of Desoto County and had no issue. The most significant figure in the area was the first born, Emile Quarles Withers (1845-1926). An alumnus of Chalmers Institute in Holly Springs, he was a lieutenant in Forrest's command, 3rd Mississippi Cavalry. Married three times, he was a board member of the Bank of Holly Springs, an important planter of north Mississippi, and a cotton factor at Memphis. Among his great-grandchildren is Sledge Taylor of Como, who has provided information.

The younger son of the Mississippi founder Sterling Withers was Sterling Adolphus Withers (1826-1852), who married in 1845 Emily Caruthers, daughter of John Paxton Caruthers (1799-1872). Natives of Rockbridge County, Va., several Caruthers brothers and cousins settled early near Holly Springs. Sam Houston's mother was a Paxton, and the man called The Raven visited his kin and connections in the town. The second Sterling Withers died as a young man, and his widow and children settled near her father, who lived in Desoto County.

John Paxton Withers (1850-1925), son of the widow, served on the Yazoo-Mississippi Levee Board and the Desoto County Board of Supervisors. He married Ada Thompson and had five children to reach adulthood and three to have issue (see the sketch in Goodspeed's *Biographical and Historical Memoirs of Mississippi* [1891], 2:1067-1068). The Withers family are identified with Lake Cormorant in Desoto, and OK plantation in Tunica County, founded by Sterling Withers (1877-1939), who never married. The Withers family and OK are the subject of *Goodbye Ole Miss* by Carroll Seabrook Leatherman (2003). I could never have written this essay were it not for the help of a son of this branch, Sterling Withers of Tunica.

The Martins in Two Counties

Hubert H. McAlexander

The Martin family made their mark in two of the Cession counties. But it is an increasingly faint mark, and here I must record what I know before all memory of them is forgotten. I take most of this material from a file assembled by my friend Charles Nunnally Dean for the 1958 centennial of the Episcopal church in Holly Springs, Christ Church.[1]

John Davidson Martin (1795-1860), along with partners Chisholm and Craig, bought the site of Oxford from Hoka, a Chickasaw woman, and donated it for the county seat in the early months of 1836.[2] That transaction would have been enough to ensure his place in our history, but he did something even more important. In December of 1841, he donated a half section of land in west Oxford for a state university.[3] For these two actions, he will always be of record in Mississippi history. But for all sorts of other reasons too, the family was important in the early years of this region.

John D. Martin built in the late 1830s the original one-story frame cottage incorporated in the Thompson-Chandler house on South 13th Street in Oxford. The complete antebellum house is the model for the Compson mansion in *The Sound and the Fury*.[4] By 1850, he had moved north to Holly Springs, where he died in 1860. His home was south of town, on Peyton Road, a frame plantation house, built at the top of a hill with a carefully terraced slope. He was one of the significant planters of the county, having a slave force of over 100. His large plantation was on the north side of the Tallahatchie. He was a sustaining member of Christ Church (Episcopal), and his rector, Joseph Holt Ingraham, a well-known literary figure in his day, is buried in the Martin lot in Hillcrest Cemetery.

In 1830 in Jackson, Tenn., John D. Martin married Sarah (1812 -1895), daughter of Col. Samuel Dickens and the sister of his younger brother's wife, Ann Vaughan Dickens. Of his many children, only the youngest, John D. Martin, Jr., appears to have had issue. His wife was a Davidson of Oxford, but not kin. They settled in Florida.

Andrew Lesper Martin (1798-1842), a younger brother, was actually the more prom-

---

1 Copy in the McAlexander Marshall County Collection, University of Mississippi.

2 C. John Sobotka, Jr., *A History of Lafayette County, Mississippi* [1976], p. 28

3 See Lowry and McCardle, *History of Mississippi* [1891], p. 425, and also the 1928 clipping from Memphis *Commercial Appeal* "Gave Oxford Acres For Ole Miss' Site," in Robert Milton Winter, ed., *Amid Some Excellent Company* [2003], p. 175

4 Thomas S. Hines, *William Faulkner and the Tangible Past* [University of California Press, 1996], pp. 54-56

inent of the Martins. He announced June 5, 1824, in the Jackson, Tenn., newspaper, that he would begin the practice of law there, and in November of that year, the newspaper carried the notice of his marriage to Ann Vaughan Dickens, daughter of Col. Samuel Dickens. Colonel Dickens was an important man, a representative of the University of North Carolina's speculating company, which bought large tracts in Tennessee.[5] Andrew Martin's Jackson mansion was later bought by Union University, and in Mississippi he built another mansion. This one was on Martin's Hill, less than two miles northwest of Holly Springs, from which, as his niece Sherwood Bonner put it, "the town could be seen like a picture in smoke".[6] The house was an "elegant brick residence of eight rooms" and two stories.[7] Andrew L. Martin died in 1842 in Philadelphia, while he was in the north on business.

Andrew Martin and Ann Vaughan Dickens (1807-1876) had seven children, six sons and one daughter: Samuel, Andrew, Henry, Gaston, Garrett, George, and Amelia Wilkinson. William Gaston Martin died in Lafayette County; his will is dated November 1857 (Packet # 986, p. 177). The executor is Dr. Charles Bonner, husband of his first cousin, and among the witnesses is William M. Strickland, a noted Holly Springs lawyer. Among his heirs is his brother, Kenneth Garrett, who married two daughters of Dr. William H. Jamison, a prominent Chulahoma physician, and his wife, Ellizabeth Nunnally. Immediately before the Civil War, Kenneth Garrett built the Miller house several miles southwest of Waterford (see Wilson Golden's "Waterford Days" in this volume).

The Andrew Martin daughter, Amelia, married William P. Mitchell of Memphis and they had descendants who lived in the Delta and in Desoto County. In 1958, Ben Ferrell Mitchell (born about 1890), lawyer of Cleveland, Miss., made a gift to Christ Church, honoring the Martins. He noted that his father, Andrew Martin Mitchell, had many old Holly Springs friends among members of the "Crawford, Rather, Featherstone, Schumacher, Seesel, Tyler, and Jones families".[8] Many of them "visited us regularly in our home near Oxford during the quail and fishing seasons."

The eldest Martin son's line gave a Southern Gothic end to the family story. Andrew Lesper Martin, Jr., married a woman named Rebecca, said to be a Peters, probably of the

---

5 Samuel Cole Williams, *Beginnings of West Tennessee* [ ], pp. 109-112

6 Anne Razey Gowdy, *A Sherwood Bonner Sampler, 1869-1884* [University of Tennessee Press: 2000], p. 171

7 Holly Springs *South*, 1 March 1882

8 BFM to Charles Nunnally Dean, 24 May 1958, copy in McAlexander Marshall County Collection, University of Mississippi

family of the jealous husband who shot and killed General Earl Van Dorn.[9] In 1903, Mrs. Rebecca Martin left Martin's Hill to her grandson, Andrew Huffman. Tradition has it that, as she was dying, he sold the house brick by brick. He also dug up the family cemetery on the place and used the stones as building blocks.

In addition to John Davidson and Andrew Lesper Martin was a younger sister who also settled in Marshall County. Ruth Martin Wilson (1800-1845), is important because of the history of two descendants — her daughter, the murdered Sallie Wilson Coxe, and her granddaughter, the writer Sherwood Bonner. In the middle 1820s, Ruth Martin married Samuel D. Wilson, a well-heeled Tennessean, who settled near Chulahoma soon after the Chicksaw Cession land sales. He died in 1844, leaving her with two daughters. The older, Mary, married in 1846 Dr. Charles Bonner, an upright Holly Springs physician who served as executor of William Gaston Martin's will.

The younger Wilson daughter, Sallie, met a tragic fate. Against her family's wishes, at the age of sixteen she married Robert R. (Toby) Coxe, son of a very rich and hot-blooded clan. Sent over by their parents from Lexington, Ga., the Coxe brothers were socially prominent and notorious. During a brief visit with her sister Mary Wilson Bonner and her family, Sallie received a message from Toby begging her to return home. Despite tearful remonstrances from Mary's children that she should stay, when her carriage arrived at the house, she left. That night Toby killed her and then himself. On February 6, 1856, the Memphis *Eagle* carried this story under the headline "Horrible Calamity":

> Mr. R.R. Cox[e], who resided about twelve miles from Holly Springs, Miss., in the vicinity of Chulahoma, on Wednesday last, shot his wife, killing her instantly, and then shot himself through the head. When the servants broke into their room, both were found dead. Mr. Cox[e] was at times partially insane. He formerly resided in this city, in South Memphis, at a place known as the "Swiss Cottage." He was a most worthy young man, and the awful calamity just recorded can be attributed only to insanity, with which his friends believed him to be afflicted for some time previous to this melancholy affair. His wife (Miss Wilson of Marshall County, Miss.) was a bride of but six weeks.

The article continues by giving more background;

> Mr. Cox[e] is the third male member of a worthy family who has died a violent death within the last eight of ten years. One in a fit of insanity threw himself from the deck of a Mississippi steamer, and was drowned; another was slain by the accidental discharge of a double-barreled shotgun when starting on a camp hunt; and now we have to record the death of still another, and that of his fair young wife, by his own hands.

---

9 See Hubert McAlexander's *Strawberry Plains Audubon Center: Four Centuries of a Mississippi Landscape* [University Press of Mississippi, 2003], pp. 59-61, 97-99

In my youth, some still remembered hearing of two hearses drawing up before the Episcopal church, and only one was taken in, before both resumed their progress to the cemetery.

One of the tearful children who watched their aunt Sallie Wilson Coxe get in her carriage and drive away was Kate Sherwood Bonner (1849-1883), who married David McDowell. She provided the region with still another shock. In the fall of 1873, she abandoned both her husband and her eighteen-month-old child and fled to Boston to establish a literary career. Becoming Henry Wadsworth Longfellow's protegée, she cut quite a dramatic figure before her early death. Bonner's *Like Unto Like* (1878) uses the Coxe murder-suicide, but gives it a feminist cast.[10]

---

10 See Hubert McAlexander's *The Prodigal Daughter: A Biography of Sherwood Bonner* (1981, reprinted 1999)

Dr. Weldon Jones and General Wheeler's Granddaughter

Bobby J. Mitchell

One frequently reads highly exaggerated statistics of the wealth of some of the families in the county; however, none approach the actual wealth of Dr. Weldon Jones. There are many stories of the vast numbers of slaves held by some families, whereas the truth falls far short of the myths.

"Large Slaveholders of 1860 and African American Surname Matches from 1870", a very large research site prepared by Tom Blake, includes Blake's considerable work on the two censuses. One can access his work at the MSGenWeb "African American Resources" website. His work shows that in 1860 in Marshall County there were only seven slaveholders who held more than 100 slaves. Among those were Col. John D. Martin, William H. Coxe, Eben N. Davis, William B. Lumpkin, Alexander M. Clayton, and J .P. Hardaway, the last two of whom lived in what is now Benton County. The seventh of those on the list, according to Blake, was Dr. Weldon Jones, the only slaveholder in the county to hold more than 200 slaves, with a total of 223.

The census of the time was more intrusive than one would expect in today's world. One such question asked how many acres of land, improved and unimproved, one owned, and what it was worth. Jones answered that he had 2,500 acres of improved land and 1,877 acres of unimproved land for a total of 4,377 acres, most of the land lying in the very southern portions of the county. This is the largest plantation in the county for which I could find records. In all of Mississippi in 1860 there were only 481 farms of more than 1,000 acres.

Earlier in the county history there were speculators who, either individually or as land agents of various land companies, had acquired vast land holdings in the Chickasaw Cession, but as speculators, they quickly sold it at inflated prices. Such men were James Fort, who soon acquired nearly 27,000 acres, or Weldon Jones himself, who had 19,650 acres, and his brother John P. Jones in Lafayette County, who had more than 33,000 acres. Samuel McCorkle of Holly Springs had more than 21,000 acres and Joseph Matthews, one of the government land surveyors sent in to survey the lands, and who was later governor of Mississippi, had nearly 45,000 acres, but none of these were farmers; they were only buying and selling land, not using it. The acreage shown for these speculators includes only land directly patented from the U.S. and does not include other private purchases, for instance the land Jones owned in Marshall was all privately purchased except for one quarter-section of 160 acres.

Another question on the 1860 census required one to reveal the value of his property and assorted investments. A report of Weldon Jones to the census taker showed that he was worth $804,000. An Internet-based inflation calculator indicates that the amount he had in 1860 would be in excess of $21 million today.

Even with all his wealth and connections, he could do nothing about the cataclysm of the Civil War, during which he was ruined financially. While I was working on deeds for this essay, Beverly Hurdle, in a role reversal, took advantage of my youth and inexperience in using deed searches and quickly found a couple of references for which I had searched fruitlessly for an hour. With her find in hand, I saw that as early as 1864, if not earlier, Jones' lands were being lost for delinquent taxes. The losses continued into 1868 and later.

By 1870 Jones was living in Lawrence County, Ala., with his brother Richard, and worth a total of $23,000. He died in 1875, nearly 85 years old, and is buried in the Wheeler Family Cemetery there. He left what estate he had left here to his niece, Daniella Jones Wheeler, who in turn left it to her daughter Lucy Wheeler, who died in 1924. With Lucy's death in 1924, her sister Annie Early Wheeler inherited what remained of the Jones property in Marshall County.

Annie Wheeler did not file her sister's will with the court in Marshall County until 1935. Beverly pointed out that when a will such as this one is filed years later, it usually means that preparations are being made to dispose of all or part of the estate. Congress passed the Flood Control Act of 1936 with Sardis Dam being the first approved on the Yazoo Headwaters Project. The United States had to acquire title to the lands along the proposed flood control project, and it is possible the Wheelers knew of the proposed legislation, and were anticipating the sale to the U.S. government of their property. In 1938 Annie Wheeler did sell 725 acres to the government for $6,900, or about $9.50 an acre. The land she sold was just west of the Tallahatchie River Bridge, between the old Oxford Road and Whiskey Hill Road. Wheeler may have had other small properties to dispose of, but this transaction essentially was the end of the old Weldon Jones lands.

Annie Early Wheeler was one of the most famous women in Alabama history at the time of her death in 1955. She had worked with Clara Barton in Cuba, and then went to the Philippines, where she worked in a military hospital during the Philippine Insurrection. She went to Europe during World War I with the Red Cross, and worked with the Red Cross in Alabama during WWII. She established schools on her plantation, paying the teachers personally for years, and led to the introduction of home economics in Alabama schools.

Major Stephenson's Nursery

Hubert H. McAlexander

My forebear Maj. J.P.M. Stephenson (1806-1863) owned a large nursery in Marshall County, five miles north of Holly Springs at Mack. This was an unusual undertaking in our cotton-growing region, and one remembered for a long time. My great-grandfather's 1933 obituary, written by historian John Mickle, spoke of it thusly: "his grandfather Stephenson operated before the Civil War a nursery on the plantation that was widely known in the Mid-South, and certain varieties of apples that he developed were especially noted."[1]

Miss Martha Moseley, living at the adjoining plantation, Strawberry Plains (now an Audubon property), recalled Stephenson Seedling apple trees growing there until the severe ice storm of 1920. My great-uncle John McAlexander, who owned the Stephenson place at Mack after his father, remembered delicious Damson plums and recalled an orchard of apple trees planted in a semicircle by the cemetery near the pond. In my youth, only one gnarled pear was left of an orchard south of the house.[2]

Among the remaining books in the major's library was a tantalizing one—*Coxe on Fruit Trees*, published in 1817. My research of Marshall County history turned up other references. Major Stephenson bought his plantation in September 1836 (Deed Book B:317), and the first possible evidence of the nursery came almost four years later when on March 2, 1840, the county governing committee, the Board of Police, ordered, "that Major Stephenson be allowed to change the Holly Springs & Mount Pleasant road around his garden." (Board of Police Minutes, 2:10). The next piece of evidence is clear and wonderfully detailed. The editor in the November 14, 1846, issue of the *Holly Springs Gazette* commented that: "Major Stephenson has our thanks for the handsome present of some of the finest and best flavored apples we have ever tasted. These apples were raised by Major Stephenson, who has upwards of ten thousand fruit trees of every quality, variety, and description by sale."

In an 1855 letter to the *Southern Cultivator*, the primary Mid-South agricultural journal, Dr. Willis M. Lea, of Wildwood plantation west of Holly Springs, commented enthusiastically on the Stephenson Seedling. All this evidence pales before a recently discovered let-

---

1 Obituary of E. L. McAlexander, Holly Springs *South Reporter*, March 2, 1933.

2 Interview with Martha Moseley, June 16, 1965, and with John I. McAlexander, November 22, 1967.

ter in the Old Courthouse Museum Library in Vicksburg. Among the holdings is an 1852 letter from Major Stephenson to Jefferson Davis that accompanied a shipment of apple, pear, peach, and plum trees. The letter includes instructions for planting. If that document provides as much as we will ever know about the Stephenson orchard, that is enough.[3]

3 Willis M. Lea letter, of 1855, *Southern Cultivator*, 13:131.

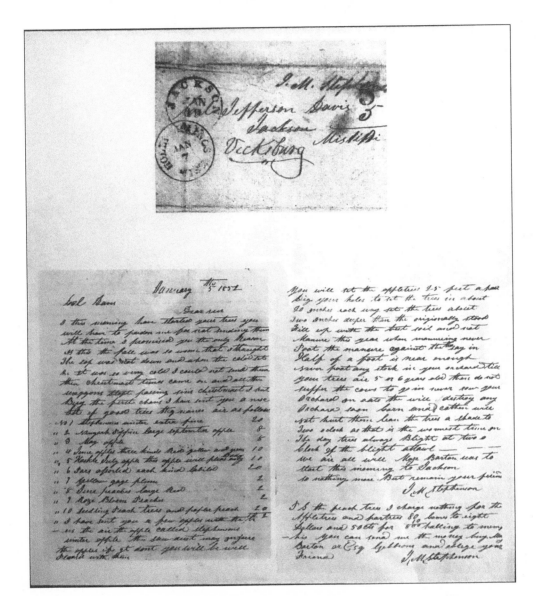

Major Stephenson's letter to Jefferson Davis
Old Courthouse Museum Library, Vicksburg, MS

The fields of Marshall County were still white with cotton,
which was harvested primarily by sharecroppers now. Smith Collection

The Slaves of "Strawberry Plains"

Hubert H. McAlexander

Chapter 4 from *Strawberry Plains Audubon Center: Four Centuries of a Mississippi Landscape*, by Hubert H. McAlexander. Jackson, Mississippi, University Press of Mississippi, 2008. National Audubon Society.

According to the 1860 slave schedules of the U.S. census, E. N. Davis at Strawberry Plains in Marshall County owned 114 slaves. The census taker came on July 16, when the field hands were cultivating the crops, and the slave count is divided into four sections: 16 house servants and skilled workers; 45 children under the age of thirteen; 27 male field hands, aged thirty to thirteen; and 26 female field hands, aged thirty-four to thirteen.[1]

At that particular day the slave children would have been under the care of a mature nurse and several older slave girls. These nurses would have been included among the eleven female slaves in the group of house servants and skilled workers. Others of the eleven women servants, who ranged in age from fifty-four to sixteen, filled the positions of cook for the family and the house servants, cook for the field hands, housekeeper, house maid, laundress, and head nurse for the children of the big house. The five males in this first group, varying in age from sixty to twenty-five, would typically have included a blacksmith, a carpenter, a carriage driver who probably also oversaw the stables, a gardener, and a servant with general duties inside the big house. The names of only a few of these servants have been passed down. Aunt Sarah was the big house cook, Aunt Margaret Lee was the Davis children's nurse, her husband Frank Lee was a house servant, and Edmund was the carriage driver.[2]

The house servants were considered the privileged group among the slaves. They were the best dressed, and they ate the most varied and delicate fare that was served to the family. Some, in violation of Mississippi's slave laws, were taught to read by Martha Greenlee

---

1 Slave schedules of the 1860 U.S. Census for Marshall County, Mississippi, 40.

2 John Hebron Moore, *The Emergence of the Cotton Kingdom in the Old Southwest: Mississippi 1770-1860* (Baton Rouge: Louisiana State University Press, 1988), 108; Eugene D. Genovese, *Roll, Jordan, Roll: The World the Slaves Made* (New York: Random House, 1974), 328; William H. Duncan, "A Brief Account of the Life of Martha Trimble Greenlee Davis (1823-1906)," written in fall 1979 for a graduate folklore course at the University of Arkansas, Little Rock, in the Audubon Mississippi/ Strawberry Plains Finley Collection, Special Collections, John Davis Williams Library, University of Mississippi (hereafter abbreviated as AM/SPF); Robert Milton Winter (ed.), *Our Pen Is Time: The Diary of Emma Finley* (Lafayette, California: Thomas-Berryhill Press, 1999), 70. I have also drawn upon my own article, "Strawberry Plains: House of History" published in the June 19, 1958 Holly Springs *South Reporter*, and corrected some mistakes made there almost fifty years ago.

Davis. They lived on the ridge across the ravine from the front of the big house. According to the testimony of slaves on comparable Marshall County plantations, all slave dwellings were like the Finley's frontier cabin, "good log houses with dirt and stick chimneys." Beds were what the slaves called one or two-legged "aggies" with one end fastened to the log walls. Mattresses were "pretty comfortable, with ticks stuffed with shucks and rye." These houses across the ravine, together with the clusters of cabins for field hands to the northwest and to the east, numbered twelve buildings. Some were one-room affairs, but married couples with a number of children were given double pen log houses. Large planters typically set aside space by the slave cabins for small vegetable gardens. We know that at Wood-cote plantation nearby, a patch was provided to the rear of the cabins for the slaves to grow tobacco for their own use. Many of the slave yards there also had chicken houses and, at the neighboring Clopton plantation, the "thrifty women sold many chickens and eggs — thereby making their 'change.'"[3]

Census records reveal the identities of two of Eben Davis's overseers: in 1850 William A. Andrews, a twenty-six-year-old Alabamian, and in 1860 Booker Flippin, a twenty-four-year-old Virginian and the first cousin of neighboring Richard O. Woodson. Among the Strawberry Plains papers is Davis's contract with Flippin, a rare surviving document in northern Mississippi:

> Article of an agreement made & entered into by & between E. N. Davis of the first part and Booker Flippin of the second part, To wit:
>
> I Booker Flippin of the second part hath agreed to attend to the business of E. N. Davis as an Overseer for twelve months. I give my entire service to the said Davis for the said specified time. I agree to stay with & attend faithfully to the hands & see that their work is properly done. To treat the slaves as humanely & kind as their own conduct will allow. To attend to the stock of every kind to see that they are properly fed and salted regularly. To attend to all the geare and tools of every kind to keep them in good order and in their proper places. To attend to the slaves & see that they have the proper attention on the part of the other servants. See that they keep their bedding and wearing apparel in good order, washed & mended & observe that each slave shall keep their person cleanly and hair combed once a week. I agree to attend to all the business appertaining to the duties of an Overseer & farthermore [sic] I agree to make up or deduct all loss time either by sickness or otherwise. Said Davis agrees on his part if the said Flippin shall continue with him for twelve months

3 Moore, *Emergence of the Cotton Kingdom*, 108; McAlexander, "Strawberry Plains"; narrative of Aaron Jones in George P. Rawick (ed.), *The American Slave: A Composite Autobiography*, Supplement Series I, vol. 8, *Mississippi Narratives* (Westport, Connecticut: Greenwood Press, 1977), 1185-1186; William Kaufman Scarborough, *Masters of the Big House: Elite Slaveholders of the Mid-Nineteenth Century South* (Baton Rouge, Louisiana State University Press, 2003), 201; Clara Clayton Fant, "Away Down South in Dixie," 1885 manuscript, photocopy in McAlexander Collection, University of Mississippi; Seymour Carpenter, quoted in Edwin Sawyer Walker (ed.), *Genealogical Notes of the Carpenter Family, Including the Autobiography and Personal Reminiscences of Dr. Seymour D. Carpenter* (Springfield, Illinois: Illinois State Journal Co., 1907), 96.

as agreed to do the said Davis is to pay said Flippin four hundred dollars at the rate of thirty-three dollars 33/100 cents per month & if either party shall become dissatisfied we can separate by the said Davis paying said Flippin for the time he may have been in service. Given under our hands Jany 17th 1860.

   E. N. Davis

   B. Flippin

Serving immediately under the overseer would have been one or more slave foremen (or drivers). The overseer's contract begins to convey to us some of the reality of chattel slavery, and the strange status of these human beings who were also regarded as possessions, like the stock and tools.[4]

Flippin commenced his job soon after the harvest. As is true of all farming operations, work at Strawberry Plains had a seasonal rhythm. The first three months of the year were devoted to maintenance and repair and indoor work. Each slave had "his own task," Callie Gray, a former slave on the Fant plantation west of Holly Springs, told a WPA interviewer. "Some hauled wood to last all year, some plaited corn-shuck mule collars, and split rails and mended fences and bottomed chairs and lots of other things." Some women, she said, "sewed all the time after Miss Liza cut out the clothes, and they sewed with they fingers 'cause they warn't no sewing machines. They spun the thread and dyed and wove it too. They dyed it with walnuts and shumake and oak bark, and copperas wuz put in the dye too."[5]

From late March through late April, field hands were engaged in planting corn, oats, wheat and vegetable gardens, as well as cotton. From late spring until August, hands labored cultivating the crops. "August," as one Marshall County resident recalled, "was a transition month — too soon to harvest and too late to plant or cultivate — a time to rest if such were possible in the heat and humidity." Another upland man who had himself labored in the cotton fields left a more lyric description of August: "It gave us a fine feeling to look out over our well-tilled fields and to see the heat radiating upward in dazzling waves, to see cotton blooming and the corn tasseling out. August was cotton-growing weather, and the hotter the better — cotton liked the blazing heat, chilled now and then by a short sudden August shower. The fields blossomed like islands in the South Seas, white and red hibiscus-like cotton flowers on the green cotton plants that spread away in long curving rows across the silky vermilion of the fields." Both writers note that this

---

4 Henry Morton Woodson, *The Woodsons and Their Connections* (Memphis, Tennessee, 1915), 301, 465; Booker Flippin contract, AM/SPF; Genovese, *Roll, Jordan, Roll*, 305-306; Eben Davis's granddaughter Martha V. Moseley had apparently confused "overseer" and "driver" when she told me in the 1950s that Strawberry Plains had a slave overseer.

5 Rawick (ed.), *The American Slave*, vol. 8, 804.

hot month of rest was reserved for the annual religious festivals at camp meetings. In the Strawberry Plains neighborhood, a large camp meeting was held at Wesley Campground, a six-acre tract lying in Section 26, Township 2, Range 3, on the northern bank of the Cold-water River. The Clopton tutor Seymour Carpenter remarks that it lasted for a week. "The colored people held their services in a shed about a hundred yards from the white people," he tells us, "and I have never heard more moving music than their singing, especially at night, when, as they said, 'The power got hold of them.'"[6]

The August revival bolstered the faithful for the yearly routine of religious obser-vances. We have already heard Carpenter's description of the slaves attending services at Wesley Chapel along with the Clopton family. Clara Clayton Fant's memoir of Wood-cote plantation adds more to our knowledge of slave religious life. Located ten miles to the northeast of Strawberry Plains, Wood-cote was a comparable land holding, supported by the labor of 140 blacks. Wood-cote slaves went twice a month to the master's church for a service just for them. Clara Fant notes their restrained, respectful attention to those sermons, and comments, like Carpenter, on the beauty and power of the singing. "Their whole hearts found utterance in the singing. They had remarkable voices, the men espe-cially, and though altogether untaught, they sang with perfect time and harmony. As they neared the end of the hymns and their emotion increased, they would meet each other in the aisle, with a hearty and prolonged shaking of hands, but with no noise or confusion to disturb the music. In addition to these services at the white church, there were also reli-gious observances at Wood-cote conducted by African American preachers on Sunday eve-nings, which were much more impassioned and emotional. The slave services mentioned in memoirs of Strawberry Plains were likely at of the same order. Church was probably held in a shed or a barn or under a brush arbor that the slaves had constructed.[7]

After the time of rest and revival came fall, the season of unremitting labor from dawn to sundown. Throughout the work week during the winter and the spring planting, work-ers assembled at the plantation kitchen for all meals, eaten under large trees in fair weather or within doors around the huge fireplace. But during cotton-picking season, the midday meal was brought to the workers in the fields, and all hands (men, women and the older children) did not return for supper until dark. All year round, provisions were given to

---

6 E. N. Davis to James D. Davidson, 9 April 1856, and 14 Aug 1858, Davidson Papers, McCormick Collection, Wisconsin State Historical Society, Madison; James M. Power, typescript of memoir of his moth-er, McAlexander Collection, 93, 102; Ben Robertson, Red Hills and Cotton (New York: Alfred A. Knopf, 1942), 222-223; sectional index for Section 26, Township 2, Range 3, Deed Book O, 44, Chancery Clerk's Office, Marshall County, Mississippi; Walker (ed.), *Genealogical Notes of the Carpenter Family*, 98.

7 1860 Marshall County, Mississippi, slave schedules, 95 B; Fant, "Away Down South in Dixie," 4; McAlexander, "Strawberry Plains."

slave families for Sunday, when they cooked their own meals in their cabins.[8]

The end of the cotton harvest was celebrated with a barbeque. It would have been, with seasonal variations, like the annual plantation barbeque given to celebrate the Fourth of July, when the slaves at Wood-cote feasted on "whole Shoates and mutton," fresh peaches, and early watermelon. Not long after the harvest celebration came Christmas, the "grand holiday of the year," the Wood-cote mistress called it, and other observer confirm its importance in the yearly cycle of slave life. The occasion was likely observed in a similar fashion at Strawberry Plains. "There was no work for four days, and dancing and feasting lasted through the whole. How they did enjoy the dancing! The banjo and the fiddler were played as fast as fast could be, but never too fast for the untiring feet, and the 'pigeon wing' was cut and the 'double shuffle' shuffled in a manner wonderful to beold. At Christmas too were distributed new shoes, hats and clothes. There were great good boxes of them, and each person was allowed to try on till suited. Then my father made a small gift of money to them, giving most liberally to the hardest workers." Here Mrs. Fant's account lends support to historians like Eugene Genovese, who chronicled so well this enslaved race's amazing capacity for both faith and joy under a repressive institution. It also puts in context the old Strawberry Plains story that one year Eben Davis, as a special reward, presented his workers (perhaps only the "hardest workers") with top hats.[9]

Throughout the year, there were other special occasions, like the marriage between two slaves noted in Emma Finley's 1818 diary: "There is to be a wedding tonight — the happy couple James & Julia Ann; — the wardrobe almost completed, & cakes, pies, chickens, meats generally are in a state of preparation." Though denied the legal bonds of marriage by state law, slaves of the more religious masters and mistresses were sometimes joined in a ceremony performed on the steps of the big house, followed by a wedding feast. "I remember well when my nurse, whom I loved dearly, was married," Clara Clayton Fant wrote. "The bridal party came up to our house and stood in one of the porticoes; the bride dressed in a pretty white Swiss muslin, that fitted nicely her neat figure, with a single rose in her hair." At Wood-cote slaves were married by the family minister, whereas on the Finley and Davis plantations, the masters probably read the service. But at none of the three, apparently, were slaves married by the folk ceremony of jumping the broom stick.[10]

Simple recreations were enjoyed on Sundays and during lulls in the farming year. "De

8 Moore, *Emergence of the Cotton Kingdom*, 104.

9 Fant, "Away Down South in Dixie", 5; McAlexander, "Strawberry Plains"; Duncan, "A Brief Account"; AM/SPF

10 Winter (ed.), *Our Pen Is Time*, 12; Genovese, *Roll, Jordan, Roll*, 475-481; Fant, "Away Down South in Dixie"; 4-5.

pleasures de slaves had," one former slave commented to a WPA interviewer, who was prone to broad dialectic transcriptions, "wuz things lak fishing, hunting, an' frolicking." Sundays and the slow periods in the agricultural cycle offered time for fishing and for hunting during the day or at night. Mrs. Fant ranks "possom hunting as the male slaves' 'chief amusement.'" She recalls, "On a bright moon light night the sounding of the horn and the barking of the dogs could be heard on the hills till far into the night." The "frolics," or dances, were so popular that when one was held on any plantation in the vicinity, neighboring planters would often provide passes so their slaves could go to them.[11]

Within the hierarchy of the plantation, a responsible, humane mistress contributed greatly to the health and welfare of the slaves. The eulogy of the "ole mistress," or "ole miss," of Wood-cote strikes the same notes sounded often in the descriptions of the duties and skills of Martha Greenlee Davis: "It was she who visited and watched over the sick, saw they were well nursed and the doctor's directions followed. It was she who superintended the work of the women, the weaving, the spinning (for their clothes were made at home and the wheel and loom were always going), the cutting out, the sewing, and the knitting, and saw that every man, woman, and child was well clothed." By all accounts, Martha Greenlee Davis filled conscientiously and ably the responsibilities of the mistress of a large plantation. The measure of respect felt for her is suggested by the loyalty of her servants during and after the war.[12]

Some others with whom the slaves were in close contact did not get such high marks. Former slaves expressed great bitterness toward the patrollers, who policed the neighborhoods trying to catch slaves who had left the home plantation without a pass. Stories of slaves eluding or escaping from them run throughout the area's WPA slave narratives. But the scorn evidenced for the patrollers was no match for the loathing expressed towards overseers. As one Marshall County slave voiced the feeling, the overseers "was death and gaul… common white trash." John Hebron Moore's history of antebellum agriculture, *The Emergence of the Cotton Kingdom in the Old Southwest*, documents a decline in corporeal punishment by the mid-nineteenth century and finds that "progressive planters [instead] resorted to incentives during the later decades of the slavery era in an effort to obtain a maximum of labor from their slaves." But a few, Moore acknowledges, "abandoned the use of the whip altogether," and whippings are reported in Seymour Carpenter's account of life on the Clopton plantation in 1846. Like the recruit, whose hostility is focused upon the drill sergeant rather than the company commander, slaves naturally hated most the

---

11 Sylvia Floyd, quoted in Moore, *Emergence of the Cotton Kingdom*, 104; Fant, "Away Down South in Dixie," 6-7.

12 Fant, "Away Down South in Dixie," 7.

overseer, the man who administered the lashes. Still, in the WPA narratives, former slaves were often candid in judging masters, as exemplified in the testimony of Jerry Howell of Marshall County, who judged his own master "mighty good," but the owner of the adjoining plantation "unmercifully cruel."[13]

The only surviving documentary evidence of Eben Davis's place on the scale of masters is the clause he wrote into the 1860 overseer's agreement requiring that Flippin "treat the slaves as humanely and kind as their conduct will allow." The clause, of course, is subject to various interpretations. But one thing certain is that, in the mid-1850s, the rhythm of labor changed at Strawberry Plains and the hard labor required of the strongest among the slave force increased.

In February 1855, Eben Davis reported to James Davidson in Virginia that there is "a great feeling manifested by the planters of the hill county to go to the bottom lands, for our hill county is exhausting so fast." Davis had purchased 10,000 acres in Arkansas for nineteen cents an acre, and in the fall of 1854, he had signed the first contract to construct part of the levee along the eastern bank of the Mississippi in exchange for land patents in the "Mississippi bottom," as the Delta was then called, for the patents evidently totaling 30,000 acres. He cited as provocation that year's "poor crop which drove me into this speculation to give employment to my hands." Only male field hands were used for this heavy work, and after a few months Davis was asking Davidson's help in securing "some 6 or 8 negro men & boys."[14]

In early April 1850, he wrote Davidson that he had finished the levee, which he referred to with pride: "It is a grand piece of work." But he had met the terms of his contract only by keeping all his "efficient hands" at the river until the middle of March. Then bringing his work force back to Strawberry Plains, he had planted corn, but would not start planting cotton until late April.

In the ensuing years he continued to counterbalance the demands of Strawberry Plains with his levee building, constantly moving slaves between the river and the Marshall County plantation. Two growing seasons later, in August 1858, Davis wrote he was anticipating a record crop, while in the midst of another levee contract with "some 30 odd hands Leveeing on the Miss. river." He planned to bring them back to Strawberry Plains by October 1 to harvest the crop, and he commented, "Then nothing but Sickness, Sundays & rainy days will stop us."

---

13 Rawick (ed.), *The American Slave*, vol. 8, 1187, vol. 6, 204-205, vol. 7, 350-351, 366; Moore, *Emergence of the Cotton Kingdom*, 110; Walker (ed.), *Genealogical Notes of the Carpenter Family*, 100; Rawick (ed.), *The American Slave*, vol. 8, 1186, vol. 7, 365-366, vol. 8, 1052.

14 Davis to Davidson, 17 Feb 1855, Davidson Papers, McCormick Collection.

Oxford courthouse with tents of federal troops around it.

Part III:
Flames of War

The Yankees Are Coming

Courtesy, Arthur Palmer Hudson

From *Strawberry Plains Audubon Center: Four Centuries of a Mississippi Landscape*, by Hubert H. McAlexander. Jackson, MS: University Press of Mississippi, 2008, Chapter 8. "Devastation" pp. 66-68.

Originally published in *Specimens of Mississippi Folk-Lore* by Arthur Palmer Hudson. Printed by Edwards Brothers, 1928, 344 pages.

The Marshall County countryside was anything but a haven. The Alexander Civil War diary bears witness to the continued uncertainties of living under the threat of invasion, with the only hope of protection from the Union troops being the Confederate cavalry company of Capt. Billy Mitchell, raised in the Coldwater countryside and active locally through much of the conflict. The constant menace the citizens faced was even voiced in a local song, "The Yankees Are Coming," sung to the tune of "The Campbells Are Coming."

Nine of its ten stanzas were preserved in the ledger of a country store a few miles west of Strawberry Plains:

The Yankees are coming! Away! Which Way?
Who saw them? Do tell us. And what did they?
Are they infantry, cavalry? How many? How far?
Fifteen hundred, they say and are at Lamar.

The Yankees are coming! They'll be here by daylight,
Until the brave Mitchell shall put them to flight,
Or ambush and whip them, as often he has done,
With his handful of men and the double-barrel'd gun.

The Yankees are coming! Did you hear the drum?

Hark! Boom goes the cannon! They surely do come,
With Matches! They'll steal the last mule that we have,
For thieves they are all, up to Grant and his staff.

The Yankees are coming! Send the news round and round,
They're many, says a courier, but three miles from town.
Oh mercy! they are here. You may run if you will,
But yonder they rise o'er the top of the hill.

The Yankees are coming! See, they dash through the street.
Some are looking for mules, and others for meat.
Bang. Down goes the door, and out go the mules
With saddles and harness and all sorts of tools.

The Yankees are come, vile thieves that they are.
Thus are old men and women to wage such a war.
They spoil all our gardens; not a chicken they spare,
To an old sitting hen and the clothes your babes wear.

The Yankees are come! Yes, alas it is true,
Each one of them breeched in his sky blue.
I hear their sabers. Clatter, clatter! they go.
How fiendish they look. They are jayhawkers, I know.

Now Yankees are come — yes, the worst of the crew,
From Iowa, Kansas, and Illinois, too.
To restore the blest Union at Abraham's call,
The negroes set free and drive Secesh to the wall.

The Yankees are come! How madly they rave!
The rebellion they'll crush and Vicksburg they'll have.
In their efforts they say they will never relax
Till Pemberton's whipped, or they die in their tracks.

Van Dorn's Raid

Mrs. Carrington Mason (née Maria Boddie)

Typed copy of original at Marshall County Historical Museum

Over the entrance of an ancient library was this inscription, "And much remains unsung."

This is not more true of the songs than of the deeds of the people.

The world is full of heroes — the fame they acquire is a matter of accident or opportunity. An admiring nation may kneel at their altar of sacrifice, or the smoke of conflict may hide the brave deeds, while the dust licks up the blood they freely shed for their country. The world's history of its great men and its lessons, the record of their self-sacrifice and devotion to principle.

Abraham is not known as the father of a mighty nation, but as the "father of the faithful." We think of George Washington not as receiving the sword of Cornwallis, but as "Washington crossing the Delaware."

Our war with Spain furnished one of the most brilliant episodes in history. With a straight uncomplicated fight, the world for spectators, the home country greedy for news of the battle, and unlimited telegraphic facilities to herald every day's doings, the incidents of the war were of unusual interest and completeness. The daring feat of Admiral Dewey, which has thrilled our nation and challenged the admiration of the world, brings to my remembrance an unrecorded, but not less brilliant, victory in which a band of 1,600 ragged Confederate cavalry brought about the disastrous retreat of an army of 60,000 men commanded by General U.S. Grant.

In "The War of Rebellion: A Compilation of the Official Records of the Union and Confederate States," published under the direction of the Honorable Russel Alger, Secretary of War, I find no mention of this raid so splendid in its execution and so disastrous in its results to the Federal Army. On page 34, series 1, vol. LII, there is a letter from General Grant to General Hallick, written from Oxford, Miss., on December 14, 1862, referring to certain promotions in which he says incidentally, "The people of Mississippi show more signs of being subdued than any we have heretofore come across. They are very cordial in their reception of federal officers and seem desirous of having trade resumed."

Grant is back in Memphis on January 2, 1863, and writes to have a regiment of heavy artillery from St. Louis report to him. He wants six companies at Memphis and six at Corinth, Miss.. There is no word to explain why Grant was at Oxford, Miss., on December 14, and back at Memphis on January 2. The only light thrown on the matter from a Confederate source is a letter from General Joe Johnston to Jefferson Davis in which he says, "Grant is still on the Tallahatchie so that the remainder of Loring's and Price's troops cannot be removed from Grenada. From his halting, I suppose he is repairing the railroad. The force at Grenada (about 11,000 men) is too weak to do more than delay the passage of the river by the enemy. My hope of keeping him back is in Van Dorn, under whom I propose to unite all the available cavalry when Forrest and Roddy can be found."

The Confederate Army, under the leadership of General Earl Van Dorn, had on the 3rd, 4th, and 5th of October, 1862, been thrown against the fortifications of Corinth, Mississippi, a place of great strategic value, being at the junction of two important railroads and the scene of the battle of Shiloh. The Confederate forces had met with a terrible defeat, General Price having lost one third of his command of 7,000 men. The army was completely demoralized and disregarding all discipline, they straggled cold, hungry and dispirited into the neighboring towns and farm houses.

They came into Holly Springs, Mississippi, a town of about 2,500 inhabitants, by twos and threes, all of a cold, rainy October day, many of them barefooted and in shirt sleeves. Some of them had begged pieces of rag carpet from the farmers' wives, and cutting a hole in the middle through which they thrust their heads, thus combined tent, overcoat and umbrella.

The people made great fires in their houses and laid them along on the floors; it was the best they could do, the blankets had long ago been sent to the boys in the army. In a few days, the soldiers were gathered into two encampments, one consisting of about 7,000 men at Hudsonville, six miles north; the other of 6,000 Missourians under General Stirling Price at Lumpkin's Mill, four miles south of Holly Springs.

While they were in camp, I rode out to see a review of General Price's command. It was a sorry sight. Many of the men were bareheaded and barefooted, and all were shabby. They had requested to be allowed to march in the original companies in which they had come out from Missouri. In some of the companies there were barely enough men to furnish the necessary officers, and some of the flags didn't carry silk enough to make a handkerchief. Yet, the sun of Indian Summer shone kindly down on their broken ranks, and I do not remember ever to have seen a despondent soldier. We think the soldier's life a trying one and so it is, but it contains one element which more than counterbalances all its hardships. It is freedom from responsibility. It is not labor, but care and anxiety that spoil the life and rob us of our rest. The soldier has only to obey and to take one step at a time. The private is really freer than the General who commands him.

In the meantime, the blackest of war clouds was gathering on the western horizon. General Grant was collecting his troops at the Grand Junction, the intersection of the

Memphis and Charleston and Illinois Central railroads. The government had tried in vain to open the navigation of the Mississippi River. The batteries at Vicksburg still offered an impassable barrier. Grant determined to raise an army large enough to overcome all opposition, and with the Illinois Central Railroad as a means of transportation to cut off Vicksburg in the rear and to starve it into surrender.

One night in early December, General Price and his staff were spending the evening at my house. At eleven o'clock, an order came from General Van Dorn to begin the retreat at once as the Federal cavalry was advancing from the Grand Junction, only 25 miles away. Between midnight and day Van Dorn's entire command passed through the town, and when morning came, we found ourselves inside the Federal lines. The sound of the bugle broke the stillness of the morning and before we could say, "The Yankees are coming," the cavalry dashed into town.

It was a sore sight to Southern eyes, but numbers, style, and elegance of equipment in comparison with the shabbiness of the Confederate cavalry offered a fascination which could not be resisted. The bluegrass paddocks of Kentucky and Tennessee had supplied the officers with the finest of thoroughbreds and the splendid uniforms and gay flags presented more the effect of a pageant than an army.

The next day the infantry began to arrive. My home stood at the end of the street on which they came into town, so that they turned to the west in front of the house, marched one square, then turned south again into the Oxford road, so I believe I saw every regiment in the army for although the sight was heart-breaking, it was magnificent.

First would pass by the regimental band playing always "The Girl I left Behind Me," then marching four abreast in handsome new uniforms, come the infantry, and as the music of one regiment died away, the next could be heard in the distance, and so on and on for three days they came, as we thought, a great blue monster, going to swallow up the devoted victims of the Confederacy.

The wagon train was five days long.

I wanted very much to see General Grant and suposed his escort would be specially distinguished, but either because they were all so elegant or he was so modest, I failed to recognize him.

But we soon learned that this was no passing show. General Grant had determined to make Holly Springs his headquarters, and the depot of supplies for his army, the Illinois Central Railroad furnishing a long line for transportation both North and South, and communication with the Mississippi River being easy through Memphis. It is astonishing what immediate and complete possession any army takes of a town when one settles down upon it. All the public buildings are seized for headquarters and army offices, and the best dwelling houses become hospitals and homes of officers. Livery stables, warehouses, depot buildings, and a large armory where the Confederates had tried to make guns, were filled with magazine stores, provisions, and the winter clothing of the troops.

And the sutlers, that curse of the army, came by hundreds. All the little old shops on the public square which had nothing but the sleepy comfort of good times, were crammed to their utmost capacity with whiskey, canned goods, and cheap clothing, til they fairly shook with a delirium of excitement. The negroes, liberated by the coming of the Yankees, swarmed in the streets, spent their money, and got drunk in celebration of their freedom.

Three weeks passed away; the main body of the Federal Army had gone as far south as Oxford, Mississippi, their advance had reached Coffeeville, and it seemed as if nothing short of a miracle could turn them back. The Confederate Army had apparently melted away; there was not even a skirmish to relieve the monotony.

In the meantime, Uncle Sam was pouring into the little town of Holly Springs a wealth of provision for the "Boys in Blue." Many officers' wives had settled themselves for the winter in the homes of the citizens, who true to their Southern traditions, were offering them a kindly if compulsory hospitality.

On the morning of December 20, as I lay in bed, I heard a sound which I thought was the singing of the wood fire, but on going nearer it, I found that the sound came from a distance. Raising the window, I cried out, "Oh, it is the Rebel yell I hear firing out at the railroad station!" In a moment there dashed up the street a squad of most disreputable-looking fellows, who cried out "Got any Yankees in your house," but before they could reply to my "What's the matter?" they were gone.

The firing grew more and more furious, and untrained as I was to the noises of battle, I thought a thousand men must be falling at every explosion. In a little while, another squad of men went dashing by, but they called out that Van Dorn's cavalry had captured the town. I ran down to the public square and rushed into pandemonium as never enacted except in a captured town.

Citizens, negroes, yankees and rebels were stirring around in inextricable confusion; squads of Federal prisoners were being brought in faster than they could be patrolled; and there were not Confederates enough to guard them. The sutler stores were being rifled while officers were having the heads of whiskey barrels knocked in for fear the soldiers might get drunk. The post office seemed to promise a rich booty, and many negroes sat all day opening letters with the hope of finding money.

Many of the citizens were delirious with joy, and for a moment, indulged the hope of a permanent occupation by the Confederates, but we soon learned that Van Dorn's entire force consisted of but 1600 men who with their horses were exhausted from several days and nights hard riding, and that they must "fire and fall back."

The warehouses and depot buildings where the clothing and commissaries of the Federal Army were stored were half a mile away, and soon great columns of smoke floating over the town told that the work of destruction had begun. The greatest difficulty encountered by the Confederates was getting rid of the magazine stores. They were backed in brick livery stables on the public square and to have set fire to one of them would blow up the entire town. So the principal occupation of the soldiers and citizens was to take the ammunition out, make it into small piles in the streets. and set them off one by one. A stable which was not entirely emptied by the soldiers was set on fire after they left, and the explosion broke almost every windowpane in town.

It must have gone hard with the hungry, ragged rebels to burn all those warm clothes and good rations, but they dared not overburden their tired horses, as they had a long, dangerous journey before them. But the prospect of frostbitten feet was too much for them and nearly every soldier had a bunch of wool socks tied at the back of his saddle.

When all was over and the Confederate troops were drawn up in a line for their departure, it was almost impossible to realize that such a body of men, so ragged and worn, riding horses that were little better than skeletons, could have conceived a feat so brilliant and have executed it with such consummate skill and daring. They had left the city of Grenada, ridden more than a hundred miles, and made a wide circuit around the Federal Army. The men had been in the saddle day and night almost without food, rest or sleep. Their pants were worn off to the knees, and their horses reeled as they ran.

Van Dorn had found on the road three men who had what are called trading passes. Three of the soldiers took their clothes and passes and going into town at night discovered the location of the troops and pickets. They ran into town at daybreak, General Sam Jackson of Belle Meade, Tennessee, leading the advance. As they captured the pickets, no alarm was given, and the surprise was so complete that no resistance was offered. Most of the officers were in bed.

It was evident that General Grant had counted too confidently on the weakness of his enemy. An attack in the rear was a contingency for which no provision was made. And millions of dollars worth of valuable stores had been piled up in Holly Springs, but not a single breastwork had been thrown up, not one bale of cotton had been placed on another for defense in case of attack. There were thousands of soldiers in the town, but they evidently never expected to be awakened by the Rebel yell.

The casualties were ridiculously small so far as I could learn, there was not one man killed. A Federal soldier, running from a Confederate, looked back with his mouth open and a rebel took aim and shot right into it.

There were many officers' wives in town, but though terribly shocked and frightened, they were entirely unmolested. General Grant's family were boarding in the home of Mrs. Pringle [Push] Govan, a beautiful and cultured woman, a daughter of Bishop Hawkes of

New York. Mrs. Grant had gone to Oxford to spend the day with the General, but she returned to find all of her belongings safe with her hostess, only her carriage had been burned along with other "munitions of war." It is said that when the Confederate soldiers came rushing in hoping to capture General Grant's war papers, Mrs. Govan met them at the head of the stairs and said, "Soldiers, it doesn't become a Southern gentleman to enter a lady's bedroom." They all turned back leaving the coveted prize in a bureau drawer.

The Confederate soldiers formed in line about four o'clock in the afternoon and vanished as suddenly as they had appeared, leaving nothing but smoldering ruins and taking only the consciousness of a glorious victory.

Penetrating still further into the enemy lines, they broke up the Memphis and Charleston Railroad at LaGrange, Tennessee, and proceeded north on the Illinois Central as far as Bolivar, burning bridges and trestles in every possible way, obstructing operations of Grant's army. These men were in the saddle 17 days alternating a ride of eight hours and rest of four, day and night. They carried all their ammunition on their persons, slept on the ground without blankets and shared their scanty rations of corn only with their horses.

Never was there a greater vicissitude of fortune from the height of triumph to the depth of despair than befell that little border town as night closed in on that December 20, 1862. The 2500 paroled soldiers swarmed like a hive of angry bees. Defeated, hungry, and houseless, they declared they would burn the town and were only prevented by the instinctive generosity of the people. Seeing the sad plight of these men, the citizens to the utmost of their capacity, took them into their homes, and these soldiers rewarded their hospitality by affording them much needed protection in the dark days that followed.

The burning of millions of dollars of Government stores was a heavy blow, but the consequences of their destruction was far more disastrous. That splendid army had been gotten together at great expense, and many weeks had been consumed in carrying them into the heart of Mississippi. Now the railroad was broken up, the stores burned, the country through which they had come was devastated, and there was nothing left to do but beat a hasty retreat. A march of a hundred miles for a big army almost without rations was a situation which might well perplex the wisest of generals, and it was one to which Uncle Sam's army was altogether unaccustomed. But General Grant, imperturbable in defeat as in victory, marched his army back to Memphis, and so far as the records show, the world never knew that he had sustained a disastrous defeat, he merely changed his tale.

The dashing and ill-fated General Earl Van Dorn
Mississippi Department of Archives and History

General Earl Van Dorn and Faulkner's Use of History

Hubert H. McAlexander

Originally published in *The Journal of Mississippi History*, 40 (Fall 1977), 357-61.

"I dont care much for facts, am not much interested in them," William Faulkner wrote in a 1946 letter to Malcolm Crowley. "You cant stand a fact up, you've got to prop it up, and when you move to one side a little and look at it from that angle, it's not thick enough to cast a shadow in that direction."[1] The statement, which was specifically a defense of the inconsistencies between *The Sound and the Fury* and the recently written appendix to the novel, stands as the most revealing of Faulkner's many comments on the relative value of the factual. And it articulates particularly well his attitude toward historical fact.

This feeling evidently had its roots far back in Faulkner's past. Questioned in 1938 by Robert Cantwell on the sources of his historical knowledge, Faulkner replied: "'I never read any history… I talked to people. If I got it straight it's because I didn't worry with other people's ideas about it. When I was a boy there were a lot of people around who had lived through [the Civil War], and I would pick it up I was saturated with it, but never read about it."[2] Corroborating such remarks are interviews with Phil Stone, a friend during Faulkner's early years, in which Stone contrasts his own interest in the Civil War "from a historical point of view" with Faulkner's attraction to "local legends, heroic anecdotes, 'smart-cracks,' and tall tales."[3] One should not take these statements to mean that Faulkner was not also interested in written history, especially that of the Civil War period."[4] But the direction of his interest is clear: Faulkner was attracted to history, not as the factual matter of the past, but as the story of the past. He was always drawn to the human dimension, not just of those who lived those far-off events, but of those who told them. Of greatest

---

1 Malcolm Cowley, *The Faulkner-Cowley File: Letters and Memories, 1944-1962* (New York, XXX.

2 Robert Cantwell, "The Faulkners: Recollections of a Gifted Family," *William Faulkner: Two Decades of Criticism*, ed. Fredrick J. Hoffman and Olga W. Vickery (New York, 1960), 57.

3 H. Edward Richardson, *William Faulkner: The Journey to Self-Discovery* (Columbia, Missouri, 1969), 39.

4 From many of his public statements, one can usually gauge the breadth of Faulkner's reading in history. In addition, Joseph Blotner's *William Faulkner's Library—a Catalogue* (Charlottesville, 1962) reveals that the library contained twenty-three volumes devoted to the history of Mississippi and the South.

importance was the cast shadow, and as an artist Faulkner was constantly changing the prop of historical fact to achieve just the kind of shadow he wanted.

Perhaps nowhere is this creative process more clearly displayed than in his use of the career of the famed figure from his area's Civil War past—the Confederate general Earl Van Dorn. The relevant "facts" are these: on December 20, 1862, Van Dorn made a daring raid on General Ulysses S. Grant's base of supplies at Holly Springs, Mississippi, destroying a million dollars worth of material. Five months after this event, perhaps the pinnacle of his career, Van Dorn was shot and killed by a physician in Spring Hill, Tennessee, who thought that the general had been partner to his wife's infidelity.[5] Faulkner must have listened to many accounts of the raid in this town only thirty miles from his own, one of the most exciting events of the war in Mississippi and an incident still vividly preserved in local memory. Equally well preserved is the story of the general's subsequent fate.[6]

Faulkner was obviously fascinated by Van Dorn's history, finding him both a dramatic and a representative figure. He was to use the figure of Van Dorn initially, in fact, when first he turned squarely to his native materials in *Sartoris*, though here Faulkner employs the general merely to fill in the historical dimension of Colonel John Sartoris' career.[7] Subsequently, however, Faulkner found more interesting uses for the Confederate leader. In *Absalom, Absalom!*, the narrative voice speaks of Confederate generals "who would whip three separate armies in as many days and then tear down their own fences to cook meat robbed from their own smokehouses, who on one night and with a handful of men would gallantly set fire to and destroy a million dollar garrison of enemy supplies and on the next night be discovered by a neighbor in bed with his wife and be shot to death."[8] Here Faulkner has foreshortened, transmuted, and propped his facts; and it is the prop of his own perceptions that casts the shadow, as he contrasts the courage and military genius of the Confederate leaders with their impracticality and moral laxity.

But this is not the only shadow that can be cast, as one notes from the 1938 interview with Cantwell. The two were driving through the town of Holly Springs when Faulkner commented on the famous raid. "'This was just a country lane when Van Dorn rode down and burned Grant's stores,'" he said. "'Van Dorn burned Grant's stores and kept Grant from getting into Vicksburg from the rear.... That was a pretty gallant thing to do. But about

---

5 Robert G. Martin, *Earl Van Dorn* (Nashville, Tennessee, 1967).

6 Colonel William C. Falkner and his family had known Van Dorn. Donald Philip Duclos, *Man of Sorrow: The Life, Works, and Influence of Colonel William C. Falkner 1825-1889* (University of Michigan, 1961). It is probable that young William Faulkner early heard a lively version of the General's career.

7 *Sartoris* (New York, 1929), 223, 226.

8 *Absolom, Absolom!* (New York, 1964), 346.

a week later some fellow caught him in bed with his wife and killed him. He might have been good for a dozen more victories. But honor meant a lot to them.'"[9] Here the shadow is cast from a different angle as Faulkner uses the same material to show the husband's putting personal honor above good of country. Though this view of the Van Dorn story never found its way to the fiction, the conversation offers evidence that Faulkner was constantly turning historical fact in the light in order to reveal as many meanings as possible.

These examples suggest the variety of Faulkner's perceptions of a set of historical facts. A third instance involves a more complex use of the Van Dorn material. In *Light in August*, Faulkner ironically reduced the general's fatal experience by having Gail Hightower's grandfather, a private, shot during the gallant raid by someone whose chickens he was stealing.[10] The grotesque shadow cast here is determined by Hightower's perception of the incident. "Any soldier can be killed by the enemy in the heat of battle, by a weapon approved by the arbiters and rulemakers of warfare," Hightower argues. "Or by a woman in a bedroom. But not with a shotgun, a fowling piece, in a hen-house."[11] To Hightower, "This is beautiful… that fine shape of eternal youth and virgin desire which makes heroes."[12] Here Faulkner dramatizes something which he may well have learned through listening to those historical accounts of his youth: that history for any one man becomes essentially what he perceives it to be. Here indeed is a perceived shadow grossly incommensurate with the facts.

With its full presentation of the relation between fact, shadow, and perceiver, the strange story or Private Hightower and his grandson constitutes Faulkner's richest artistic use of the ill-fated Earl Van Dorn. And, taken together, these three uses of the Van Dorn material form a consistent and highly suggestive pattern. Clearly they serve to suggest, as definitely as does a novel like *Absalom, Absalom!*, that Faulkner's subject was never history in an academic sense, but history as it was perceived, sometimes distorted, but always open to a variety of interpretations. The use of the Van Dorn material further serves to give us a glimpse of the continuing creative process in which Faulkner was involved. For Faulkner, though historical facts possessed no sanctity, they were always waiting in his artist's "lumber room" to fit "the particular corner [he was] building."[13]

---

9 Cantwell, 57.

10 One can observe the progressive transmutation of the Van Dorn material in Faulkner's unpublished short story "Rose of Lebanon." There Charley Gordon, a regimental commander, has met his death stealing chickens on the night of the raid. The raid is given its true setting, Holly Springs; in *Light in August* it is set in Jefferson. Michael Millgate discusses this story as preparatory to *Light in August* in *The Achievement of William Faulkner* (New York, 1971), 130-131.

11 *Light in August* (New York, 1968), 459.

12 *Ibid.*, 458.

13 *Faulkner in the University: Class Conferences at The University of Virginia 1957-58*, ed. Frederick L.

Mitchell's Cavalry

Hubert H. McAlexander

The distinguished folklorist Arthur Palmer Hudson included in *Folksongs of Mississippi* (1936) a local ballad, "The Yankees are Coming." To the tune of "The Campbells are Coming," county residents sang this song bitterly during the War Between the States. Following are the first two stanzas:

> The Yankees are coming! Away! Which way?
> Who saw them? Do tell us. And what did they?
> Are they infantry, cavalry? How many? How far?
> Fifteen hundred, they say, and are at Lamar.

> The Yankees are coming! They'll be here by daylight
> Until the brave Mitchell should put them to flight,
> Or ambush and whip them as often he has done,
> With his handful of men and their double-barrel'd gun.

If the exploits of Mitchell's daring company were famed in their day, then we today should know something about them.

Mitchell was William F. R. Mitchell (1840-1879), who grew up on the Salem Road, near a community then called Cotton Grove in extreme eastern Marshall County. His grandfather Littlebury Lesueur was a rich planter, leaving at his death in 1841 several hundred acres, including his home plantation on section 17, T3, R1; 43 slaves; and 140 shares of Mississippi Union Bank stock. His oldest daughter, Tabitha, married William H. Mitchell. In 1850 their plantation was large enough to support an overseer. By 1860, the widow Tabitha Lesueur Mitchell was head of a household that included Issac Littlebury Mitchell (1842), Napoleon Hamilton Mitchell (1852), and her oldest son, William, and his new wife, Elizabeth A. Cocke, daughter of Nathaniel James Cocke and his first wife, Frances Pleasants, living north of Rossville, Fayette County, Tennessee.

William Mitchell (called Billy or Billie) had a long connection with Fayette County that preceded his marriage in August 1860. It was in Fayette County that he joined the Confederate Army in May 1861 and was almost immediately elected a second lieutenant. After the Battle of Shiloh, in April 1862, the unit was reorganized, and Mitchell was not reelected to his lieutenancy. His year enlistment was also over.

In August, he was appointed captain of a company of Partisan Rangers, and he began recruiting volunteer cavalrymen from the region. This was the period of his fame. Mitchell's company was a constant irritant upon the federal troops in northern Mississippi and along the Tennessee border. On December 5, 1862, Colonel A.S. Norton wrote his commanding officer from La Grange, Tenn.:

> Mitchell's band has made another raid upon the forces below us, killing one of the Twenty-ninth Illinois Volunteers. His band is increasing daily and will have two pieces of artillery here within a few days. Now is the time to bag him. We could do it easily with the help of 40 or 50 more cavalry for a few days, and if we should neglect now his annoyance will be constant. (*Official Records*, ser. I, vol. 17, part 2, p. 387.)

Norton's request was not met, and the annoyance and the sorties remained constant. From this period comes this roster of Mitchell's cavalry company:

Roster of Company A, 18th Mississippi Battalion
W. R. Mitchell, Captain
Mills E. Brittenam, 1st Lieutenant
H. A. Reynolds, 2nd Lieutenant
Geo. A. Powell, 3rd Lieutenant

Then follow the names of nine non-commissioned officers and 109 enlisted men. Among the enlisted men are a number from Mitchell's own Marshall County neighborhood. Three Beck brothers are from near Salem and the first cousins of Forrest. No. 52, John Hubbard, is evidently not John Milton Hubbard, whose memoir of service under Forrest was published as *Notes of a Private* (Memphis, 1919). No. 78, Isaac Mitchell, is Captain Mitchell's younger brother Isaac Littlebury (Bud) Mitchell, who was captured twice and sent to a Union prison. Sim and John Marsh were grandsons of Squire John Record, whose plantation was just up the road from the Lesueur place. Alumni of the University of Mississippi, both had originally joined the University Greys. Ben and J.A. Sigman were from the same neighborhood. No. 121, William Wall, is evidently the confirmed bachelor Billy Wall, who lived with his sister at Sunnyside plantation near Sylvestria Church.

On October 7, 1863, Mitchell was promoted to major, in the command of Lt. Col. Alexander Chalmers, of Byhalia (OR, series I, vol. 30, part 4, p. 732). It is obvious from a survey of Mitchell's military records that he was fiercely independent and resistant to authority. Though a skilled commander, he was often in trouble with his superiors. Mitchell's service record reveals that he was demoted to captain May 28, 1864. On the back of that sheet it is noted in pencil that he is dismissed from the service in June 1864 by the military court, Forrest's Cavalry.

On August 24, 1864, Maj. General Nathan Bedford Forrest ordered, "Arrest Mitchell.... He has no authority from me" (*OR*, series I, vol. 39, part 2, p. 799). Even after this, the *Official Records* show that in late August 1864, Federal Maj. J. M. Graham reported that "there is a force destroying the railroad between [La Grange] and Holly Springs under Mitchell, reported to be 300." (*OR*, series I, vol. 39, part 2, p. 302).

After the war, Billie Mitchell returned to his wife and family. In 1866, another son was born, whom he named for two great Confederate cavalrymen, Morgan Stuart (or Stewart) Mitchell (1866-1942), grandfather of Bobby Mitchell, president of the Marshall County Genealogical Society. In all there were five children.

Littlebury Lesueur and Penelope King also had five children who lived to maturity. Near in age to Tabitha Lesueur Mitchell was Charles Marion Lesueur, a graduate of Chalmers Institute in Holly Springs and Cumberland College in Princeton, Ky., a Cumberland Presbyterian institution. He moved to Texas and was prominent. Other children were Martha, a graduate of Cottrell's Girls School, who married Charles Powell; Susan, also a graduate of the Cottrell school, who married Augustus H. Branch; and David H. Lesueur, who married Elizabeth A. Powell. The Lesueurs were Cumberland Presyterians, who probably attended church in Tippah County, the line then just a mile from where they lived. But Bettie Cocke had grown up in Pleasants Christian Church in Fayette County, Tenn., and therefore the Mitchells were active in that denomination at Colbert, founded in eastern Marshall County after the war.

The bachelor brothers Isaac Littlebury (Bud) and Napoleon Hamilton (Poly) had a large farming operation. The 1929 obituary of Poly Mitchell quotes a "well posted financial authority" as saying that, "while not as wealthy as some," Poly Mitchell "could have raised more ready money, through money in bank and convertible securities, than any man in town or county." Poly, the last of the children of William H. Mitchell and Tabitha Lesueur, had died at the old Lesueur plantation near Colbert. The obituary, written by local historian John M. Mickle, notes that

> There were three [actually four] Mitchell brothers, the eldest, Capt. Billie Mitchell, attained some reputation as a Confederate raider in this section during the war of the sixties. He died many years ago. (*South Reporter*, April 7, 1929)

But that was not the last contemporary reference to the captain. The next year a man working in the Holly Springs High School, William Baskerville Hamilton, wrote his University of Mississippi master's thesis on the early history of the town (published 1984 by the Marshall County Historical Society). He included as an appendix some Civil War correspondence of Cordelia Scales of Scales Depot (Hudsonville). In a letter dated January 27, 1863, she reported that a federal army colonel left Oakland, her plantation home, with two companies and two wagons to "plunder and destroy" at the Widow Mitchell's place. After Mrs. Mitchell had chided them, they left when she said,

> "Yes, Billy Mitchell is my son & I am proud of him. He is doing nothing but his duty & I hope he will continue & Sir as long as I have a crust of bread that crust will be shared with him and his company."

Billy Mitchell, Miss Scales commented, "is such a brave fellow." And so the captain has come down to us.

Oxford after the Union troops burned it

The Burning of Oxford

Elizabeth Pegues

This Pegues family letter of August 26, 1864, is the best first-hand account we now have of the burning of Oxford. No direct military engagement led to the event. Union troops burned the town merely because of its use as headquarters by Confederate General Nathan Bedford Forrest. General A. J. "Whiskey" Smith, drunk and maddened by Forrest's cavalier foray into Memphis, gave instructions for the burning. An excellent treatment of the event is Don H. Doyle, *Faulkner's County: The Historical Roots of Yoknapatawpha* (2001), 246-251). Doyle also draws from the letter.

We have added paragraphing to the version in "Pegues Letters and Diaries." The reader must remember that the letter was written by an adolescent, thus the strange juxtapositions. This letter was sent by Lizzie (Elizabeth) Pegues (1845-1889) from Oxford, Miss., to her relative Bettie Pegues in Dallas County, Ala.. Lizzie sent it from the Pegues compound at the top of North Lamar.

Two prominent Pegues cousins, great planters and public men, held vast acreage out in Lafayette County and a 100 acre tract in Oxford, where both planned to build mansions. Shortly before the Civil War, Thomas E. B. Pegues employed local builders using the design of architect Calvert Vaux to build a great Italianate villa. His cousin and brother-in-law, Alexander H. Pegues (Uncle Sandy), never built his mansion, but there were evidently two structures on the tract that constituted a kind of Pegues compound.

For knowledge of the existence of this letter I must thank my old friend Will Lewis. And for its use here, I want to thank Guy Turnbow, both of Oxford.

Oxford Miss. Aug. 26, 186[4]

My dear Bettie

Uncle Sandy requested me to write to you today as he has so much business to attend to he cannot possibly do so himself. He has gone to his plantation to gather up the remains. I was much obliged to you dear Bettie for your nice letter. It is the only one I have received since I came home. We have had no mails in four weeks. Now I must begin and give you a full account of all our troubles. It is a great pity Charley and I did not remain in Alabama three or four weeks longer. We got home in time to be robbed.

Monday morning on the 22nd August about eight o'clock the Yankees entered Oxford. The morning passed very quietly, most of the citizens had guards till 12 o'clock. About that time they heard Gen Forrest was in Memphis and they only wanted an excuse for doing so the whole town was given up to the soldiers. Every house was plundered and several burned. Mrs. Thompson's, Mrs. Butler's, Mr. Kendall's, Dr. Branham's, Col. Brown's, the whole Square, Mr. Turner's work shop and all the depot buildings. The Square is a horrid sight. It would break your heart to look at it.

All our friends have suffered more or less. Mrs. Roscoe lost a great deal and her house was set on fire three or four times, but she managed to put it out. Mrs. Quinche, Mrs. Harrison, Mrs. [unreadable], Mrs. Sheegog, Mrs. Evans, Mrs. Jones, and in fact all our friends have suffered about as much as we did. Miss Julia lost nearly all her clothes and a great many of Mrs. Longstreet's things. A hogshead of fine bohemian glass, and another of china, papers, books, letters. Her house was fired twice but put out. We thought we were escaping finely for no Yankees came into our house till between four and five o'clock, then about 100 rushed into the back yard screaming for sugar. They tore down the old smoke house and dragged out Aunt Rebecca's half barrel of sugar. We had bolted the front door and all [unreadable] on the back doores [sic]. They came up and demanded meat. We told them we had none and begged them not to come into the house but it was no use. They just pushed us out the door and came pouring in. None of us know how many there were but somewhere between 150 and 200 I think. Mother says there may have been more.

They took whatever they wanted, tore open trunks, took off books. Every book is gone out of the parlor—and about 12 or 15 of Aunt Rebecca's. I hardly know what they were yet. They brought about 20 bushels of dirt into the house. It was fearful indeed. I hope that I never pass through it again…

Uncle Sandy says he had not lost near as much as he expected at the plantation. None of his wheat was taken. Eight of your negroes went off—Amos & Silvey, Kate, a younger Sister, and four children. The gin house was burned, also the house Mr. Gist lives in. Mrs. Gist is now staying with Mrs. Winn. Fortunately they did not get to our plantation, but they made up for it by plundering us in Oxford. I have written you quite a doleful letter dear Bettie. How much I wish I could see you again. It is a great pity Charley and I left when we did. Charley sends his love and a kiss. He wrote to you the other day. We all love him very much. Give my best love to Sister Princil and Fan and to Aunt C. I will write to Prissie before too long. Tell her to get my brilliance night gown and keep it for me. You know Pa [Thomas E. B. Pegues] is in the State Service at Grenada. Bud is with him. We are all very cheerful and don't complain. Give my love to every body particularly Aunt R & Ella, Lizzie.

P. S. Tell Nick [Ellerbe] I have been looking for my letter a long time. Give my very best love to him. I intended to made him a nice blue cravat but the plagued Yankees got the silk. Forgot to tell you the new house was set on fire in four rooms. Mother C, Lill, Katie, and I put it out with the help of four Yankees. There is a great hole burnt through the floor upstairs and another in the kitchens. Charley says you must write to him. I think I would die if the Yankees should ever come back.

Zizzie

FROM '60 TO '65

SHERWOOD BONNER

This piece was originally published in the October issue of 1876 *Lippincott's*, 58:500-509. It is now more conveniently available in Anne Razey Gowdy, ed., *A Sherwood Bonner Sampler, 1869-1884* (Knoxville: University of Tennessee Press, 2000), 164-179.

Readers of this volume should read the essay "The Martins in Two Counties," which covers some of the people and places that Katharine Sherwood Bonner McDowell fictionalizes. In addition, let me tell you more of what she uses. The little Southern town, Hollywell, is obviously based on Holly Springs, Miss., her native place. The Jones-McIlwain Iron Foundry, which made rifles during war time, is transformed into a place manufacturing cannons. She draws upon her own aunts as characters. Mrs. Herrick, the blockade runner, is her great aunt Sarah Dickens Martin, and her aunt Ellen Hopeton is Anne Vaughn Dickens Martin, the wife of Andrew Lesper Martin. He was long dead, and his widow lived at Martin's Hill, about two miles northeast of the village, from which "the town could be seen like a picture in smoke."

Before, during and after the war I lived in a little Southern town called Hollywell, almost on the boundary-line between Mississippi and Tennessee. The life of the dead-and-gone yesterday is divided by such sharp lines from that of to-day that its very memory is growing dim, even to those who talk most loudly of its idyllic contentment and peace. But of the four years between we all have stories to tell — years of peril and disaster; of hardship and suffering, yet they held all the fascination of romance, the splendid excitement of passionate tragedy.

Twenty years ago Hollywell was a sleepy, prosperous little town — so pretty that the country papers called it the "City of Flowers," and never tired of extolling its exquisite gardens, spacious, handsome houses, and dainty park where the young folks walked on summer evenings and fed the tame squirrels or made love to each other on the "swinging seats" under the linden trees. But the fire of '63 left ruin behind it, and the vacant spaces have been but poorly filled. The Beautiful is no longer cultivated by a people who describe themselves as "poverty-stricken," and have to struggle sharply for the bare comforts of life. The park has been utilized as a court-house square, and is ornamented by a row of wooden posts with perpendicular teeth, over which the country people throw their mules' bridles when they come to town to do their trading or "tend court." The court-house in the centre resembles a particularly bad style of frozen music, and is a blot upon the fair face of Hollywell. The gardens have lost their look of cultivated order, for the Uncle Neds and Caesars who used to care for them are perplexing their simple souls with questions or supply and demand and problems of political economy. The untrained honeysuckles stretch long detaining arms across your path; seed-pods hang on the rose-bushes, skeletons at the feast of the opening buds: heartsease and snapdragon, lily and larkspur, spring up intertwined as though some wanton fairy had flung them to earth in her flight; violets have grown over their beds and are crushed under your feet with red japonica blossoms and the fragrant petals of the Magnolia fuscata. In all this there is a sweet disorder and a wantonesse not without its picturesque charm, but to the people of Hollywell it speaks only of desolation. Those among them who had reached middle age when the war began find nothing that is good in the life of to-day. They are fond of contrasting the old times with the new. Society lines "in their day" were clearly defined. The planters — as lords of lands and men — held the highest social rank; the professional men came close behind them; the tradespeople and mechanics fell naturally into their places. To-day things are mixed in a dreadful way. The sons of our best people are clerks for petty shopkeepers; one of our college-bred youths has opened an ice-cream saloon; and, crowning humiliation! we have to accept the quondam tailor of the village as its aristocrat, for he made a fortune at blockade running, and spends it "like a gentleman."

Nevertheless, I am disposed to think that vaunted life a dull one. Mothers and grandmothers gossiped placidly at "early teas" or solemn dinner-parties. Daughters went to church, rode horse-back, and read Richardson and Scott, with occasional longing glances toward Fielding and Smollett on the high shelves — sealed books to them until they were married. The wild excitement of a tournament sometimes varied the monotony, and at election times there was much dissipation in the way of barbecues and torchlight processions. Now and then a party of young folks on horseback or in an old lumbering family coach might be seen looking on at a "bran-dance" or a "gander-pulling;" these unique sports being indulged in by that class of the population called by the negroes "po' white trash." They owned no slaves, and lived in log houses through whose chinks sun and rain entered freely; the men supplied the larder by hunting and fishing: the women dipped snuff, moulded tallow candles and "raised" tow-headed children who rejoiced in princely and historic names.

On the whole, the darkies had rather the best time of it. After the work of the day they danced "old Virginny breakdowns" until midnight, with an active enjoyment I have never seen equaled. To them the fascinating circus offered its manifold charms. The dearest joy my childhood recalls is a visit to the mysterious tent where the elephant and clown improved the shining hour, holding fast by the hand of my dear old "granmammy," both of us in an ecstasy of delight. Sunday was their great day. They lighted the long white streets with a picturesque glow as they poured forth from their afternoon church, laughing and chattering with the effervescent flow of spirits natural to the race. Their high voices were not unmelodious, and in their extraordinary combinations of color they nearly always managed a harmony of effect. Their air of self-conscious dignity was amusing, and prominent alike in the venerable aunties with their glossy faces surrounded by turbans of rainbow hues, the men in the cast-off swallow-tails and stovepipes of their masters, and the children of various sizes and complexions tricked out with ribbons and beads, and stepping daintily along like important little paroquets. There was a wide difference between the town and plantation negroes. The former had a more cultivated taste, used better English, and could often read and write, the children of the house delighting them as pupils. They were proud of the family name, and they were treated with a love and consideration that their fidelity abundantly rewarded. They had a manifested idea of their own importance, and were rather apt to look down on their country relations. As an old aunty of my acquaintance once expressed it, "'Dey put on airs enuff ter stock de kingdom o' heaven." The plantation negroes, with the ignorance and uncouthness of their African ancestors, retained many of their superstitions. Foremost among these was the strange belief in Voudooism or Hoodooism, as it was indifferently called. The planters forbade the open practice of its repulsive rites, but they could not prevent the wild orgies of secret midnight meetings nor destroy the influence of the Hoodoo priests. These men held an extraordinary power. Even the negroes who were Christians and affected to scorn Voudooism feared them as much as their most abject followers, and were no less eager to win their favor by propitiatory offerings of spring chickens, scaly-barks, and the finest yield of the melon-patches.

To the men of Hollywell, life was never dull, for it had an unfailing source of interest that, like the widow's curse, never ran dry. They all talked politics. The planter and the merchant, as the one ordered and the other measured jeans and linsey for the hands; the young men in broad-brimmed hats and negligent neckties, who lounged at the street corners and arranged the details of fox-hunts and game suppers; the village great man and the village loafer, had all the same common interest. To them the science of government was the only one worthy of the serious attention of the mind. The very schoolboys squabbled fiercely over political questions, and the boundary of ambition for each was the Congressional hall. The women had no part nor lot in this matter. They wore the cockades or medals presented by husbands or lovers, and echoed their opinions with honest fervor. But the wisest of them had not much more knowledge of the subject than was displayed by my intimate enemy; a rival at school, who wept when Fillmore was defeated, and poisoned my life by the remark that she never knew a Democrat who didn't have red hair. The Southern men liked this ignorance, and thought it lovely and feminine. They cannot reconcile themselves now to the lively interest in the affairs of the country felt by the women of to-day. Some years after the war an eminent politician turned against his party and joined "the Radicals." Hearing that a lady friend was deeply indignant at his course, he said with a sneer, "I had hoped that the day would never come when Southern ladies would attempt to understand political questions."

As the years went by improvements came to Hollywell — gas, railroad connections and an iron foundry. Property increased in value, and a new air of prosperity was given to the little town. But the social life remained much the same. Against this faint gray background was thrown the red beacon of the coming war. The people sprang from lethargy. They saw not in its glow a prophecy of disaster, but a promise of victory.

The first cannon made in the South was moulded at the Hollywell foundry. It was a great day when the work was begun. Crowds of people were outside the building, and as many as were allowed to enter were within. Standing there among the din and whir of machinery; while the sooty-faced workmen hurried hither and thither and the great furnace roared and reddened, the hour was pregnant with grand significance. As the melted ore poured forth[,] a woman's hand held under it the great iron ladle and emptied it into the mould with the solemnity of a priestess assisting at a holy rite. Every woman and child followed in turn. It was our consecration to the cause — an hour that I cannot remember now without a thrill of emotion akin to that which thrilled me to the very centre of my being as I clasped my hands around the iron handle and felt that in that moment I sealed my devotion to the South.

The next excitement at Hollywell was the presentation of a flag to the first regiment made up in the town. Eager groups of people assembled at an early hour in a large grove east of the town. Here were the ranks of soldiers in their spotless gray uniforms, the platform gay with ribbons and vases, the colonel with his plumed hat and scarlet sash, the gorgeous banner whose silken folds fluttered around the slight figure of a dark-eyed girl upon whom all eyes were turned. She was the heroine of the day, for she had been chosen to present the flag. Her address was a wild appeal to Southern passion and patriotism; at its close she sang the Marseillaise hymn, which had been adapted to Southern words, in a voice of thrilling timbre. The effect was electrical. People threw themselves into each other's arms, wept, laughed, clasped the hands of the excited soldiers, and in every wild and extravagant way gave vent to their emotion. If there had been any cooler souls who had hung back when the secession fever was raging over the land, they resisted no longer, but were swept along by the current of popular feeling. It was some time before any realization of war came home to us. General Price made Hollywell his head-quarters for a few months, and we gave ourselves up to patriotic dissipation. Ah, those golden October days! Who among us can forget them? Houses were thrown open, and around every table gathered the gray-coated officers. Young girls taken from the school-room blossomed into belles and coquettes. Picnics, balls and reviews made every day "run to golden sands."

General Price was a gallant old officer with a square, portly figure, a bluff, hearty voice and a straightforward simplicity in his use of words. He took advantage of his position and kissed all the pretty girls. They submitted right loyally though deep in many a little rebel's heart lurked the wish that the son stood in the father's shoes, for Celsus Price, youngest son of the general, was a hero with whom all the girls were in love. He had a prim little delicious way of saying "my father" that showed his pride in the old soldier's glory; but affectations aside, he was an elegant young fellow, with a handsome face and a handsome head covered with waving locks as beautiful as the clustering curls of the young Antinoüs. One night at a small party a pretty romp essayed to pull his hair. To her horror, it all came off at her touch, and a round light poll under it blushed "celestial rosy red" at the sudden exposure. Celsus, it seemed, had been sick of a fever and had lost his hair. The wig was borrowed from an old major on his father's staff, who retired into his night-cap while Celsus displayed his borrowed plumes, only claiming that the captain should take his turn in obscurity at the jovial dinner-parties that the major delighted to honor.

Heroes were so plentiful that we could afford to be fastidious. General Van Dorn was second in rank only to General Price, but he did not enjoy the same popularity. Hollywell was a strait-laced town, and Van Dorn was separated from his wife. Added to this, he had lost a recent battle by his unskillfulness as an infantry commander, and the people were embittered against him. But his friends were devoted, and the officers of his staff loved him as tenderly as men love women. Indeed, I know of no Southern officer who inspired such passionate attachment as the gallant and ill-fated Van Dorn. He seemed to live in an atmosphere of romance. When he showed his dark, haughty face in the ball-room, not a girl among us would have refused him as a partner in spite of the warning looks of mammas and chaperons. But he felt that he was under a ban, and made little effort to gain the good-will of matron or maid.

Those were the bright days of Hollywell. Into a few short months we crowded the gayety of a lifetime. No fear shadowed our pleasure, for we had absolutely no doubt as to the result of our struggle. It is pathetic now to look back upon that childlike confidence and unreasoning hope.

It was a sad day when the army left, for we bade friends good-bye to prepare for foes. Boxes of silver were buried at night under flower beds or ashheaps; gold-pieces were secured in leather belts; doors were locked and windows barred. Then we waited until one bright morning in December, when frightened negroes came flying in from the country round with the dread news,

"The Yankees are coming!" They came, with the sound of music and the beating of drums, into a silent town. From behind closed blinds we listened to the tread of their advancing feet or peeped timidly at the blue ranks marching by. Before sundown the pleasant groves of Hollywell were dotted with white tents, the stars and stripes fluttered from a high flag-pole, and from the park the inspiring strains of "Yankee Doodle" seemed to mock our impotent anger and bitter humiliation.

We had just grown accustomed to the presence of our unwelcome guests when a wilder excitement than any we had yet known came to Hollywell. General Grant, with the main body of his army, had passed through the town "on his way to the Gulf," as he said, leaving only a few regiments to guard his ammunition and commissary supplies, which were stored in our foundry. Van Dorn seized the opportunity to make a raid into Hollywell. The day — "The Glorious GLORIOUS Twentieth," I find it called in my diary of that date — has become forever memorable in the Hollywell annals. The Confederates dashed in early in the morning, surprising the sleeping camp and gaining a surrender without a fight. The people were frantic with joy, ready to make an idol of the general they had condemned so bitterly. The air was alive with the shrill cry, "Hurrah! Hurrah for General Van Dorn!" A Federal colonel had chosen our house as his head-quarters, and Van Dorn had paid him the compliment of a call. He had a very handsome sword that had been presented to him by the ladies of his native place, and he bit his lip angrily as he gave it up. Van Dorn handed it back to him with a courteous bow, to the surprise and gratification of the irate colonel, who from that moment accepted things with a good grace. His wife, however, was furious enough for two: never were frowns so black or tones so sharp; her pale anger as she snapped out remarks about "rebel devils" was a joy to my Southern soul. I innocently inquired why her people had come South if they did not want to be so badly treated!

"To make you *behave* yourselves; and we're going to *do it*, too," said she fiercely.

I waved my hand toward the road where a squad of blue coats was passing, escorted by a rebel guard, and said in a melancholy voice, "It looks like it; it does indeed!" This joke cost me dear, for two days later we were turned out of our house through the colonel's representations, but nothing could take away the satisfaction that had been mine for one perfect day.

Many of the negroes had been won over to the Northern side and the most devoted were wearing the blue breeches given them by their soldier friends. Seeing the Southerners triumphant for a day, they thought it for ever, and quaked with fear for their lives. So they turned coat — or pantaloons — literally, and as easily as the vicar of Bray changed his principles. Skulking behind trees or under doorsteps, they tore off the offending garments and put them on again wrong side out, reappearing with faces of conscious integrity and legs clothed in virgin white, the blue seams down the sides the only remaining streaks of their disloyalty.

As the day wore away the Confederates prepared to leave, first firing the buildings that held the army stores. It was sad to think of the destruction of the delicate food needed by so many; and negroes and whites together tried to save something from the flames. The burning buildings were not far from our house. We could feel the hot wind against our cheeks as we watched the great blazing pyre where flame and smoke struggled together; and in whose very midst the daring wreckers were at work — soldiers filling their knap-sacks, negroes loading wheelbarrows and baskets, — all fighting with the greedy fire that was licking up so many treasures. But for my mother's watchful eye, I should have joined the crowd and rushed to the scene of the action. As it was, I had to content myself with sending my brother, a lad of ten, with instructions to bring me the biggest jar of pickles he could lay his hands on. Ruth yearned for cologne and letter-paper, while even the gentle mother owned that a few cans of pickled oysters would not come amiss. That boy of ours was gone until after sundown; at last he appeared marching triumphantly over the hill. Our disgust can be imagined when we saw that the youthful pillager, as the result of his efforts in behalf of a hungry family, dragged behind him a battered canteen and a broken bayonet.

The destruction of his stores forced Grant to bring back his soldiers. They wreaked their vengeance on Hollywell as they passed through it a second time, and then left it to its old quiet. For the next six months I was at boarding school in Montgomery, Alabama. Here again I saw the bright side of the war. To be sure, our preceptor had an unpleasant way of holding up a slice of beef on the end of his fork and telling us how much it cost, and we had to give sixty dollars a pair for very ill-fitting shoes; but these were minor evils that we bore with the easy philosophy of youth. The city was delightfully gay; General Joe Johnston was there a part of the time with his staff and, school-girls though we were, we had more than an occasional glimpse of our military heroes in concert or ball-room.

In the summer I went back to Hollywell, and not until then did I realize the desola-tion that follows in the track of war. The town was cut off from communication with the outside world, except for a hand-car that ran between the towns on the Mississippi road. It was managed by a blind man, a cripple, and two negroes. In the afternoon of a long hot day I stepped off the car at the village station. I found a young soldier-cousin who was at home on a furlough awaiting me in a broken-down buggy that creaked mournfully at every turn of the wheels. I should never have recognized in the dreary village the once prosperous, comfortable little town. Rank weeds grew everywhere, and desolation hung over all things like a funeral pall. Where the town-hall had stood was now a shapeless heap of brick and mortar overgrown with nettles and dog-fennel. The door of the old church where we had worshiped from one generation to another had been torn away, and, looking in, I saw the organ bereft of its pipes, the pulpit of its cushions. The seats were broken up, and not a pane of glass was left in the windows. Even in the graveyard the destroyer had been at work; the gravestones were toppled over, and upon the white columns yet standing were scrawled rude jests and caricatures. The flowers were dry and dead: a few melancholy cows were cropping the weeds that had overgrown the once sacred graves. Here and there a mouldy coffin-lid was thrown out upon the upturned sod. The school-house was leveled to the ground, but its red chimneys stood, like faithful sentinels, over the ruined pile. Private dwellings, too, were gone, and in their stead were hastily-erected cabins through whose open doors we caught glimpses of black-robed figures. The square was deserted, except by a company of small boys, who were marching round it in soldier fashion, and a few old men with long white hair, who were dozing in the sun.

As we turned down the street leading to my home we met an ox-wagon holding three bales of cotton, on top of which a woman's figure was comfortably perched. She wore a green sun-bonnet, a faded calico dress and brown cotton gloves.

"That's Mrs. Herrick," said my cousin, with a nod in her direction.

"What?" and I gave such a start that the crazy buggy almost tipped over. Mrs. Herrick was the wife of one of the richest planters in our State, noted for her pride and aristocratic prejudices. I had seen her last at a dinner-party given in honor of General Price. She wore black velvet and pearls, and her languid beauty had never produced more effect.

"She is one of our best blockade-runners," said my cousin in a matter-of-course sort of tone — "on her way to Memphis now with her cotton. She brought me these cavalry-boots — tied 'em to her hoops, you know. The Yanks have the women searched now as they pass the picket-lines, but they can't get ahead of a first-class smuggler like Mrs. Herrick."

My aunt, Mrs. Ellen Hopeton, lived alone on a small plantation three miles from Hollywell. At the first rumor of the approaching raid she came for me to stay with her during the troubled times. My bravery was recommendation in Aunt Ellen's eyes, and my only one, I regret to say; for I was a most imprudent young rebel, and thought it my bounded duty to proclaim my patriotism in season and out. Far be it from me to say that at heart Aunt Ellen was not as much devoted to the cause, but she tried to play the part of England in the fight and keep in with both sides. To the Yankees she would talk of "my nephew, Charles Hopeton, in Sherman's army," with a more than maternal fondness, when the fact was that this youth was a degenerate and far-off relative whose face she had never seen. With the rebels she was safe for "'my son, Colonel Albert Hopeton," was well known through the country, and his mother's loyalty was never doubted in spite of her politeness to the enemy. Her plan was to treat her foes not only as men and brothers, but as gentlemen and scholars. She occasionally got a rebuff from some rude fellow, but on the whole she succeeded well in her efforts to keep the peace. She was by nature and education the most timid person I ever knew; and I am disposed to rate very highly the moral courage she displayed in preserving under all circumstances, her calmness and dignity. I, in my imprudent youth, scorned her polite little speeches; yet, dear old lady! She was fighting a battle no less gallantly than the soldiers in the field — fighting to keep the old home for her boys. And what a beautiful home it was! A great white house, with dormer windows and queer little porches jutting about in all directions, set high on a hill from which the town could be seen like a picture in smoke. A green lawn sloped down to the road, dotted over with flower-covered mounds, in which white rabbits burowed. A hawthorn hedge enclosed the place, and mimosas and magnolia trees made it an Eden of sweetness. Such a home was worth the fight Aunt Ellen made, yet the strain was terrible, and sometimes Nature was too much for her. I remember an amusing instance of this. It was when the army first entered the town — a time of peculiar change on account of the mischievous stragglers who would break from the ranks. Aunt Ellen determined to keep them out of the house. There were two gates, the big gate and the little gate, the one being the entrance to the grove, the other to the front yard. Aunt Ellen had our chairs brought to the little gate, and here we prepared to "receive."

"Take a book with you," she said, "it will look more tranquil."

I was in no tranquil mood. I liked to do battle in my own way, and my weapon was sharpened for the fight. But in spite of my sauciness and rebellion Aunt Ellen managed me as she did everyone else; so I tucked Hyperion under my arm, put on my blue sun-bonnet and followed her to the gate. She took some soft knitting-work with her, and we sat there in the sunlight, a white kitten in the folds of Aunt Ellen's black dress, a little mulatto girl holding a parasol over her gray head.

Soon they came straggling in through the big gate, up to the little gate where we sat in invincible repose. Aunt Ellen was all suavity and sweetness; she might have supposed them angels unawares, from the gentleness of her manner. Things went on delightfully. They were evidently impressed. Aunt Ellen spoke of her nephew, Charles Hopeton, and asked with innocent naïvetè if any of the gentlemen were acquainted with him. (The gentlemen in question were a villainous-looking lot: one rough fellow had five diamond rings on his grimy forefinger.)

In an unlucky moment the conversation turned to retaliation. The soldiers approved it loudly, one of them declaring that "Scripter said an eye for an eye and a tooth for a tooth."

Aunt Ellen seized the opportunity to give a lesson in love. "I don't believe in it at all," said she, in her gentle tremulous voice. "Don't you know that the New Testament tells us that a soft answer turneth away even a Yankee?"

Of course, she intended to say, "turneth away wrath," but out of the abundance of her heart her mouth spake, and she smiled placidly upon us, quite unconscious of the novel turn she had given to the sentences of peace. The soldiers saw this, and greeted her mistake with a roar of good-natured laughter, in which even I joined, and felt more friendly in consequence.

It is amusing to look over my diary and read my fiery accounts of these Degraded Beings, as they are usually called in pages black with underscorings and exclamation-points. The blackest and bitterest and funniest pages contain a humiliating account of a slight flirtation with one of those Degraded Beings, which, although it did not progress beyond shaking hands and singing rebel songs to him, seems to have filled my soul with anguish. "He is a Lieutenant Meeker," I say in a heart-broken way; "and certainly has the most beautiful dark eyes. The facts seem very bad." I can remember the groan with which I wrote the words. "If the girls knew of this they would judge me very harshly. Yet any sensible person can see that there are many extenuating circumstances. He is officer of the picket-stand in the lane, and being lonely comes up to the house often. Of course I have to be polite to him, for suppose any harm should come to dear Aunt Ellen through my imprudence."

But my own soul resents this flagrant hypocrisy; and further on in a magnificent burst of magnanimity I give utterance to the rank heresy that a Yankee may be a gentleman, and Lieutenant Meeker is one; and moreover, that "I have come to the conclusion that a man may be in the Northern army and yet be an honest man."

Yet I felt myself guilty of a miserable weakness, and could only even things by treating all the other officers with whom we were thrown with extra civility. Aunt Ellen was in constant fear lest my heedless tongue should undo the effect of her smiles. But on one occasion even her politeness was put to a sore test. The regiments had all left Hollywell to join forces in the south. One day we noticed a small company of men down by the old picket-stand. They had on gray jackets, and we jumped to the conclusion that they were Confederate guerillas. Uncle Wash, Mrs. Hopeton's colored factotum, was called, and after a prolonged look he said, in an oracular tone, "Dem's our folks." This settled the question. We were wild with excitement. Not only were we anxious for news — there was fighting down on the Tallahatchie — but the very sight of Southern soldiers was "welcome as stars and flowers to prisoned men." Too impatient to wait, we started to meet them — Aunt Ellen and myself, a dozen or two darkies, and Uncle Wash in a dignified trot at our head. We ran down the hill at full speed, waving hats, bonnets and handkerchiefs, beckoning eagerly to our friends to come.

Come they did at a rapid gallop. As they neared us I noticed that the leader bore a singular resemblance to a Yankee captain whom we had met a few weeks before. I stopped as if I had been shot, staring with eyes that grew bigger every second. Need I say that it was the Yankee captain with his company? And can any one but a Southerner know how I felt as they greeted us with delighted surprise at our sudden loyalty? Aunt Ellen changed color several times; then with marvelous self-possession she responded to the captain's cordial greeting and invited him into the house. I walked by their side with averted face and swelling heart. Reaching the house, I bolted myself in my room and found relief in the bitterest and angriest tears I had ever shed.

As a rule, the Southern women were very frank in their expression of rebel sentiment: if they professed loyalty to the North, their truth was doubted by the very men with whom they hoped to win favor. An old lady and her daughter living in the country gave up part of their house to some federal officers, whose goodwill they were anxious to gain so that their property might be protected. Hence they were loud in their protestations of loyalty and personal friendliness. One night there came a low knock at the door. Mother and daughters stood in parley.

"Who's there?"

"Hush! Speak low. We are gray guerillas: open the door, quick!"

The door was thrown open, and the gray-coated soldiers drawn in to the dimly-lighted hall. The mother hastened off to prepare a supper from her hidden stores, while one of the daughters seized one of the soldiers by the arm, and pointing up to the officers' rooms, cried in a low, fierce voice, "Run up the stairs and kill the devils!" A loud laugh was the response to her frantic appeal; and, stepping into the light, the rebel guerillas showed the faces of the Federal officers, who had got up this masquerade to test the sincerity of their Southern friends.

It is pleasant to remember that we often met with the utmost kindness from officers and men. Aunt Ellen had a pair of mules that were her sole dependence for the coming winter, as Uncle Wash drove them in a wood-wagon, and in this way earned money enough to supply the family with necessaries. These mules she managed to keep, one commander after another giving her a protection paper. One Sunday afternoon I had a fight for them. The soldiers had just been paid off and were ripe for mischief. We were sitting on the back porch with nearly fifty of them around us. Some were drunk, all were disposed to be noisy and quarrelsome. Aunt Ellen, trusting in her peace policy, proposed that I should read the Bible aloud. "I am sure these gentlemen would like to hear you," she said with her pathetic smile, "it will remind them of home."

At the least show of anger or fear the men would have broken all bounds. I did not dare to refuse, but quietly opened my Bible. A light breeze waved the boughs of the mulberry trees with which the old yard was shaded. The soldiers, with sabres clanking as they changed from one lounging position to another, sat on the cistern or well-curbing, or leaned against the time-stained pillars of the porch. Occasionally they would nudge each other and break into a laugh, but on the whole they preserved a rude respect. Aunt Ellen, in her dark skirt and cool linen sacque, sat with her back against the door she was guarding fanning herself negligently. She was a perfect picture of a well-bred, elegant old lady at ease in her own home and I could almost hear her heart beat.

Suddenly, Uncle Wash's little grand-daughter came running up from the direction of the stable: "Oh, Miss Ellen, Miss Ellen! Dey done busted de door offen de stable, an' de mules is gone dis time sho'!"

Aunt Ellen looked as if she had come to the end of her endurance. The mules must be saved. But what could be done? She dared not leave her post. I sprang to my feet: "Aunt Ellen, I will go."

For a moment she hesitated, and then, "'God help us! There is no other way," she said, her very lips turning white. I rushed off with the fearlessness of youth. There were some twenty men at the stable. They were just leading the mules out. I ran at full speed, waving the protection-paper frantically, and shouting "Stop! stop!" at the top of my voice.

They halted and waited for me to draw near with evident curiosity. As soon as my breath allowed, I read them the paper in my most emphatic tone. It was very short: "Mrs. Hopeton is allowed to keep two mules. By order of Major General Smith, U. S. A."

"Of course," said I, "you'll put those mules back, or I'll have you arrested for disobeying orders."

"I'd like to see you do it," muttered one of them. "Let me see the paper, will you, miss?"

Without thinking, I handed it to him. There was a great roar of laughter, and one of the men said, "Well, you are a green 'un! Don't you know that he can tear up that paper and do what he likes with the mules and you too?"

I was frightened enough, but my mother wit came to my aid, and I said with a smile worthy of Aunt Ellen herself, "I trust to his honor as a gentleman."

It may have been his intention to destroy it, but he handed it back with a shamefaced expression, and said, "Well, miss, you've got plenty of pluck, so you hev. If you'll just shake hands all round, we'll leave you the mules. What d'ye say, boys?"

There was a shout of approval. I very willingly submitted to the rough hand-shaking, and went back to Aunt Ellen radiant with triumph.

In addition to the mules, a small calf had been left us. One day I saw a tall soldier with a "lean and hungry look" taking long strides in the direction of the unconscious animal, which was dozing under a syringa bush. I ran to the rescue, caught the calf by the tail, and held on as he ran wildly about the yard with the soldier in full pursuit. An officer riding by burst into a fit of laughter, and called the soldier off. "And I'd advise you, miss, to hide your pet," he called gayly. "He doesn't look very tempting, I'll allow," and his gaze wandered critically over the lean, ill-fed little beast, "but the boys won't leave him to fatten."

I took his advice, and hid the calf in the cellar with a pig that one of the neighbors had sent us for safe-keeping. The few chickens and turkeys we had left were then caged in an empty room upstairs. The work was just accomplished when some officers came to take dinner with us. Our dinner was a plate of greens and hot corn-dodgers. Aunt Ellen apologized for the poor fare by a remark on her destitution. "Heaven knows," said she, "where the next week's food is to come from! Everything is swept away."

At this moment, as if suddenly possessed by some perverse imp, our "dumb animals," above and below, opened their mouths and spake. Hens clucked, roosters crowed, the pig squealed and the calf mournfully mooed. It was too much for our gravity, and we all laughed together. The officers honorably kept our secret, and we held our captives to the end.

The long summer wore away. The army left, winter came, and except for an occasional raid Hollywell was left in peace. We had no premonition that the end was near. It could not be denied that inch by inch the enemy was gaining ground, yet at the logical result we never looked. When the shock came it found us all unprepared. One spring day — the 10th of April, 1865 — the ladies of Hollywell were busy collecting silver plate to be sent to Richmond and melted for the depleted treasury. They had just left our house, and I stood with them on the brow of a hill beyond. One was a widow of seventeen, whose husband had been killed a few weeks after her marriage; the other an older, graver woman, had lost her lover as short a time before her wedding day. As we lingered for a few last words we saw Dr. Pointdexter coming up the hill. He was a man of seventy; usually slow and stiff in his movements. Now his steps were rapid, almost a run. His long white hair floated out behind him, and once, twice, he threw his clasped hands above his head with a gesture of despair. We knew that he had a son in the army, and thought at once of some disaster to him.

"Jack is killed!" cried the young widow with a burst of tears.

We drew nearer together in trembling sympathy and waited for the grief-stricken father to pass. In the wild white face that he turned toward us there was such agony as I have never seen save in the face of a soldier in the hospital who had died an unlooked-for and horrible death. He looked at us a moment in silence, then in a hollow, harsh voice struck us with the words, "General Lee has surrendered!" and passed on into the falling darkness.

Of the suffering of that after-time I have even now no words to speak. Its very memory is so terrible that I do not know how we endured it then. You, who have lost much, suffered much, for a cause that you have gained, cannot measure the suffering of those who gave their all and lost.

Part IV:
Post-War Life

From Robert Milton Winter (ed.), *Amid Some Excellent Company: Holly Springs Mississippi Through the Life and Words of John M. Mickle.* As originally published in The Holly Springs *South Reporter* (1920-1941). Holly Springs, MS: Spring Hollow Publishers, 2003.

Account of Big Tournament, Glamorous Social Event of 1866

John M. Mickle

December 20, 1934. The most glamorous social event since the close of the War Between the States was undoubtedly the big tournament that took place in July 1866 at Mrs. Powell's grove — known in later years as the Chesterman Place. Mrs. Powell was Ben Powell's grandmother.

I have never known a tournament in Marshall County on such a scale, and the object, to raise funds for a monument to the Confederate dead — the strongest appeal that could have been made. The aroma of the Old South was just the breath of war behind, the knights were heros of a hundred battles; and woman still stood on her pedestal — worshipped of all men.

The first day's tilting was interrupted by a heavy rain and the tournament was concluded the next day. A clipping from *The Memphis Daily Argus*, July 20, 1866, gives some data, but only of the second day. Only one tilt remained to be taken as two had been taken the first day. Each knight had five rings and there were three tilts.

"At or near 10 o'clock," says *The Argus*, "the marshals, headed by Gen. W. S. Featherston, mounted on the most showy charger on the ground, and the knights made their appearance and entered the enclosure. The knights after parading around the ring to the music of the band, retired to await the calling of their names.

"The bugle sounded and off dashed the first knight, the second, and so on. When the name of Willie Matthews — 'Rob Roy' — (later the Rev. W. D. Matthews of Oklahoma, now deceased) was called, he started at full speed as usual, his horse fiery, and not well trained, as few of them were. Just after passing the first ring, his horse struck a muddy place and fell, bringing the rider headlong to the earth and falling partially on him. In an instant, however, he was up and rode to his tilt." (He was uncle of Mrs. W. H. Jones and Mrs. S. R. Crawford.)

The Knights of Douglas — Eddie Walker of Okolona — took eleven rings, the highest, and won pride of place and selected Miss Anna Davidson of Holly Springs as Queen of Love and Beauty. Miss Davidson, I have heard old folks say, was one of the most beautiful women who ever lived in Holly Springs. I was too young to remember her. She married Bayliss Gray and they moved to Jackson, Tenn. She died in Nashville twenty-five years ago.

The Knights of Luxahoma (ten rings), C. S. Meriwether of DeSoto County, nominated Miss Octavia Stinson of Marshall County as First Maid of Honor.

The Knights of Twelfth Night, or What You Will (ten rings), John S. Finley (father of Mrs. Ann Craft of Holly Springs), nominated Miss Nannie Dunlap of Holly Springs (later Mrs. George J. Finley, and mother of Tom Finley).

Knight of Bull Run (ten rings), J. P. (Pitt) Humphreys of Red Banks, nominated Miss Helen Fant of Holly Springs as Third Maid of Honor.

The Knight No Name (eight rings), A. C. Brewer (husband of the late Mrs. Lida Coxe Brewer of "Galena"), being a married man, waived his right of naming the fourth Maid of Honor in favor of Henry S. Dancy, who chose Miss Jennie Llewellin of Holly Springs.

YOUTHS IN SECOND CONTEST

After dinner — they called the mid-day meal dinner then — the bugle sounded and a second contest, of youths under seventeen years of age took place. Their names and the rings they took were:

Knights of Daubers, A. B. (Bud) Upshaw, 2 rings. He and his father Col. E. W. Upshaw later were publishers of *The South*, and Bud was assistant attorney general, I think, under President Grover Cleveland. He was cousin of Mrs. Mal Williamson Smith of Dallas, Texas.

Andrew R. Govan, 6 rings. He was brother of the late Mrs. Ed Chew, and was a planter in Helena County, Ark.

Knight of Fenians, William Alexander, 3 rings. He was brother of the late Mrs. Dora Tyson.

Knight of Memphis, J. Worsham, 2 rings. He was a connection, I believe, of the late Mrs. M. F. Dunlap.

Knight of Potomac, 1 ring, Will C. Wooten (brother of Miss Nettie Wooten of Miami, Fla., and Mrs. Jackson Johnson of St. Louis). Knight of Ivanhoe, J. D. Alston, 1 ring.

Master Govan took first prize, a saddle, and chose Miss Betsy Hull (mother of Mrs. Gelon Craft, and a great toast among the younger set of that day) his Queen of Love and Beauty. Master Alexander won second prize, a bridle.

Horsemanship Contest

Following the best color feature of the tournament, a contest in horsemanship — most Southern youth could ride well then, and some of these had ridden with Morgan during the war. Contestants were:

Samuel Finley (brother of the late Mrs. M. D. Dunlap, and later mayor of Holly Springs), R. A. McWilliams (who doesn't remember old Bob, sheriff for so many terms?), Henry S. Dancy, (the Rev.) W. D. Matthews, Joseph M. Butts (father of the late Mrs. Ethel Butts Quiggins),

George M. Walthall (brother of the late Mrs. Kate Freeman), A. C. Brewer, James A. Matthews (father of Mrs. W. H. Jones), E. M. Walker, A. B. Upshaw, R. G. (Gobey) Robinson (brother of the Southern poetess, Annah Robinson Watson), L. A. Stephenson (dentist, grand-uncle of Chester McAlexander).

K. G. Martin, R. A. McWilliams, T. B. Garrett, Charles L. Brackin (brother of the late Mrs. Ella Lucas), A. R. Govan, D. Chism, W. Lea (father of Will Lea), W. J. Walker, J.R. O'Dell (kinsman of Charles O'Dell of Chulahoma), Charles Nunnally (uncle and namesake of Mayor C.N. Dean). Mr. Nunnally's horse fell in the first day's tilt, and though he continued to ride he died not long afterward from the effect of the injuries he received.

Young Ladies, Judges

Young ladies of Holly Springs who acted as Judges were Miss Susie Hull (Mrs. William Lea of Memphis), Miss Sallie Lea (the late Mrs. John Calhoon), Miss Lou Alexander (the late Mrs. T. C. Ingram of Byhalia and sister of the late Mrs. Dora Tyson), Miss Leanora House (daughter of the late Jim House), and Miss Medora Jones (sister of the late L. T. — Bunk — Jones).

"The display of horsemanship was very creditable," said *The Argus*, "not only to Marshall County, but to the state of Mississippi. Mr. Finley, who displayed some remarkable feats — such as standing up and riding at full speed, etc. — received the award of the spurs."

A grand ball and supper was given that night at the Franklin House by H. B. Miller, the proprietor. This was doubtless the old Franklin Female College, which served in its time as church, court, hotel, theater, but chiefly as a school.

The net proceeds of the tournament, $1,722, went to the Monumental Association, organized to erect a monument to the Confederate dead of Marshall County, and with $465 raised at a concert, was unfortunately loaned and lost.

The association began anew and the lower part of the monument set up in the '70s, was erected. The crowning shaft was completed only about twenty-five years ago, and the monument unveiled. Judge James M. Greer, then of Memphis, now of Tupelo, making the address.

Spires Boling was architect for the identical Holly Springs (1870) and Oxford (1871) courthouses.

From Robert Milton Winter (ed.), *Amid Some Excellent Company: Holly Springs Mississippi Through the Life and Words of John M. Mickle*. As originally published in The *Holly Springs South Reporter* (1920-1941). Holly Springs, MS: Spring Hollow Publishers, 2003.

SPIRES BOLING:
CARPENTER, MASTER BUILDER, ARCHITECT

HUBERT H. MCALEXANDER

Because of William Faulkner's works, the Oxford courthouse has become iconic. Recently, as these things slowly go, the name of the architect has been revealed. It is Spires Boling.

I have been interested in him for years. He was probably the principal architect in Holly Springs, and my removed uncle married his daughter. Finding that he was architect for the Oxford courthouse simply makes my knowledge of his career of more than local importance.

Among the many contributions of John M. Mickle, one of the most valuable in my view is his article "Old Boling House in Historic Hook-Up," published in *The South Reporter* Historical Issue of Dec. 15, 1932. Here he establishes Spires Boling's importance as a builder and attributes two buildings to him: the residence constructed in 1858 for Judge Jeremiah Watkins Clapp on Salem Avenue, a notable antebellum architectural achievement, and the three-story Masonic Hall erected in 1870 on the east side of the square, a major building project during the period of Reconstruction. The Mickle article laid the groundwork for any attempt to document the career of this figure so central to Holly Springs architectural history.

Spires Boling (1812-1880), the son of Mitchell and Nancy Boling, who are buried in a cemetery a few miles northwest of town, was apparently born in North Carolina, though census information on the Boling family is confused, inconsistent, and contradictory. He married his wife Nancy (born in Virginia) apparently in Ohio about 1833. In 1840, he was a resident of Jefferson County, Arkansas. He evidently joined his father and brother in Marshall County about 1845. Boling's sequential designations in the county censuses of 1850, 1860 and 1870 — carpenter, master builder, architect — reflect the career pattern of a number of regionally important builders in nineteenth century America. These men were frequently self-taught artisans who worked from pattern books and in their eclecticism often produced interesting variations on standard architectural styles and types.

Boling must have been a person of some substance by January 6, 1858, when he purchased from W. S. Randolph and wife four lots on the west side of Randolph Street, south of the intersection with Salem Avenue, "being the premises on which Randolph formerly resided" (Marshall County Deed Book Y, 45). Considered the founder of Holly Springs, Whitmel Sephas Randolph owned a half-interest in the partnership that originally owned the site of the town. Randolph's house on the street bearing his name burned in the mid-1850's and he moved to Panola County. Boling, however, did not erect a residence on Randolph until after February 16, 1860, when he bought from Randolph the large adjoining lot (Lot 44). He then built his house centered on the boundary line of Section Six and the township line. That line dissected his central hall. This second purchase from Randolph included the lot, "together with the right and privilege of using the water from springs on Lot No. 389 on Section 6, or so much thereof as will be sufficient for his, the said Boling's purposes, the water to be conveyed from the Spring in pipes laid under the ground, the pipes extended up to the spring house" (Deed Book Y, 44).

The springs in question are associated with the earliest history of the town. At the time that Holly Springs was selected the county seat, the county governing body, the Board of Police, agreed to make the choice only on condition that the partnership holding the site convey the title to the Board of fifty acres that the Board was to select and "also convey as Commons the ground now enclosed around the Holly Springs and the Springs known as Randolph's Springs" (Board of Police Minutes, 1:8). The Holly Springs were in the southern edge of the ravine between the old Power House and the present water tank; Randolph's Springs were located in the northeast section of Spring Hollow, behind the Randolph residence. Randolph's Springs are apparently those referred to in this second conveyance from Randolph to Boling.

John Mickle recalled that "Bolling's three story distillery, later known as Johnson's Mill, was located in the north part of Spring Hollow, which gave Holly Springs its name", and he comments, "I feel sure it was built before the war, and Mr. Boling operated it for some years after the war." This second conveyance from Randolph to Boling obviously enabled Boling to build the distillery. It is interesting to note that the species of mint still growing deep in the hollow supposedly dates from the earliest days of the town, having been planted for use in the juleps served by the taverns perched on the south and east sides of the hollow.

Boling is listed in the 1860 census of Holly Springs as a "master builder" with holdings of $17,000 in real estate and $3,000 in personal property — this latter sum most probably reflecting his ownership of three or four slaves. Once of these was Lizzie Bell, who worked as a cook for the family. She married James Wells, a man from Tippah County apprenticed by his master to Boling. This couple were the parents of Ida B. Wells, the noted journalist and crusader, for whom the new Holly Springs Post Office was named in the 1980s. The valuation of Boling's real estate in 1860 apparently included his own residence on Randolph, the story-and-a-half Greek Revival cottage with front portico surmounted by a pediment centered with a fanlight and supported by four octagonal columns, the structure now housing the Ida B. Wells Barnett Museum.

Boling's prosperity is reflected by his being an incorporator of the Memphis, Holly Springs and Mobile Railroad in 1859, along with several prominent Memphians and such leading citizens of Holly Springs as the attorneys Jeremiah Watkins Clapp and J. W. C. Watson (*Laws of Mississippi*, 1859, 51-61). On 10 August 1860, a transaction occurred that casts some light on Boling's work as a master builder. On that date, Dr. Gray W. Smith and his wife conveyed to "S. Boling & Co." the city block bounded by the present streets of Randolph, College, Maury and Van Dorn, on which stood Dr. Smith's fine brick residence (Deed Book Z, 12). We learn from a later deed (Deed Book 26, 46) that in 1866 S. Boling & Co. — composed of S. Boling, W. C Dunn and Stephen W. Gregg — forfeited title to the block conveyed by the Smiths because it had been conveyed "in return for building Dr. Smith a mansion on the outskirts of Holly Springs." The firm had been unable to complete the house because of the war, and the uncompleted structure was burned by Sherman's army on 21 December 1862, one of a number of buildings burned in retaliation for Van Dorn's devastating raid on General U.S. Grant's base of supplies in Holly Springs the preceding day.

Gregg and Dunn, ages 28 and 23 respectively, were Ohio-born carpenters living with four other carpenters in a Holly Springs inn at the time of the 1860 census. The six were most likely employed by Boling. By the close of the war Gregg, who may have been Boling's nephew, and Dunn, who married Boling's daughter Harriet in 1865, had become his partners.

Boling made a decided financial recovery during the Holly Springs building boom of the late 1860s and early 1870s. In 1866, he was a major stockholder in the Marshall Manufacturing Company, incorporated to deal in lumber and iron castings among other items (*Laws of Mississippi* 1866: 172). According to John Mickle, when the local Masonic lodge made plans to rebuild the three story Masonic Hall destroyed during Van Dorn's raid, "Mr. Boling, who was also a distiller, offered the…Lodge a turnkey job if they would give him a ten-year lease on the ground floor to sell whiskey." Though the lodge declined and financed the structure by a bond issue, Boling was still chosen contractor. *The Holly Springs Reporter* of December 7, 1871 reveals, however, that the firm Boling and Reed, Wholesale and Retail Liquor Dealers, was located in the Masonic building. The same year that he built the Masonic Hall (1870), Boling joined eight other Holly Springs citizens, including Colonel Harvey W. Walter and General Winfield Scott Featherston. in incorporating the Holly Springs Hotel Company — the major hostelries having been destroyed in the course of the war (*Laws of Mississippi* 1870:384-85).

The Boling children were very much involved in the social life of the town. Mr. Mickle remembers Walter Boling, "my classmate at Chalmers Institute," the boys' school dating back to the early days of the town, and Miss Nannie Boling, "one of the belles of the sixties and early seventies." Among the other children were Harriet Boling, who married William C. Dunn Marshall Boling, a druggist last found in the 1870 Holly Springs census; Thomas Boling, who as a child fell into a vat at the distillery, was scalded, and died in 1868; and Emma Boling, who married Dr. Lea A. Stephenson in 1871. The Stephensons, both red-haired, were an attractive and fashionable couple. In the fall of 1871, they built the Victorian cottage on the southwest corner of Salem and Walthall (occupied for much of the twentieth century by the Baird family). Nearly all of Spires Boling's children were consumptive and died early deaths. Several are no doubt buried without tombstones in the Boling lot at Hill Crest Cemetery, as is Spires Boling. The lot is marked only by a marble threshold piece carved with the family name.

Spires Boling is listed on the 1870 census as an architect, with $11,000 real property and $2,000 personal property, sums representing a good recovery only five years after the close of the war. But like a number of other citizens, he was ruined by the Panic of 1873 and the ensuing depression. On February 23, 1874, he lost the Randolph Street property as a result of indebtedness (Deed Book 36. 294). The Boling family, however, continued to occupy the family residence, as tenants of Boling's friend Judge Gordentia Waite, who had held the note on the property. Spires Boling died there of consumption in Febuary of 1880 at the age of sixty-seven (*Mississippi Mortality Schedule for 1880*, 7). On 29 December 1881, Mrs. Nancy Boling was dismissed by letter from the Holly Springs Methodist Church because of her removal to Jackson, Tennessee. In 1882, she made a visit from Jackson to the J. B. Johnsons, who were occupying the Boling house on Randolph. That is the last trace I have uncovered of the family in Holly Springs.

But Spires Boling has left his mark on the architecture of Holly Springs. No one will probably ever be able to assemble a complete list of the Holly Springs structures for which Boling is responsible. Boling's own frame residence on Randolph Street, which was standing by the summer of 1860, was replicated in the house he built for Dr. Samuel Creed Gholson on the southwest corner of Randolph and Van Dorn, begun shortly after Gholson purchased the lot in the fall of 1860 and completed after the war had begun (Deed Book Y, 252). The Gholson house, though it has undergone two renovations and a fire, still retains the old doors and millwork and attenuated octagonal columns. Even these two simple structures reflect Boling's eclecticism in the unusual proportional relation of column to portico. The original fanlights in the pediment (still extant in Boling's own residence) are a feature carried over from the Greek Revival mansions that Boling had built.

It is these mansions of the late 1850s and early 1860s that are his major contribution. In addition to the Clapp house (now called Athenia) posited by Mr. Mickle, we have documentary evidence that Spires Boling was the contractor for the grandest of the Holly Springs mansions, Walter Place, which he completed in 1860 (Deed Book 50, 8). He likely built other houses for which no documentary evidence is still extant. I suspect that he built all the Greek Revival mansions of Salem Avenue — the house of Dr. David Pointer at the eastern end of Salem Avenue (probably the first of these mansions, which burned in 1898 while housing St. Thomas Hall, a boys' military academy), the home (known now as Wakefield) of Dr. Pointer's son-in-law Joel E. Wynne, who was Boling's subcontractor for the Walter Place, and the home of Joel Wynne's close friend, Robert McGowan (known now as Montrose), erected n 1860. These structures appear to be the work of the same person. Thus Spires Boling would be the man responsible for what I have heard Eudora Welty call "those vertical Holly Springs houses," the particular Holly Springs version of the columned Greek Revival mansion.

The late 1860s and early 1870s were also evidently a productive period for Boling. In addition to the Masonic Hall (destroyed by fire in 1951), I suspect that he was also responsible for other buildings on the north and east sides of the Holly Spring square (which had been left in ashes by Van Dorn's raid). The cast iron lintels used above the windows on some of these buildings are identical to those on Walter Place, and may well be a Boling signature. The only residential project that I can tentatively assign to him is the transformation of the old Nelson place on College Avenue into an Italianate mansion for James J. House in 1870. The structure, known in this century as Grey Gables, is the only residence in town to compare in grandeur with the antebellum Greek Revival mansions. I want to attribute it to Boling for two reasons: first, the similarity of certain features (the stairway, the dining room) to those of the Clapp house, which Mr. Mickle credits to Boling; and second, the business connections between House and Boling (see Deed Book 26, 579) and between House and Boling's son-in-law William C. Dunn, who had moved to Jackson, Tennessee, with House after the latter went bankrupt. Grey Gables also has the same lintels used on Walter Place and buildings on the square.

The iconic Oxford building after additions and white paint

The Clapp-West-Fant mansion is among Boling's finest achievements.
Mary Wallace Crocker's *Historic Architecture in Mississippi*

BENTON COUNTY

HUBERT H. MCALEXANDER

"The pre-war differences between the cultures of Marshall and Tippah Counties, though often overlooked, were very real, "wrote Andrew Brown, the best local historian of his day, in his history of Tippah County. The differences, he argues," were traceable to the different types of settlers in the two areas, which in turn reflect the nature of the land itself." The soil of Marshall and western Tippah is in the loess belt that runs from the Marshall line with Tennessee through Natchez and Woodville to the Louisiana border. The loess belt is plantation country. The land to the east is "suited more to small farms." In my youth, I still heard (though as a period expression), an old Holly Springs saying, 'You look like you jus' came outta Tippah.'"[1]

The northeastern part of Marshall and the extreme western part of Tippah were taken to form a new county—Benton, created by a legislative act dated July 15, 1870. Since the region had only villages, the courthouse town Ashland had to be created. The county was named for General Samuel Benton, C.S.A., of Holly Springs, and the new town for the home of Henry Clay. Both instances are surprising for this Reconstruction era.[2]

Two of the original villages in the area became completely extinct in the 19th century. In Marshall, midway on the stage road between LaGrange, Tennessee, and Holly Springs, was Lamar. Like many places near a rail line, it was merely moved two or three miles and re-incorporated. On the other hand, Salem, just over the county line in Tippah County, was a thriving village of 200 that became eclipsed by the new town of Ashland, four miles or so to the east.

The essay "Extinct Towns" in the 1902 volume of *Publications of the Mississippi Historical Society* makes note of both places. The leading merchant and planter of the original town of Lamar was Col. Timmons L. Treadwell. The region was "a fine agricultural section," settled by a "wealthy class of planters." The list is headed by Captain. William Coopwood, Thomas Mull, Col. Charles L. Thomas, Judge Alexander M. Clayton, the Smiths, the Hudsons, the Cheairs, the Rooks, the Rhineharts, the Gormans, Dr. Cummings, Col. Andrew R. Govan, Dr. Hardaway and John, Dabney, and William Hull.[3]

---

1 Andrew B. Brown, *History of Tippah County, Mississippi; The First Century* (Ripley: Tippah County Historical and Genealogical Society, Inc, reprinted 1976), 18.

2 Robert Lowry and Willian H. McCardle, *A History of Mississippi* (Jackson: R. H. Henry & Co, 1891), 444-445.

3 Franklin L. Riley, "Extinct Towns and Vallages of Mississippi," *Publications of the Mississippi Histori-*

Salem will be long remembered in Holly Springs because it gave its name to Salem Road (later Salem Avenue), the town's longest street. The village was a destination and a center that had strong, old associations. The essay on Salem in "Extinct Towns" tells us that it boasted "twelve or fourteen business houses, two hotels and a thriving female school" and that the neighborhood was "composed of wealthy, substantial planters." The prominent men listed are, first: Col. Francis Terry Leak, Thomas Hamer, and Col. Daniel B. Wright, a lawyer who practiced in both Holly Springs and Ripley. The list continues with Col. John B. Ayres and his son, Dr. Gus Ayres, Robert McDonald, Dr. Moorman, Col. William Locke Baird, and John W. Matthews. The writer then mentions Orin Beck, proprietor of a watering place called Beck's Springs and uncle of Nathan Bedford Forrest, later the famous Confederate general. He closes his remarks by mentioning Joseph W. Matthews, the only pre-war governor of the state from north Mississippi. A similar list but given with a more nostalgic touch is conveyed in John M. Mickle's essay on Salem in this volume.[4]

Tippah County had been formed out of the Chickasaw Cession by a committee of three: Leak and Matthews, both from the Salem region, and Thomas J. Word, of Ripley, the uncle of Col. William C. Falkner. A group of Woffords and McKenzies settled near the community of Spring Hill in Tippah (later Benton) and dominated the first election. When Col. William M. Wofford died in 1846, his obituary in the Holly Springs newspaper characterized him as "an esteemed citizen of Tippah." His tombstone proclaims him as a member of the Cumberland Presbyterian Church, which had a large congregation there.[5]

Marshall County gave up the lands of some of its biggest pre-war planters to the new county. Many of them were located around the communities of Early Grove and Davis Mill, very near the Tennessee line and close to LaGrange. Early Grove had two churches marked by large cemeteries, Early Grove Methodist Church and St. John's Episcopal. But the most interesting place of the land that Marshall gave to Benton was called Davis Mill. It was established by Hugh Davis, born 1806 in Georgia, who grew prosperous and built an impressive story-and-a-half frame planter's cottage that is still standing. The community figures frequently in *Official Records of the War of the Rebellion*.

After the war, Hugh Davis sold the property and emigrated to Brazil. The buyer was Ransom Elijah Aldrich (1821-1873), a New-York-born Union army veteran from Sandstone, Michigan, with a distinguished New England ancestry. He was well established in Mississippi by 1870, and his son Jeremiah Marvin Aldrich (1864-1935) married a Tread-

---

cal Society (1902) V: 320.

4 Riley, 320-321.

5 Brown, 23. *Holly Springs Gazette*, 14. Mar. 1846.

well of Lamar. These were no carpetbaggers, but people who contributed to the tone of that part of Mississippi. Davis Mills became Michigan City and the Aldrich family helped Cavalry Episcopal Church in the community.[6]

---

6 . Some of Hugh Davis' Confederate descendants visited Holly Springs and environs about the year 2000. The information on Ransom Aldrich (1821-1873) and his family comes from descendant Sledge Taylor of Como, supplemented by what is included on Ancestry.com.

From Robert Milton Winter (ed.), *Amid Some Excellent Company: Holly Springs Mississippi Through the Life and Words of John M. Mickle*. As originally published in the Holly Springs *South Reporter*. Holly Springs, MS: Spring Hollow Publishers, 2003.

LEARNED THAT FROST DOESN'T KILL FEVER

JOHN M. MICKLE

November 26, 1931

The supernal beauty of the past fall, so long drawn out, recalls that of 1878, when the people prayed for early frost, that was supposed to kill out the yellow fever, which had afflicted the town for two months.

We now know that frost had no effect other than to thin out the mosquitoes that transmit it. Finally the first frost came in October and another early in November, and it was considered safe for me to return and open the store. I was employed at Crump, Hull & Finley's dry goods store.

I returned November 5, two months to a day from when I left. The town was crowded with strangers, doctors, nurses and helpers who had come during the epidemic; and people looking for jobs. People seemed to think that jobs would be plentiful after so many deaths, and flocked here from the northern tier of southern states and from across the Ohio River — all fever-afflicted towns had this experience.

I was decidedly in the dumps, especially that first day, meeting so few people that I knew and missing so many that I would never see again.

To make matters worse the weather had turned warm and several new cases were reported, one of whom, Bob McDermott's sister, died. I was more uneasy than on the day I left.

Walking along with my head down I ran plump into Ben Baer whom I had heard had died in Cincinnati as did John Lebolt. I met Aleck McCrosky at the south gate of the courthouse and his greeting was characteristic of him: "John, I am glad to see that you are still above the surface."

I went out (where Sam Booker lives) on Chulahoma Street — and called the cook, Aggie Yancy. She was not there, but my pointer dog, Plato, came running out. We literally hugged each other. He was a large handsome fellow, white with large liver spots.

I had reluctantly left him behind, but found him all right. The cook told me Plato would go to the Cooper Hotel, headquarters of the nursing staff, and the doctors and nurses fed him until he was as fat as a butterball.

That was a lonesome gloomy night, and I allowed Plato to stay in the room for company. I don't believe there was another white face on that street. My reflections were gloomy for in the three days before I left I had seen Fox Moore removed from William Lea's home, just across the street, and taken out to the country to die. I had seen Randle Moore and another colored man bring Charlie Chenowith home (on the site of C. C. Stephenson's house), where his brother John (Miss Lilly Chenowith's father) was already down, they both died a few days later.

Mrs. Stephen Knapp, who lived in John Wade's house, died the morning I left, and her husband a few days later. Col. H. W. Walter and his three sons, Frank, Avant and Jim, my old schoolmates at Chalmers Institute, had laid down their lives for their friends.

The town soon began filling up, though, with returning refugees, and the streets were pathetically black — due to the universal custom then of the women wearing mourning. [There] followed the memorial exercises at the different churches, and other organizations, for their dead, and the two newspapers, *The Reporter* and *The South*, were heavily loaded with resolutions.

Then, when severe cold weather had set in, the mournful journey of the dead who had died in other places, back home.

The cemetery looked like a plowed field, the graves having wooden head boards carrying the name of the dead, some marked "Unknown." In the hurried burials mistakes were made as to lots, and these bodies had to be re-interred.

After all great catastrophes, human nature attempts an effort at forgetfulness, often with an increase of dissipation, and the winter of '78-79 was an exceedingly lively one.

Colonel Harvey W. Walter (1819-1878) was at the fore
of every civic endeavor in North Mississippi for forty years.
Southern Tapestry by Hubert H. McAlexander

WALTER PLACE AND FLOODING IN THE DELTA

DR. ANNE WALTER FEARN

From Fearn, Anne Walter, M.D., *My Days of Strength: An American Woman Doctor's Forty Years in China.* New York & London: Harper & Brothers Publishers, 1939. Excerpts from Chapter 1, "Walter House and My Youth"

Note: We have already witnessed the building of the Cession's most famous mansion built with money provided by a great Cession speculator (see in this volume the essay "Colonel James Brown of Oxford and Walter Place"). Anne Walter was born there in 1867 and gives us vivid glimpses of her Holly Springs childhood and her distinguished father, Col. Harvey Washington Walter. Later she was sent away to school in Charlotte. After graduation, she had to face squarely the economic uncertainty that followed her father's death. Soon all remaining family members were advised to remove to the Delta plantation that precariously supported them. There she saw one of the great periodic floods that swept that region, and she reports it in all its power and horror.

Drama continued in her life afterward, but that took place outside the region, and we will not follow it. Anne Walter Fearn joined a group of north Mississippi feminist heroes. In the generation before was writer Kate Sherwood Bonner McDowell. She was followed by painter Kate Freeman Clark and political activist Ida B. Wells (daughter of slaves). In Oxford, the chain began with the iconic early academician Sarah McGehee Isom. Discussion of these women must wait until another volume. (HHM)

Asmall girl with cropped, curly hair was perched precariously on the edge of the veranda. Her hands were folded primly in the lap of her starched white dress and she was being very quiet because she was supposed to be safe inside the house with her three sisters and little brother. But the excitement in the air had been too strong to resist; like a magnet it had drawn her out of doors. Half hidden by a pillar she listened to the strange sounds; she heard the rush of many feet; the rising murmur of the confused crowd that filled the yard. She watched the townspeople mill around the man on the steps, imploring him to stay with them. She looked up into the man's face and thought of lions, so wonderful were his eyes, so full of power and strength.

I was that eleven-year-old child, and the man was my father, Colonel Harvey Washington Walter. That was my last sight of him, standing there with his three grown sons behind him, and telling his neighbors that as long as life lasted, he and his sons would remain there with them.

I didn't know then why the women cried, why the men walked about with faces drawn and tense. Later I was to learn. That was the summer of 1878, the never-to-be-forgotten year, when the terror of the South — yellow fever — raged all around us.

New Orleans, a constant victim of its ravages, was in the grip of an epidemic and slowly the disease had made its way northward. Holly Springs, with a higher elevation in Mississippi and heretofore immune, grew apprehensive as first Grenada, then Water Valley, and finally Oxford, the university town thirty miles to the south, were stricken. My father, the ruling spirit in Holly Springs, had been away somewhere at court. He returned to find that in his absence his fellow citizens had established a shotgun quarantine. Grieved by this seeming heartlessness, and strong in his faith in the immunity of our hills, he had induced them to raise the quarantine and welcome refugees from the neighboring towns. Soon sporadic cases appeared in our midst, and the courthouse bell tolled ominously; the epidemic was among us.

The morning after the meeting on our front lawn my mother, with the younger children, took "the last train that stopped." It was all very thrilling to a little girl who liked things to happen, whose mind was stirred by adventure then and always, and who didn't realize the seriousness of that trip or the tragedy left behind. My father and older brothers stayed on, as my father had promised, tending the sick and burying the dead. Our house was turned into a hospital. Every household was in mourning and in many cases whole families were blotted out. But it was not until the frost had fallen, the greatest danger past, and the end of the epidemic in sight that my father and brothers fell ill with the fever. Then, within one week, all four were dead.

My mother was left desolate. Of our homecoming I cannot speak.

We were in Huntsville when the first mail reached us in all those weeks of exile. Even before the news came my mother had an experience that made an indelible impression on me. I usually slept in the same room with Mother and I was awakened suddenly by her cry. My married sister, Minnie (Mrs. H. C. Myers), who had joined us there, was in the next room. She came at once and I was shifted to another room. It was not until many years later that I dared to ask my mother about that night. She hesitated before replying and then said,

"It distresses me to speak of it, but since you have asked, I will tell you that I was awakened by a light that shone about your father, who stretched out his arms to me as he said, 'Dona, my wife, it has come upon me like a thief in the night.' "

Among the letters we received in that first batch of mail was one from my father to my mother. It began: "Dona, my wife, it has come upon me like a thief in the night."

During that long, sad autumn I have fleeting memories of my mother wandering drearily from room to room in the big house which had been so easily filled by the presence of the large-hearted man who was gone. It was years before we heard her laugh again.

It was incredible to us children that Christmas should not be as we had always known it. Hospitality had been the family watchword, and Christmas the time when the house overflowed with gaiety and friends and happiness. But we learned, with sorrow and surprise, that we were not even to speak of Santa Claus, nor expect any festivities. On Christmas Eve the five of us, Irene, Pearl, Lillian, Brother Harvey, and I, Annie, were grouped on the floor around a glowing fire, ready for bed and unhappy that we were not allowed even to hang our stockings on the mantel. It was all so different from other Christmas Eves that we had little to say and sat silent until the baby, Pearl, held up a soft and worn-out shoe and said timidly, "Can't I even hang up my shoe?"

We hung them — five in a row and Santa Claus did not forget us completely.

One incident of my very early childhood remains stamped on my memory. My father was host at a large luncheon to many distinguished men. Mint juleps had been served, and after the guests had gone into the dining room, I, then a child of about five, slipped into the parlor and ate the sugar left in the glasses. How long this orgy lasted I do not know. I do remember being found on the upstairs balcony in great distress, holding my arms out toward Sally Knapp's house. Something was wrong with me. I wanted something — but what? I had always wanted Sally's house so it must be that. My next recollection was of being in bed. My mother was sitting beside me. She was crying. It puzzled me that she should cry when it was my stomach that was aching in such a surprising manner. I remember my mother's tearful words, "To think my little daughter is a drunk!"

I had never heard that word before. I had no idea what it meant. It must mean sick. If so I was dreadfully drunk.

When I was twelve, having exhausted the educational advantages of our Presbyterian Sunday School which served also as day school, I was sent to the Charlotte Female Institute in North Carolina (now a part of the Woman's College of South Carolina). There I spent three years, getting only the little learning which I could not manage to escape, although, coming from a scholarly family, I probably retained more information than I thought. However, after three years I passed my examinations and came home. Music I really loved, and my training in voice and piano was of the best. I seriously considered the stage and grand opera. To be honest, I hardly think anyone else considered it for me. I was qualified for nothing but the life of a social butterfly; a bitter disappointment to my mother and, I must confess it, somewhat of a shock to myself.

After my father's death, great changes had taken place in the family fortunes. During his lifetime, with a rich Delta plantation and a good law practice, he was counted one of the wealthiest men in the state. but his income was barely sufficient to meet the demands of an unlimited hospitality and a large and expensive family. As was the custom of the time, he had charge accounts at all the stores in town that sometimes ran for months. Periodically he would go around and ask how much he owed at each store, paying each bill without question.

My mother, the daughter of a prosperous planter and the wife of a successful lawyer, knew nothing of finance and less than nothing of economy. In our home, lavish expendi-

ture alternated with grueling economy, a practice which has been unfortunately characteristic of my own adult life.

My grandfather Brown gave each of his children several servants and a large plantation
as a part of the dowry when they married. This small, dainty girl with the very blue eyes
and very black hair, had as her portion several thousand acres of black alluvial soil for-
ty-five miles from Holly Springs in the heart of the Mississippi Delta, just across the river
from Friars Point. Its richness, increased by the frequently recurring floods, was capable of
producing great wealth; but without money for taxes, wages and the ceaseless war against
the floods, it brought us only annual deficits. Many years later its sale brought us a small
profit, but much freedom from worry.

But it was our only hope and haven for some time. My brother-in-law had served
as Secretary of State for eleven years (the first three by appointment), and was unable to
run for a third term. He suggested that we all take up our residence for a while on this
plantation, so in the autumn of 1888 we moved from our Holly Springs house to live in
what the Negroes called the White House. It was a spacious log cabin set high on a grassy
knoll, overlooking fields that extended for hundreds of acres; fields which should have
been covered with cotton and corn, but which, because of the threatened flood, were lying
idle, unworked, bringing in nothing.

The next year the rain fell unceasingly and in torrents. Day after day we watched
Brother Henry, with a look almost of desperation on his face, staring toward the sunset at
the western sky, praying for just one red streak to indicate a change in the weather. Nearly
every day brought a fresh calamity. The best mules died; a near-epidemic threatened the
cattle; and still it rained. In the evening the sun continued to go down in a sodden gray sky.

Several times each day word came. It was always the same: the river was rising. One
evening just at dusk a messenger brought word that the levee had broken forty miles away.
The Negroes, already organized into working parties, were sent to throw up private levees
around the place. All night they worked, singing, and as the water in the bayous rose,
the words of their song came to us. It was "Roll, Jordan, Roll," and we breathed a fervent
prayer that the "Mississippi" Jordan would turn and roll the other way. Late that night we
went to our rooms. All the doors were open and but for the far-off singing of the Negroes
there was an unearthly stillness.

About four in the morning we heard old Uncle Charlie shuffling to Brother Henry's
room. We heard him whisper, "Marse Henry, she's a-creepin' in."

Down to the banks of the bayou we rushed, and sure enough, she was "a-creepin' in."
Down the center of the water in the bayou, a tiny red stream, thick with sediment from
the river, was pushing its way in. While we waited and watched it widened and the water
began to rise. At six we went to breakfast and when we came out of the dining room what

had been land was a sea.

Chickens, cows, mules and pigs and fleas took refuge within our small levee, the pigs beneath our house. Our cabin on the mound and the cabins of the hands as well were built on piers. We never lost a building in flood time.

Always it was the back water coming in through the bayou which found its way to us first. But it was not long until the Mississippi was flowing past our door. Houses went down. Bellowing, struggling cattle went floating by, and an occasional bale of cotton, carrying human freight, passed us on its way to the sea. Sometimes whole families crowded on a single bale and once a small melodeon completed the outfit. One day a Negro floated by singing, "I'm gwine to join ma Savior." On another five small children were swept from one bale by low-hanging tree branches and before our eyes disappeared below the swirling yellow waters.

Those were sad and lonely days, corralled as we were upon our knoll. Occasionally we rowed in a dugout or canoe for miles and miles in the calmer waters, passing through second-story windows of deserted houses, over roofs of others. These little excursions were none too pleasant or safe. At any time a snake was likely to drop into the boat with us, for they had sought refuge in the upper branches of the trees.

Weeks passed, and at last the waters returned to the bayous and thence to the rivers, leaving behind indescribable desolation and despair. Dreadful things were found in the soil, and once or twice treasures were unearthed by the Negroes when they returned to the fields. It was a hopeless situation. The levees were breaking everywhere, as they had been doing for years, but there was no money for rebuilding or even for repair work.

The Delta was subject to periodic flooding
Sledge Taylor

Green Pryor (1796-1853) was an important planter of the Chulahoma region.
Courtesy Patsey Moore Bogen and Sam Varner

Chulahoma, Tallaloosa, Yoknapatawpha

Hubert H. McAlexander

Chulahoma was not a strange name to us. I grew up on Chulahoma Street in Holly Springs, named for what was an important destination in the old days. The thoroughway was really an avenue, but we seldom were that accurate. The name is Chickasaw, meaning "fox red." The practice in that language was to put the adjective after the noun. Thus Oklahoma means "dirt red."

As I was growing up, the familiar name brought to mind the wildness of the old days, coming down to a fiery patchwork present. The village goes back to the Chickasaw period, and appears on Henry M. Lusher's map of the domain. The Chulahoma region was probably the richest part of the new county of Marshall. And it was long the most colorful. The Coxes, Peels, Deans, and others had colorful histories, and the last time I saw Wee Tee (Theresa Totten Wittijen, Mrs. Jack Wittijen), she pointed toward another clan. "The Tuckers," she said. "What other place could have produced them?" The Rev. Jeremiah Tucker, a Baptist minister, sired 18 children, who had a memorable, often dramatically storied, progeny.

But I have been given other material that also has its interest. So we will concentrate on that. Like many things in my youth, Chulahoma's greatest days were in the "flush times," between settlement and the Civil War. For a bit longer than that, two of the important families were the interconnected clans of Pryor and Alexander. Green Pryor (1796-1853) was an early cotton planter. He first married Olivia Polk (of the family of President Polk), by whom he had three children—John Polk Pryor (1823-1901), well known journalist of the Memphis *Eagle* and Kentucky newspapers; Martha E. Pryor, who married Maj. James H. Alexander; and Mary A. Pryor, who was married in 1842, by the noted Presbyterian minister the Rev. Daniel Baker, to Fendal Wood. Green Pryor's sister Agnes married Walter S. Jenkins and they had four sons. One son, Phillip H. Jenkins, conducted an important boys school named Phidelphia, five miles north of Chulahoma. He married Mary Pegues of a wealthy family, and he was an elder at the Chulahoma Presbyterian Church.

Green Pryor was married a second time in Hardeman County, Tenn., 1831, to Jane Maria Alexander (1812-1853), daughter of Adam Rankin Alexander and sister of Dr. Benjamin Newton Alexander and Maj. James Henry Alexander. Green Pryor came to Mississippi in the 1830s, when Marshall County was known as the "Empire County." By this marriage, he had three children who lived to maturity — two sons, Adam Alexander Pryor (who married a Miss Young, aunt of Stark Young's father, and was killed in Confederate service) and Sam H. Pryor, who became a notable figure in Holly Springs, and a daughter, Olivia M. Pryor, married in 1853, by Rev. Charles S. Dod, to Dr. Christopher Smith Fenner of Memphis.

The Pryor plantation, "Luconia," was located on the Chulahoma-Laws Hill road near Laws Hill. John Mickle describes it as a brick story-and-a-half English basement house entered on the second floor, by columned porches front and rear, which were set sixteen steps above the ground (See the essay in Robert Milton Winter (ed.), *Amid Some Excellent Company* (2003), 179-180). Windows in the half story were in dormers. Extant about 1960 was part of the basement. Fifty, almost sixty years later, descendants Patsy Moore Bogen and Sam Varner have been most helpful in providing material for this essay.

Sam Pryor and his wife, Annie Patterson of Alabama, lived in the house after the Civil War. A member of the Christian denomination, Annie Patterson Pryor was instrumental in the 1870 erection of Mt. Moriah Church, a project of the Christians and the Baptists. Less than a decade later, it was there that she died of yellow fever in the arms of her closest friend, Lida Coxe Brewer of Galena plantation. Sam Pryor (1844-1900), a popular figure in both county and town, eventually moved his family of children into Holly Springs and lived in the Boling-Gatewood house (now the Ida B. Wells Museum). The girls called it "The Pryory." He served as Chancery Clerk, and his 1900 funeral was a notably large one.

The Alexanders, who are memorialized (albeit esoterically) by writer Stark Young (whose father was Dr. Alfred Alexander Young), were an important part of the village. A character in Young's *River House* (1929), recalls riding on horseback from Memphis one Christmas and spending a snowy night at the Chulahoma seat of the Alexanders. Knocking on the door quite late, he found Major Alexander "sitting alone with a glass of whiskey and Gibbon's Roman Empire" (36). He contrasts that experience with the Chulahoma of 1929.

The major's father, Adam Rankin Alexander, was a key figure in West Tennessee, building the first house in Jackson and representing that district in the U. S. House, 18th and 19th Congresses. In 1829, he was defeated for reelection to the 20th Congress by Davy Crockett. He came with his sons to Chulahoma in the 1830s.

The Pryors and Alexanders were long-time Presbyterians and pillars of the Chulahoma church. The Rev. Milton Winter's definitive tome on Presbyterianism in Marshall County, *Shadow of a Mighty Rock* (1997), gives the church history between 1839 and 1863. It is remembered as a white frame structure on the town square. The supply ministers were Angus McCallum, Almarion W. Young, James Weatherly, and Samuel Irwin Reid, headmaster of Chalmers Institute, a boys preparatory school in Holly Springs. Sustaining members were the Pryor, Alexander, Gill, and Jenkins families. The church reported 50 members in the Presbytery in 1850, as well as a flourishing Sabbath school.

Nearby was the Baptist Female Seminary (sponsored by the Coldwater Baptist Association). By 1852, it was housed in a handsome two-story brick building, with rooms accommodating a number of young ladies. Its enrollment was 100, and it was run by the Rev. Joseph R. Hamilton of Ohio. "The seminary numbered among its students," John Mickle wrote in his article on the school, "the maternal ancestry of many families still resident in Marshall County or in adjacent states—the Walls [of Wall Hill], Alexanders, Coxes, McKies, Lucases, McCauleys, Harmons, and Falkners. The sisters of the late Sam Pryor were educated there" (Winter, ed., 51-52).

Among the alumna was Eliza Malvina Jackson Anderson (1840-1930), daughter of Wiley Jackson and Harriet Teer, who kept a diary (now in the Marshall County Historical Museum) in the summer of 1863 that gives us a sense of the bustle of the village:

> 23 August 1863. I received a note to assist in a concert at Chulahoma. 24th. I went to town to practice for the Tableaux. I am in the following ones: Declaration, Faith, Bouquet of Beauty. I spent the day at Dr. Bowen's with a number of girls. The concert is a benefit for the soldiers to procure socks and clothing for those who are far away from loved ones at home. We had contributed to our concert 98 pair of socks. 440 dollars in money. 25th. I went to Mrs. Bloodworths. At night I went to Mrs. Jones and from there to Dr. Alexander's to have a rehearsal and then back to the Jones. 26th. We all repaired to the Seminary to decorate the hall for the night. We were all busy all day. We had a splendid affair, some beautiful Tableaux and exquisite Music & an entertaining charade. This ended the scenes on the night of the 26th. 27th. I was at Mrs. Lucas. The startling news came that the Yankees were close by, which was false. They went to Byhalia (copy in McAlexander Marshall County Collection, University of Mississippi).

The passage gives some idea of Chulahoma of old.

Adam Rankin Alexander had two sons, who were important in Chulahoma. Maj. James H. Alexander (1814-1911) married Elizabeth Pryor, had thirteen children, and raised a company at the start of the Civil War, but the Confederacy asked him to stay at home and raise a crop. His wife died in 1887, and shortly afterward, Marshall County lost one of its most illustrious citizens when Major Alexander moved to be near his children in Pine Bluff, Arkansas. Three of his children married into other prominent Marshall families. Dr. Henry Ludovic Alexander married his Pryor cousin Elinor Jenkins. Olivia Alexander wed, as the first of her three husbands, Thomas J. Peel, the marriage performed by Rev. Hamilton, head of the Seminary. Major Alexander's daughter, Lucy Newton Alexander, married Robert Waite McClain, who died in the yellow fever epidemic of 1878.

It is that line that has been the object of recent (2015) media scrutiny. Lucy N. Alexander and Robert Waite McLain had a son, Gordentia Waite McClain, who was living in Jackson, Tenn., in 1932 (Winter, ed, p. 390). McClain is remembered best locally for his second marriage to Miss Strachan Mickle, sister of the Marshall County historian John

Mickle. But his first wife, to whom he was married briefly, was also a countian, Harriett Roberts (daughter of Levi Roberts and Margaret Boxley). She and Waite McLain were divorced, but they had a daughter, Margaret Roberts McClain (b. 1895). She married Lawrence Lester Roberts about 1917 in Washington, D.C., and they moved to New York City. They are the great-grandparents of the movie actor Ben Affleck, who, in connection with the Henry Louis Gates PBS series, denied any slave-holding ancestry.

Tallaloosa — the name casts a spell. I grew up with it in my mind. Now it reminds me of the shadowy historical past looming in my youth. The word in Chickasaw means "rock black." Knowing that the adjective always came after the noun in Chickasaw helped me understand many aboriginal place names. But the very sound of "Tallaloosa" is haunting. It must have influenced a member of the Johnson family (from Holly Springs and founders of the International Shoe Company in St. Louis) to give that old name to the Best Place, a pioneer dwelling to the north of the extinct village of Tallaloosa. The Johnsons gave the place the name in the 1930s. That structure, a log dog-trot dwelling, still stands, and so the name survives in Marshall County.

No one knows how far the name goes back. We find it first in 1836, attached to a village of the new county. "Tallaloosy," it was called, in a list of Marshall County polling places set on March 14, 1836 (Board of Police Minutes, I:13). The Franklin Riley treatment of the place under "Extinct Towns and Villages of Mississippi," (*Publications of the Mississippi Historical Society*, 1902, V:356) places the village "about eight miles southwest of Holly Springs, on Pigeon Roost Creek." Riley reports that "it contained two or three small stores and a few families at the time of its greatest prosperity" but comments that "it was surrounded by a good agricultural section." In 1931, John M. Mickle, the historian of old Marshall, lists the "fine citizenship" living in the vicinity as "the Joneses, Nunnallys, Echols, Glovers, Woods, McClatchys, Hursts, John Williams, McRavens and Wootens," ("Pioneer Families of Marshall County: William Jones," in *Amid Some Excellent Company*, ed. by Robert Milton Winter [2003] p. 157). In his essay, Mickle discusses the region extending to the west as far as Marianna. That puts the extinct village in the general region of the Love settlement. The Loves are the noted mixed-blood Chickasaw family. See "The Saga of a Mixed Blood Chickasaw Dynasty" in this volume.

In my youth, there were still a few houses near the site of the village of Tallaloosa. The home of John Hamilton McClatchy, a postbellum wooden structure with a long porch across the central portion and a wing on either end, survived until a few years ago. It was south of the Pigeon Roost Road, facing south, a few miles to the east of the village. Other structures had vanished long before. An exception were two houses four miles west at Marianna, a much later community. At that intersection, on the southeast was Woodlawn, the plantation home of the John Wooten family, a long, low-frame structure in a stand of tall cedars laid out in three avenues. The house stood until the seventh decade of the 20th century. Still extant is the fascinating structure on the northwest corner near the Marianna store, a two-story log house. Over time, it received an outer layer of clapboard and Greek Revival woodwork. Named Oak Grove, it was built by Mallerb Jones, who in 1841 married Clementine, daughter of wealthy planter Brantley Sugg. About the time of World War I, it was bought by the McClatchys, who own it today.

When one looks for traces of the extinct town of Tallaloosa today, the most striking reminder is the old cemetery across from the village. On section 7, T4, R3, Tallaloosa stood on the western edge of a lake ending at the foot of what is probably the county's highest hill. The hill was owned by an early settler named William Taliaferro, who buried several children there before he sold the land in 1860 (see Bobby Mitchell's essay "Jewish Merchants of Holly Springs," the following essay). Taliaferro excepted the cemetery on Tallaloosa Hill (or Rhine Mountain, as it later became known). About 1900, Martin Andrew Greene, an entrepreneur whose first wife lies in the cemetery, drained the lake and made a vast, fertile cotton field. The view from the old burying ground is spectacular.

The name "Yoknapatawpha" I didn't encounter until high school. The first William Faulkner novel that I read was *Intruder in the Dust* (1948). I became a devoted reader for life, and I taught his works for fifty years. But I had already driven through Lafayette County north to south for all of my childhood. Leaving Holly Springs bound for my mother's hometown, Grenada, Miss., our 1948 Pontiac took Highway 7. First, between Holly Springs and Oxford, we went across the Tallahatchie River (Chickasaw for "rock river"). About four miles below Oxford, Highway 7 crossed the Yocona River on the way to Water Valley. Faulkner used the old, full Chickasaw name of that river for his fictional county.

In his 2007 study, *Native American Place Names in Mississippi* (Jackson: University Press of Mississippi), Keith A. Baca discusses the name as a derivation of the Chickasaw *yaakni* — meaning "land." He notes that the original name has various transliterations "including Cushman's (1999, p. 492) 'Yoconapatawfa' and 'Yak-ni-pa-tuffh'" (p. 134). Horatio B. Chushman's *History of the Choctaw, Chickasaw and Natchez Indians* was originally published in 1899 by the Headright Printing House of Greenville, Texas. William Faulkner may well have seen that volume. The old, full name (in various forms) also appeared on old maps. Of course readers worldwide are now familiar with the old Chickasaw name.

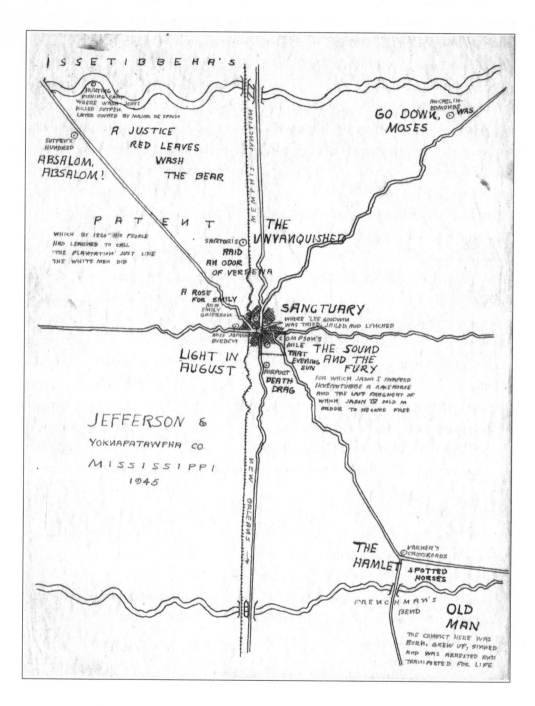

Faulkner drew this map for the Modern Library edition of *Absalom, Absalom!* The railroad here followed our family's route on Highway 7 from Holly Springs through Oxford to Grenada

Jewish Merchants of Holly Springs

Bobby J. Mitchell

In the latter half of the 19th century and well into the first half of the 20th century there was a significant complement of Jewish families residing in Holly Springs. Many of these families added to the tapestry which represented life in this community, participating in various clubs and fraternal organizations, being the dominant merchant entrepreneurs, serving on the boards of directors of financial institutions, and schools.

Although there were many Jewish families there, their numbers were insufficient to support their own synagogue and most went to Memphis for the religious holidays, and when there was a death among their faith, most were interred in the Jewish Cemetery in Memphis. In those days in Holly Springs it was common for Jewish merchants to close for Christmas and Easter, and the other local merchants would close for Jewish Holidays.

Any list of our Jewish families would probably begin with Isaac C. Levy, and then, in no particular order, the Behrs (Baer), M(e)yers, Grosskins, Leibsons, Seesels, Blumenthals, Oppenheimers, Capt. Sam Franck, brothers Isaac and Solomon Rhine, the Shumacker brothers, Lebolts, Kohners, Schneider, and others, including Marcus Louis, who was murdered in his store by an axe-wielding assailant. Louis's brother-in-law, Jacob Rosenfield, was a Confederate veteran who came here from Georgia after the Civil War. With the exodus of the Kohner family, not long after the tragic drowning of Junior Kohner in the pool at the old country club, the last of the old line Jewish families here was extinct. Several of the names of these old families are perpetuated by having their name associated with some building or landmark. Thus the I. C. Levy Store; the Nathan Seesel memorial water fountain near the entry to the Marshall County Historical Museum; the "Shumacker Bros." name, which is imbedded in the entry tile to the present day Angie's Boutique, at 111 E. Van Dorn; then there is Rhine's Mountain several miles west of town. On the high bluff of the mountain, overlooking what was at one time a large lake, is an old cemetery.

I first visited the cemetery with Gus Smith more than 30 years ago. Some call it the McClatchy Cemetery and others call it the Rhine Cemetery, even though there are no Rhines buried there. From whence did the name Rhine come to the mountain?

Solomon G. Rhine was a native of Bavaria, born about 1829. He left Bavaria, and traveling alone, arrived at the port of New York, in September 1845. He had come to the United States to live with his brother Isaac Rhine. In the 1850 census for Marshall County, Isaac is listed in the Williamson Hotel in Holly Springs with others of his family, and on the next page of the census, Solomon is listed as also living in the Williamson Hotel. The Williamson Hotel was on the north side of the square between Market Street and Center

Street. As recorded in the Marshall County circuit clerk's records, Solomon Rhine filed a declaration to become a naturalized citizen of the United States in July 1850 and received his order of naturalization on January 31, 1851.

He soon went into the dry goods/hardware/cutlery and notions business, his store being beneath the hotel. In 1858, Solomon married a woman from Baltimore, Md. By December 1860 Rhine was prosperous enough to purchase from William Talliferro all of Section 8, Township 4S, Range 3W, except the cemetery mentioned above, which introduced the Rhine name to those bluffs. The area is now practically inaccessible.

Another prosperous year followed and Sol Rhine had an increase in wealth as did other merchants, but with the coming of the Civil War, things became more complicated for merchants. Banks as we know them had not yet been established, and wealth had to be protected. There was no place to safely deposit money and have it remain secure until it was needed, and by 1862, the Federal Army was moving farther south each month. Many were afraid that Confederate money might become worthless, so businessmen wanted the money they handled to be specie, gold or silver. The specie would hold its value, but there was still the problem of securing it to prevent it being stolen. They would swap Confederate money at a discount for gold.

Sol Rhine normally went to New York or Philadelphia for his store's goods each year in January, but by 1862 he had a surplus of cash and was looking for a way to invest it and make a profit, rather than having so much cash at home. He went to New Orleans and even though he did not have a grocery store, he invested in sugar and molasses, and had it shipped by boat most of the way to Holly Springs. It was stored in the cellar of his store.

Among the goods Sol Rhine purchased in New Orleans that spring were: 85 hogsheads of sugar, each averaging 1050 pounds, for a total of 89,250 pounds of sugar; three hundred barrels of molasses totaling 12,000 gallons; 200 half-barrels of molasses totaling another 4,000 gallons; and 300 bushels of wheat. Altogether, the goods were valued at more than $35,000.

When the Yankees came to Holly Springs, they took all of Sol Rhine's stock and left him financially ruined. He filed a claim with the Southern Claims Commission in 1871, stating he had been a loyal Union man and should be reimbursed. Mr. Rhine was out of town when the Union troops took his supplies, but Mrs. Rhine was present and watched them steal the store's goods. When the claim was filed, the Rhines could not remember the exact date of the theft, but Mrs. Rhine mentioned Van Dorn's raid. This would have coincided with General Grant's orders for his troops to live off the land and take what they needed from civilians, as their supply base at Holly Springs had been destroyed in the raid. Following some witness interviews, his claim was denied. His wife testified that she had been a loyal Southerner but that her husband was a loyal Union man, and the "other

Israelites" in town had berated him for voting as a Whig, rather than a Democrat. When she told the commissioners what the "other Israelites" had done, they wanted to know if she and Mr. Rhine were Israelites also. I have wondered if the government denied his claim because he was Jewish.

With their business and money all gone, the Rhines left town separately. After a brief period of living in Baltimore and Minnesota, they each subsequently landed in Memphis. Isaac Rhine had previously moved to Philadelphia. Solomon was unable to pay the taxes on his property at Rhine's Mountain and it was taken by the state for delinquent taxes. In 1870, he was able to buy his property back from the state at a tax sale, but in 1874, for some reason his brother Isaac acquired the property from Solomon. Isaac Rhine kept the property until 1898, when it was sold to Martin Greene, another large landowner and businessman.

Solomon and his family were living in Memphis in 1878 when the yellow fever epidemic began. Unable to escape from Memphis because of various quarantines against citizens of Memphis, he moved into the countryside to avoid the illness. However, it was too late, as he came down with what the newspaper called "malaria" and died on August 29, 1878, at the age of 49.

I want to thank my friend Eileen Rhine, of Santa Fe, N.M., for contributing the information about the claims against the government.

Gunshots in Tunica County

Hubert H. McAlexander

Walker Percy once said that Mississippi was closer to Dodge City than to New Orleans. Nothing demonstrates that better than the shootings on the streets of Tunica in 1908. The local newspaper, the *Delta Democrat*, documented the incidents well.

The Houstons, a family well established at Vaiden in the hills, settled in the Mississippi Delta and established a cotton dynasty in the golden age of King Cotton. The oldest of the four Houston brothers, Percy Marion Houston (1861-1908), reached a pinnacle by his election to a highly coveted office on the Yazoo-Mississippi Levee Board. It also sealed his fate.[1]

The *Delta Democrat* of March 31, 1908, carried this story:

> A very sad and deplorable affair occurred on our streets Monday afternoon, March 30th when Hon. J.T. Lowe shot and killed Mr. P.M. Houston, Secretary and Treasurer of the Yazoo-Mississippi Levee Board.

J.T. Lowe was arraigned, posted bail, and was released to await the convening of the grand jury. He resumed his usual life about town. But the populace received another shock on the morning of June the tenth:

> When Mrs. Una Mai Weinstein, the oldest daughter of Mr. P.M. Houston, passed Hon. J.T. Lowe on the street, she turned and drawing a pistol from her handbag fired point blank at Mr. Lowe, the ball entering just below the right shoulder blade and coming out the center of his breast about three inches below the neck, striking the pearl stud in the front of his shirt.

It was later reported that when Lowe drew out his pistol, turned, and saw Houston's daughter, he said, "I cannot shoot a lady," and lowered his weapon.

John Thomas Lowe (1864-1915), also from the hills, had married well. His wife, Amanda Idella Irwin, was daughter of Robert Clell Irwin, and her sisters had married Abbays (a clan among the earliest settlers of the Chickasaw Cession), Mangrums and Leathermans, major planters. So the families and connections of all involved in both shootings

---

1 This incident has been treated in Hubert Horton McAlexander, Richard Douglas McCrum, and Dan Morse Woodliff, *Francis Fontaine The Builder, 1715-1785, His Ancestors and Descendants and Their Connections* (Baltimore: Otter Bay Books, 2007), 115-120.

were prominent.[2]

Lowe recovered, and no one was ever charged in the affair. Una Mai Houston and her sisters soon moved from Tunica, and the remaining Houstons and the Lowes remained close friends over the decades. In nearby Holly Springs in my youth, murderers of prominent families were sent to the state insane asylum at Whitfield.

2 Telephone interview with John Hayes Pritchard III, October 7, 2016.

Little Wilson being held by Mary Hampton

Little Wilson being put on a
horse by Jack Thompson

Gene Lanier and Constance Harris
The Martin-Miller place

Wilson Golden standing
by the distinctive stairway

Waterford Days

Wilson Golden

Introduction by Hubert H. McAlexander

In my day, as Peter Taylor has a character say in a short story, there were still people you knew out in the country. Readers of this present volume have already been exposed to the southwestern part of Marshall County, from the Oxford road to the Tate County line, roughly the region known to us city dwellers as the Chulahoma section. It was still colorful, and to us town-children, exotic.

I had access to it through boys in my grade. First, in the lower grades, through Ben Earl Fore. He lived in an old house (the old Jeffreys place) in Chulahoma, where I spent one weekend. Then later, Gene Lanier moved to the old Miller place, between Laws Hill and Waterford, when his mother married again. Waterford was the extreme eastern boundary of southwest Marshall.

Gene and Wilson's mother was Constance Harris, the most charismatic presence in the county of her generation. As a student at Stephens College, she had married Eugene Banks Lanier, her high school teacher and later a dashing major in the U.S. Army. He was killed in 1943, and she was a beautiful widow living in town with her two children, Gene and Constance Ann. In 1946, she married Woodrow Wilson Golden of the Miller Place, out in the country. To me, they were like movie stars—she, vivacious and warm, and he, handsome and forceful. I visited Gene out there many weekends for many years. Big Wilson (by then there was a little Wilson) lived (in the words of a town lawyer) like an Indian Chief. Certainly there was a lot of hunting and drinking out there. Gene, handsome and magnetic, was smart, a good hunter, and a good rider. Later he had his own car, a Studebaker Golden Hawk.

Amid all that went on out there, those of us who visited hardly noticed the two little children of the second marriage. I went to my first football game with the Goldens — Ole Miss versus Maryland — in 1950. Those glamorous times came to an end when the marriage broke up about 1962. Constance and her children (two from each marriage) moved back to town, and my family knew them well through the Presbyterian church. As an English instructor at Ole Miss, I taught little Wilson in 1966. Now he is retired from an important position in Washington, lives near me, and I have gotten him to write this fine essay, which brings back those days.

On a blustery fall day in October 2014, I found myself standing at the speaker's podium of a rural black church just off Laws Hill Road in rural southwest Marshall County, Miss., not many miles outside the small town where I was born in February 1948. Nearby were the communities of Galena and Chulahoma where my Harris and Smith kin had lived in the 19th century, connected by modern Mississippi Highway 4 to the county seat of Holly Springs. My bittersweet role that day was to celebrate the life of the deceased in this sacred place. The crowd was packed shoulder-to-shoulder into every pew and standing along the walls around the sanctuary of Mt. Peel Missionary Baptist Church. Surrounded by mourning family and friends, I absorbed the pathos of the remarks of a succession of inspirational and powerful ministers, vocalists, and laity. Looking out across the sea of mostly black faces, I prepared to deliver a brief eulogy to my lifelong friend Jack Thompson, gone to his final reward at age 93. I was swept up in memories of my early years, seeing in those faces the vivid images of Jack and his large and loving family. Many of the males of several generations before me bore a striking resemblance to the man lying in repose in the casket beside which I stood. I had lived my first 13 years on a nearby farm with many of these good people before moving into town on the day of John Kennedy's inauguration in January 1961. Among the mourners were my sister Emmy and my step-mother, Coy, widowed by my father's death nearly 40 years earlier in 1975. As the only son of Woodrow Wilson Golden, born in the Mississippi Delta 99 years earlier in November 1915, just for this one day—the first time since I was a child—I was "Wilson Jr." again.

Over 66 years earlier, my unborn self was bouncing on a mid-February Sunday morning in the back seat of my father's Willys Jeep along a gravel road made treacherous by severe winter weather. Passengers included my shivering mother, Constance, in early labor, my soon-to-be first-time father, Wilson, in the front passenger seat, nervously looking straight ahead, and longtime farm manager Jack Thompson at the wheel. She was 27, Daddy 33, and Jack had just turned 27, all living in the same, yet very different, post-Workd War II rural Mississippi world into which I was about to be born at the leading edge of what would come to be known as the Baby Boom. Navigating the tricky Oak Chewalla Creek bottom less than a half-mile from our house in the direction of the small community of Waterford was nothing new to Jack. He'd driven this old road and farmed and hunted in these bottom lands all his life. But never before had he driven the boss's very pregnant wife ("Miss Constance") on an emergency baby delivery mission to the county hospital some 15 miles away. Although Jack always took great pride in recounting his role in assuring my birth didn't take place in the back seat of that Jeep, I learned years later that in fact he got us to the North Mississippi Hospital with time to spare for the delivery of a healthy baby Golden boy. While I can't be certain of the state of my hair at birth, my mother delighted in saying that I sprouted so much curly blonde baby hair it wasn't until I reached four years old that she finally had it cut after so many people complimented her on her beautiful little girl!

On this October day of Jack's funeral those many years later, I truly felt like his "special family."

My sister and I were greeted as returning relatives, as both of us had maintained fairly close contact with Jack and his family since moving away in 1961. This was especially true for me, when I made holiday visits to the area from Washington, D.C., and from the Mississippi cities I had lived in since graduating from college. At the conclusion of Jack's service and burial in the adjoining cemetery, we shared a traditional meal with his widow, Bettie, and other Thompson family members and friends, warmly embraced by many as we reminisced and posed for pictures at the request of fellow mourners. One of Jack's grandsons even asked that I send him old photos and memories of Jack and my early life at Golden Acres living in the "big house."

Special, too, was the relationship between the Golden and Thompson families that traced its roots to the 1920s, when my father was a towheaded youngster and Tarther Jack Thompson was born on a nearby farm on New Year's Day, 1921. Over time, Daddy and Jack developed a business relationship to operate the family farm, known locally as the "Miller Place." Our families also grew close over the years in the paternalistic way that existed between many white land owners and black tenants in the Jim Crow segregation culture of pre-World War II. In the 1930s, Jack had gone off to Chicago to attend the Naval Training Station at Camp Berry. Writing to "Mr. Wilson," Jack told of how he was about to be "turned…over to the red cross" and that he wasn't "doing anything but sailing around" without pay. He wanted Daddy to "do all you can for me and soon I will be home." The bond between these two men evidenced by this letter was always strong, and in time Jack returned to start his own family, marrying Bettie Pryor in March 1944 in a union that lasted 70 years and produced 10 children.

Jack's funeral program stated that "for many, many years…he was employed by Wilson Golden, Sr.," but the relationship ran much deeper, such that the program declared that among Jack's survivors were "his special family: Wilson Golden, Jr. and Emmy Jarjoura." When it came my turn to speak, I offered "all praise to God and appreciation for the honor of speaking on behalf of Jack's special family," noting that my father had been born nearly a century earlier and that he and Jack shared over 50 of those years of labor and devoted friendship. I then described the unique role Jack had played in my own life, from the famous 1948 Jeep ride to the time after my beloved caretaker, Mary, died when I was just five, as Jack took my little hand and solemnly walked me into her Mt. Comfort Church funeral service. As Jack and I walked down the aisle, I was completely surrounded by the black mourners while my parents sat outside in the car in the sweltering summer heat. As I gazed up into the casket at my lifelong companion and caretaker, Jack made sure I wasn't scared, marching me back out of the church and down the stairs to my waiting parents. I said that was a day I would never forget, just as I would never forget this day.

I spoke of the abiding importance of family to Jack—his wife Bettie, 12 children, 41 grandchildren, 104 great-grandchildren, and 31 great-great-grandchildren. I shared that I had only one month earlier become the grandfather of a grandson, thus carrying forward the Golden name, and how on visits Jack always asked about my family and delighted in each bit of news about graduations, weddings, grandbabies and other family happenings. I then related the Jeep story, saying that Jack had been right at my side at birth just as he had been at my father's side at his passing in 1975. I concluded by saying that a great point of pride was that near the Thompson residence and my childhood home is the intersection of "Jack Thompson & Wilson Golden" Roads, a reminder of the two families' deep connection every time I drive to or from Jack's home.

Jack and Mary will forever live in my memory, but to fully appreciate the setting of those early days I must return to the distant past, as is so often necessary with Mississippi stories. Almost exactly a century before my birth, three Miller brothers—John, William, and Ethelred—came from Virginia to settle near each other in southwest Marshall County. All became prosperous from growing cotton. By 1890, John H. Miller's farm numbered 900 acres, with the addition in the early 1860s of the adjoining Martin place, on which recently had been constructed a frame Greek Revival plantation house that upon their marriage in late 1946 became my parents' home.

Originally planned as a four-over-four room structure, it was modified to a story-and-a-half dwelling when construction was halted during the Civil War. The house was built with a classic central hallway entered from the north through a large doorway with pilasters, transom, and sidelights. With high-ceilinged double parlors on the west side, the house was distinguished by a turning staircase that rose on the west wall as a suspended section ending at the top on the east wall. There a landing led to the two second-floor bedrooms. A third upstairs bedroom was added as a dormer in the early 20th century. The house featured four working fireplaces and an open porch, later enclosed, that spanned the entire back of the house. At the southeast corner of the main house was attached a one-story kitchen (serviced by a large outdoor cistern) and on the west end a store building dating from the late 19th century in which my father and his foster brother Paul Johnson operated a commissary during the 1930s and 40s. The store building and a freestanding cook's house at the back of the main house are now preserved at the Bill Fitch Farms several miles to the west of their original location. My childhood room was the bedroom at the head of the staircase, which included one of the four fireplaces, walled up long before my time. My Aunt Warrene told me that the farm manager Fred Weber, who had picked up my three-year-old father from the Palmer Orphanage in 1919, had previously occupied this room. I still have the pine twin beds purchased for my room sometime before I began attending school in 1954. Out my east-facing window I could see the small house occupied by my beloved caretaker, Mary Hampton.

Any story of my youth must include how, in the early spring of 1919, my father came to live at RFD Route 2, Box 21, Waterford, Miss.. Mollie W. Miller was born May 10, 1866, the only daughter and last born of the children of John H. and Mary Susan Harris Miller. Mollie must have been an unusual woman. After two marriages and no children, she became foster mother to two children, first Paul Johnson (1902-1995) and, later, my father. As was often the case in isolated rural 19th-century farm communities, interfamily marriages were not uncommon, the close knit families living on self-sustaining farms inaccessible by muddy dirt roads impassable much of the year. "Miss Mollie" was such a person, married to two Miller cousins (thereby making her "Molly Miller Miller Miller"). She married her first cousin Daniel W. Miller (1850 — 1911), son of the pioneer William P. Miller, upon whose death she married first cousin, once removed, Dr. James Miller, son of James Alfred and Mamie Graham Naylor Miller and grandson of Ethelred H. Miller, one of the three Miller brothers who originally migrated in 1848 from Virginia to Marshall County. Mollie's first husband, Daniel, was a leading citizen, serving a term as sheriff of the county and owner of a former livery stable in Holly Springs that ultimately became the site adjacent to the Post Office building where M. A. Greene's livery stable was built and thereafter, the area Ford dealership that I can recall from my youth. We know little about Mollie's second husband, Dr. Miller, a few years her junior, except that their marriage ended in divorce.

Many of my earliest memories are refreshed by family stories and old photographs, one in particular taken of me at about age three being embraced in the arms of Mary Hampton (whose last name I only learned from Jack in recent years). In the picture I am scowling at the camera as we posed in front of the store porch with our mailbox in the foreground and the rear of the big house visible behind us. I have this picture framed on my desk today. Unsmiling but loving, Mary was taking care of "June" (as she called me) just as she had for most every day of my young life. She lived just a few yards behind the big house in a small frame house out the rear kitchen door. In a conversation with Jack a few years ago, we calculated that Mary was around 80 when she died, making her birth just a few years after the end of the Civil War and slavery. I was, of course, oblivious to such things and only knew that Mary was my constant companion and caretaker, a part of my family without any of the distinctions imposed by society. My young world was colorblind, which no doubt framed my views about black and white issues as I grew older. I can't recall ever hearing a single word that made me feel better than anyone else, certainly not people like Mary and Jack, a fact which I consider to be one of the greatest gifts of my childhood. I just knew that I felt loved by all the people who surrounded me.

Tragedy struck our family in early December 1952 when my grandfather Hamilton Harris was murdered in cold blood as he sat drinking his afternoon Coca-Cola in the store next to his own on the southwest side of the Holly Springs town square. At the time, I was just shy of five years old and my sister Emmy was an infant of only three months. Since we had no telephone, news came in person on this chilly Friday afternoon, with family and neighbors appearing in droves, soon filling our large back yard. Our grieving mother was inside with the adults and none of us children was told why all these somber-faced people, many in tears, were suddenly showing up. I recall my brother Gene Lanier speculating to my older sister Constance Ann and me that perhaps our Great Aunt Thelma ("Big Sister") had suffered a stroke—or who knew what. Would that the horrid reality had not been true! An indelible mark was made on the entire community, with some people clearly remembering details of the murder and subsequent trial more than 60 years later. Hamilton Harris was a much-beloved man in the community, revered in our family. I have honored my grandfather's memory by giving each of my sons, Wilson Harris and Lewis Hamilton, one of his names.

Far happier memories of life growing up on a farm, with no telephone and the only way to town by gravel road, included the excitement generated by the daily arrival of the mail; the sound of the mailman's vehicle on the gravel road could be heard at the house from far down the road, always the highlight of my youthful Waterford days. I also looked forward to monthly deliveries by the "rolling store" and the "Rich Plan" trucks which stocked our pantry with canned goods and staples and an Admiral freezer with frozen food products. That freezer, which my sister Emmy still owns, was acquired just after her 1952 birth and held the fruits of many of my father's deer and bird hunting excursions. It's still working, Emmy declares, after all these years! Fall brought the harvest of our cotton crop and I was sometimes invited by my father to accompany him on trips to the cotton gin in Chulahoma. The array of machinery and noises in the huge tin building, with flying lint as the cotton was sucked from the trailer up into the gin, was a source of great wonderment to my young senses, but not nearly so much as the miracle of a cotton bale coming off the line at the end of the process. How exactly did that happen?

Summertime was filled with Scout and church camps and vacation Bible school at the Holly Springs First Presbyterian Church. I was a "cradle Presbyterian," and my family had been members there for at least three generations, with deep roots in my grandmother's Hudsonville church, where an ancestor, War of 1812 veteran Capt. Ebenezer Kilpatrick, had been a founder in the mid-19th century. The Holly Springs church was among the town's most imposing structures, situated on Memphis Street a block south of the town square as its third successive house of worship in the same block dating to the 1830s. Tradition holds that during the Union army's occupation of the town in the fall of 1862, General Grant outraged the congregation when his horses were stabled on the ground level of the not-yet-completed structure. No doubt from sympathy for this degradation, northern churches contributed to the church's completion following the Civil War. Another late summer religious experience came when I was four or five, my Uncle Paul Johnson, an ordained pastor of the Christian Church, took me along to a tent revival in Laws Hill. Imagine a scene straight out of Elmer Gantry with a big tent, glaring strings of naked light bulbs and, of course, sawdust under our feet. Writhing worshippers shouted in response to the preacher's admonitions of hellfire and damnation. This was certainly no First Presbyterian Church! These family traditions and rich history have been carried into my own adult life.

I entered the first grade in September 1954, completely oblivious to the profound impact of the U.S. Supreme Court's *Brown v. Board of Education* decision the previous May. Life in Holly Springs and its segregated public schools was unaffected, and not until my senior high school year in 1965-66 did "freedom of choice" integration occur. A fond early school memory is of my second grade train trip for a picnic in New Albany (cost: 50 cents!) and the annual parties when my mother took me and a handful of school friends to Memphis for the Barnum & Bailey circus, which coincided each year with my mid-February birthday. The circus was highlighted by the "human cannonball," who was projected nearly to the top of the arena by a massive and very loud and smoky cannon. How did that man do that?

Although mornings during the school year began in the dark around 5:45 A.M. when Cleveland Culver's school bus picked me up. I looked forward to the time spent a few miles into the journey at Lucille Fesmire's little store in Laws Hill waiting on the transfer to Fonta Odell's bus that took us the rest of the way into Holly Springs. At Lucille's, I often bought a candy bar and Coke — definitely not so great for the teeth, especially the day when I was in the fourth grade and an older boy's arm accidentally bumped the bottom of my 10 ounce Coke bottle and knocked out half of a front tooth. I still live with the consequences of that simple pleasure. I well remember those long bus rides into Holly Springs, the occasional rousting by the older neighborhood boys, many of whom wore farm work clothes that smelled of the smoke of wood burning stoves. It was on one such ride when I was in third grade that an older boy told me there was no Santa Claus. I was devastated!

Sometime when I was near twelve, my friend and distant cousin Mahon Jones was out for a visit around Christmastime. We decided to check out the former cook's house in the back yard, by then a storage building for garden supplies and other miscellany. The house was locked, so we hoisted up to look through a window. Lo and behold, there we observed what was obviously my loot from "Santa Claus." Being the naïve child I was, I immediately went and told my mother of our discovery. I shall never forget her response: "When you quit believing in Santa, he quits coming." Rest assured, never another word was uttered on the subject (and he kept coming). Family legend has it that my wiser older brother Gene professed belief in Santa Claus right through his high school graduation!

Although I can't be certain, it's probably accurate to say that politics (which, in one form or another, became my life's work) was always "in my blood" due to the many politicians in my family. Politics was a main topic of discussion at family gatherings throughout my youth. My maternal grandfather, Hamilton A. Harris, was a Holly Springs alderman in the 1920s and a longtime supporter of Dennis Murphree, who twice rose from the lieutenant governorship to become Mississippi governor upon the death of Governors Whitfield and Johnson Sr. As evidence of his activism, "Big Daddy" Harris attended the 1936 Democratic National Convention in Philadelphia as an FDR supporter. Family holiday gatherings were always spiced with tales told by my Great-Uncle "Dutch" Erwin, who served as the Memphis city treasurer and a city council member, and my Great-Uncle Sam Coopwood, a longtime mayor of Holly Springs after serving as the sheriff of Marshall County.

My father served three elected terms as supervisor of Marshall County District Four, serving during the 1950s as board president, before losing a 1959 race for sheriff, during which I learned valuable lessons at the tender age of 11 that have served me well in many subsequent election contests. I cherish a letter dated August 5, 1959, addressed to my father and mother from a prominent Holly Springs citizen and newspaper columnist. Writing the day following my father's defeat for sheriff, she expressed disappointment at his loss, saying that in a future race, "…if everyone works as hard as Wilson Jr. did, I am sure you will come out with flying colors. Everyone…was amazed at how well he kept his tally sheet and we were all asking him for figures before it was over. He was a mighty good little sport and I am sure you are proud of him." From thence no doubt sprang my lifelong passion for politics. My mother also shared in my indoctrination into the political process during the 1960 presidential election, when she allowed me to mark her ballot (for whom, I shall not reveal). Apparently the election officials at the old Laws Hill school didn't pay much attention to voters who were accompanied by their young children. Little did they know that I was no ordinary twelve-year-old, since I had followed the Nixon-Kennedy race closely, even watching their debates on television.

A distinct benefit of being a county supervisor's child was the annual beach trip to the summer convention of the Mississippi Association of Supervisors, in those days held at the Hotel Buena Vista along the Gulf Coast in Biloxi. I have many happy memories of those family vacations in the coast area, subsequently devastated by huge hurricanes like Camille in 1969 and Katrina in 2005. The site once occupied by the grand Buena Vista is now a casino along an interstate highway access ramp. Another benefit of my father's position was having a county equipment shed and old-fashioned glass cylinder gasoline pump in the front of our house, not to mention a huge bull dozer and road grader. These were big hits with my friends when my mother hosted my Cub Scout den.

I don't recall much about my father as a public servant, but among the family archives is a letter handwritten in pencil on lined school paper dated May 29, 1951, just as his first re-election campaign was beginning. The author, a member of a large family in our supervisor district, wrote that he needed "a cow to milk for my childrens. My Baby Mity Sickly." He pleaded that if my father has a cow, "would you let me milk one. Please I have ask Every one But you now I am asking you...if you can let me no at once will you, my vote and my wife are for you. I sure am going to help you if I Live." I sincerely hope Daddy rose to this worthy request.

My father's political support was often sought by statewide officials, it being the era when county supervisors were among the state's most powerful local office holders. His files contained personal letters from governors and would-be governors of the 1950s and early 60s. Then-Lt. Gov. William Winter, on whose State Senate staff I served, told me at the time of my father's death in January 1975 that he had a memory of being dispatched by Senator John Stennis to "go by to see Wilson Golden" to firm up his support for the Senator's re-election. Winter said he spotted my father out in the field driving a tractor, crossing the field to shake his hand on behalf of Stennis.

Although my father was in many ways quite worldly, my mother recalled that once on a vacation trip, a Florida state trooper pulled them over and asked him where he was from. My father looked up and simply responded "Waterford." Of course, where else? On a visit to Waterford, Ireland, a few years ago, I recalled this story with a smile. And so on the day of Jack's funeral in 2014, these and so many other memories flooded my consciousness. Wilson Jr., as it turned out, had never really left these good people nor this special place.

Jacob Thompson (1810-1885), the foremost citizen of nineteenth century
North Mississippi, provided the idea for Faulkner's Jason Compson.
Library of Congress

PART V:
HISTORY, RACE, YOKNAPATAWPHA

THE THOMPSONS, THE CHICKASAW CESSION, YOKNAPATAWPHA

HUBERT H. MCALEXANDER

Jacob Thompson, secretary of the interior under President James Buchanan, was a notable figure in north Mississippi. A dominant family in the Chickasaw Cession, the Thompsons were one of several Caswell County, N.C., clans drawn to this cotton frontier. The Leas, Malones, and Pointers all made their marks. But the Thompsons were probably the first and the most dramatic.[1]

After receiving his legal training in Greensboro, N.C., Jacob Thompson set out for Natchez, Miss., to settle there and begin his career. As he was riding out of Columbus, Miss., bound for Natchez, he was hailed by a familiar voice. Amazingly, it was his older brother Dr. James Young Thompson, who had come to the lower South before him. During the ensuing reunion, the brothers decided that the land office that the government had created up to sell the Chickasaw lands was a place they must see (Oldham, 20). Thus they entered the Cession.[2]

Before going further, let's sort out this branch of the Thompson family of Caswell County. The father of the two brothers, Nicholas Thompson, "accumulated something of a fortune in the businesses of farming, tanning, and leather and harness making." The forebear of eight children who lived to adulthood, he was staunchly Presbyterian and a model of industriousness. He sent five of his sons to the University of North Carolina. The oldest child, Joseph Sidney, and the youngest, George Nicholas, remained in the home county;

---

1   Throughout this study I have drawn upon and quoted Jane Gray Buchanan's Thompson family history (*Thomas Thompson and Ann Finney of Colonial Pennsylvania and North Carolina* (Oak Ridge, TN, 1987). Besides presenting the intricate connection of several families, it does a very good job in locating and quoting from family letters and journals.

2   Dorothy Zollicoffer Oldham, history master's thesis, 1930. Oldham is William Faulkner's sister-in-law.

the other children settled in the Cession.[3]

Saving Jacob until later, we begin with Dr. James Young Thompson (1808-1867), who ended up settling in the far eastern part of Cession, not far from where the brothers met on the road. In 1837, he bought 170 acres two miles north of Cotton Gin Port in Monroe County. To that he added 750 acres to the west, across the Tombigbee River. His country house, now on the National Register, was in Monroe County, and his very productive plantation was across the river in Chickasaw County, a part of the Cession. Dr. Young Thompson, the most politically prominent scion after his distinguished younger brother Jacob, served in the Mississippi House of Representatives, 1842-44 and 1850-52, from Monroe County. Dr. Thompson died in Okolona. "Strikingly handsome, engaging, and witty," the very young man had a relationship with a woman, which his father paid his way out of and sent him off to the University of North Carolina. Popular there, James Young Thompson also made a distinguished record, received medical training, and emigrated immediately to Alabama, where he married in 1834. He was the father of six children, who had distinguished descendants.[4]

Four other of Jacob Thompson's siblings settled in the Cession, probably at his urging. Dr. John Thompson (1816-1876) was graduated from the University of North Carolina and the University of Pennsylvania in medicine. He came to Lafayette County and began a practice in 1842. He served in the Mexican War and married Laura Hunt, daughter of a wealthy planter in Panola County, the next county west. Ann Eliza Thompson (1812-1850) married Yancey Wiley of Caswell County. He became a wealthy planter in Lafayette County and built a two-story frame plantation house at "Cedar Hill Farm,"north of Oxford, purchased and renovated in the late 20th century by Jimmy Faulkner, William Faulkner's nephew. Sarah McAlister Thompson (1821-1899) married Abner Snowden Lewis, also a graduate of the University of North Carolina. They came to Mississippi and built a similar impressive house near the Wiley place. Their daughter Lydia married as her second husband the widower Dr. Alfred Alexander Young, father of writer Stark Young by his first marriage.[5]

Next to Jacob, the family member best known to the Yoknapatawpha chronicle creator was William Thompson (1818-1902). Like most of his brothers, he was educated at

---

3 Jeannine D. Whitlow (ed.), *The Heritage of Caswell County, North Carolina* (1985), 536,

4 National Register of Historic Places Form, July 13, 1990. Robert Lowry and William H. McCardle, *History of Mississippi* (Jackson, 1891), 542. Copy of partial manuscript of Joel Williamson, "William Faulkner and Southern History," pages 198-225, sent to Tom Hopson of Mobile, Alabama, November 14, 1997.

5 Goodspeed's *Biographical and Historical Memoirs of Mississippi* (Chicago: Goodspeed Publishing Co., 1891), II:902.

the University of North Carolina. He read law locally and in 1845 came south and settled in Pontotoc. The next year, he volunteered as a private in the Mexican War and fought in the Battle of Buena Vista. He returned to Mississippi and settled in Oxford.[6]

Now we come to the Jones family of Virginia and Georgia, into which two Thompson siblings married. The Joneses deserve their own essay, but this paragraph must do. Harrison Jones (1757-1841) and his wife Anne Ligon had seven sons, all of whom did exceedingly well. The youngest, Richard, settled in Alabama and had two children. The daughter, Ella Jones, one of the wealthiest women in the South, married the second time General Joseph Wheeler of the Confederate Army. They had six children, including a daughter Lucy Wheeler, who was the heir of her great uncle Dr. Weldon Jones, the largest planter in Marshall County, the county adjoining Lafayette on the north (See Bobby Mitchell's essay in this book). Another of the Jones sons, John Peyton Jones, was one of four men appointed commissioner to create Lafayette County in the Chickasaw Cession. A man of great wealth, he was the father-in-law of Jacob Thompson. This is not the only connection with the Thompsons. John Peyton Jones' brother, William S. Jones, lived in Panola County, where in 1860 he owned over a hundred slaves. William S. Jones was the father of Martha Jones, who married William Thompson, the lawyer of Oxford and brother of Jacob.[7]

The Jones plantations in Lafayette County were northeast of Oxford on the rich soil of Woodson's Ridge amid the Martin and Pegues operations, but the important Yoknapatawpha influence was the William Thompson house in town. In the early 20th century, it was occupied by the Thompson daughter, Maria Lucretia (Luly), and her husband, Dr. Josiah Chandler and their family. A year before William Faulkner's death in 1962, an Emory University English professor got a Lafayette County countryman to give his thoughts on Faulkner's fictional world. Oxford citizens, he wrote, could "easily identify" the source for Benjy Compson. The family, he notes, "were related to the family of Jacob Thompson, a name very close to Jason Compson." In his 1963 reminiscence *My Brother Bill*, John Faulkner adds that "one of our oldest families" had an afflicted son, kept in the yard behind an iron fence.[8]

So, many people would have known the Thompson/Compson connection early on. But it was not until 1984, when Jack Case Wilson, in *Faulkners, Fortunes, and Flames*

---

6   Joseph Karl Menn, "The Large Slaveholders of the Deep South, 1860," Ph.D. Dissertation (Ann Arbor, Michigan: Xerox University Microfilms, 1974), II: 1,049.

7   James Edmonds Saunders, *Early Settlers of Alabama* (New Orleans, 1899), 217-221.

8   Goodspeed's *Memoirs*, I:537-538. John B. Cullen, in collaboration with Floyd C. Watkins, *Old Times in the Faulkner Country* (Baton Rouge: Louisiana State University Press, 1961), 79-80. John Faulkner, *My Brother Bill: An Affectionate Recollection* (New York: Trident Press), 1963, 271-272.

made the explicit connection between Edwin Chandler and Benjy Compson, and went on to cite Edwin's death by fire in 1948 and the reference in *The Mansion* to Benjy's burning. Just the next year, in an interview with Albert I. Bezzerides, the Faulkner collector Louis Daniel Brodsky included this exchange:

AIB:...He [WF] showed me the fence where the idiot prowled.
LDB: He took you to see the Chandler house?
AIB: Yeah, and he told me about the idiot who lived there and how he had incorporated him into the story. That really was a story about himself, his cousin Sally, his brothers, his mother and father, and grandparents.

So the creative process was gradually revealed. And we see that this branch and Oxford's noted family had a crucial role in the shaping of *The Sound and the Fury*.[9]

Now we come to the notable and controversial Jacob Thompson (1810-1885). His career exhibits many twists and turns, many instances of controversy. We will not go into them here, but only note his possible influence on the creator of Yoknapatawpha.

We have already seen the first honor man in his graduating class at the University of North Carolina, now a trained lawyer, enter the Chickasaw Cession to see the government land office at Pontotoc. There he remained for a couple of years, establishing himself and making his name. In his travels over north Mississippi, a favorite stop was the Lafayette County plantation home of the wealthy John Peyton Jones. Dorothy Oldham's 1930 thesis describes the house as:

the most hospitable and delightful place in [that] part of the country. It was built of logs chinked with mud mixed with white clay. The building was an immense one-story affair surrounded on all sides by broad verandas. The chimneys and the giant fireplaces were constructed with native rock and like the logs, were held together with the mud-clay mixture.[10]

In this structure, typical of the "great house" in the early Cession, occurred an unusual and now mythical romance. The daughter of the place was Catherine Jones, called Kate, a fourteen-year-old girl "famed for her rare beauty all over the countryside." In 1838, when she was 16, Jacob married her. Less than a year later, their only child, a son, was born.[11]

---

9   (Nashville, Annandale Press, 1984), 68-69. Louis Daniel Brodsky, "Reflections on William Faulkner: An Interview with Albert I. Bezzerides," *Southern Review* (1985) 21: 393

10   Oldham, 35

11   Buchanan, 71.

Legend has it that Jacob sent her to a convent in Paris to complete her education and make her ready for Washington. This is probably a gilding of the lily, but somewhere she did receive more education. Jacob served in Congress from 1839 to 1851, and when he took her to Washington, she was widely known for both her beauty and her cultivation. Be that as it may, the important point is that William Faulkner grew up in the shadow of this great man who had a great love.[12]

"For a quarter of a century before the war," proclaims the 1930 DAR History of Lafayette County, "Jacob Thompson was the leading politician and statesman from North Mississippi." After his marriage, he settled in Oxford and built a grand house near Faulkner's Rowan Oak. He followed twelve years in the U. S. House of Representatives with a position in the cabinet of President James Buchanan. He resigned after Lincoln's election, but controversy followed about his financial dealings in Native American issues during his tenure as secretary of the interior.[13]

When he left Washington, he went home to Oxford to his imposing twenty-room frame house, set on a high brick foundation, with "halls, verandahs, and galleries." He joined the Confederate Army for a time, represented Lafayette County in the Confederate Congress of 1863, then was sent to Canada on a secret mission. When Union Gen. A. J. Smith burned Oxford in August of 1864, his first targets were the courthouse and the Thompson residence. When the war ended, the Thompsons were still in Canada. With a price on his head, he settled with his wife in England. After several years, they returned, rebuilt the Oxford house as a cottage for his son and his family, and moved to Memphis. Contrary to the economic straits experienced by most Southerners, Jacob Thompson was still a wealthy man. He must have invested all of his money abroad, including the supposed ill-gotten gain. He continued to cut quite a figure in Memphis, and at his death in 1883 left $10,000 to the University of the South.[14]

Now we come to another possible, though whispered and gossiped, link to the creator of Yoknapatawpha. Faulkner's maternal grandfather was Charlie Butler (b. 1848), the youngest son of Lafayette County's first sheriff. He was made city marshal in 1876 and served in that office until he absconded from Oxford and his position in the last months

---

12   Buchanan, 71.

13   The copy of the DAR history reads on its cover page " Presented to the Library of the Public Schools of Oxford, Mississippi by the David Reese Chapter, N. S. D. A. R, May 30th 1930." It is actually a collection of essays (most of them signed) on historic topics. I have drawn from two essays —"The Jacob Thompson-Elliott House," followed by the initials M. R. S., and the essay "Jacob Thompson" by Mrs. A. J. Bondurant. *Goodspeed's Memoirs*, II: 899-901.

14   Mrs. A. J. Bondurant, "Jacob Thompson," DAR History of Lafayette County (1930). Arthur Ben Chitty and Elizabeth N. Chitty, *Sewanee Sampler* (1975), 140-141.

of 1887. Anne Percy's *The Early History of Oxford, Mississippi* traces his last years in north Mississippi, through his killing of the drunken editor of the Oxford newspaper. William Faulkner's wife, Estelle Oldham Faulkner, told Joseph Blotner in a 1966 interview that Charlie Butler left with the "beautiful octoroon companion of Mrs. Jacob Thompson." The distinguished Faulkner scholar Joel Williamson of the University of North Carolina was obviously driven wild by this revelation. In his 1993 study *William Faulkner and Southern History*, in the early pages (64-71) he had already presented and traced Col. William C. Faulkner's "shadow family" by the slave Emeline. Now here was more racial mixing on the maternal line. But though Williamson tried valiantly both in a published work and in an unpublished draft to prove the charge, he could not. It was hard for him to admit that Southerners are inclined to gild the lily. Yes, Charles Butler absconded, and, yes, he was married to a difficult woman. That makes it likely that he found another partner. But there is no proof that Mrs. Thompson had a companion, much less a "beautiful octoroon." Still, William Faulkner no doubt heard that bit of scandal. Southerners loved to bring any romantic public figure into their gossip, and in addition, such a story offered great erotic appeal. Perhaps the mixing of race in illicit sexual encounters in his own family, real and rumored, did indeed help lead to his complex exploration of race in the Yoknapatawpha works.[15]

Thus did the Thompsons figure prominently in many aspects of the early history of North Mississippi and also in the creative mind of William Faulkner, the great American writer of the next century.

---

15   Anne Percy, *The Early History of Oxford, Mississippi* (Oxford, 2008), 189-208, 227. Blotner, *Faulkner, A Biography*, I:57, note page 31. Joel Williamson, *William Faulkner and Southern History* (New York; Oxford University Press, 1993), 128-132. On November 14, 1997, Joel Williamson mailed a copy of his original manuscript pages 198-225 to Tom Hopson of Mobile, Alabama. Hopson sent a copy of this material to his distant cousin, William Lewis, Jr., of Oxford, who provided this copy for my use. Quotation is from p. 208.

Sherwood Bonner (1849-1883), regionalist and feminist, was
an early part of North Mississippi's literary legacy.
Southern Tapestry by Hubert McAlexander

Faulkner, Young, Williams, and Bonner

Hubert H. McAlexander

"These blue hills," William Faulkner called his landscape. Those hills produced four major writers before the mid-20th century: Faulkner, Stark Young, Tennessee Williams, and Sherwood Bonner. Williams, though born farther south in our state, spent some of his childhood in a Delta county of our region, Coahoma County. After 1950, other writers from the region appeared, but here we treat just these four.[1]

Of the four, Faulkner is alone in treating the landscape. Williams and Young are primarily dramatists, and Bonner was trying to be a local colorist, conveying dialect and other regional oddities. But all are shaped by this Chickasaw Cession region, its peculiar social order, and its heat and sensuousness.

William Faulkner is a great genius, a great writer. The others must take a back seat to him. Within the first ten pages of *Flags in the Dust*, the first novel to be set in Yoknapatawpha, his fictional north Mississippi county, he has this landscape description:

> This was upland country, lying in tilted slopes against the unbroken blue of the hills. But soon the road dropped sheerly into a valley of good broad fields richly somnolent in the leveling afternoon. This was Bayard Sartoris' land, and as they went on from time to time a negro lifted his hand from the plow handle in salute to the passing carriage. Then the road approached the railroad and crossed it, and a partridge and her brood of tiny dusty balls scuttered in the dust before them; and at last the house John Sartoris had built and rebuilt stood among the locusts and oaks where mockingbirds were wont to sing.[2]

Faulkner may not have capitalized "negro," as one should the name of a race, but the first mention of a person of color in the house is the word "mulatto." This is truly significant. Despite the reference to mockingbirds, this begins a picture of a different fictional South, not the usual romantic one. Because of Faulkner's immediately introducing a mulatto character, we know that he had begun the brooding about race that is a part of his genius and of a full representation of the region. In his great works William Faulkner engages the complexity of the issue.

Many connections exist between Faulkner and Stark Young. As a teenager, Young (1881-1963) moved to Oxford, Miss., the town that Faulkner (1897-1962) was to make

---

1 The phrase is taken from "Mississippi Hills: My Epitaph," quoted in Joseph Blotner, *Faulkner: A Biography* (New York: Random House, 1974). I:373-374.

2 William Faulkner, *Flags in the Dust* (New York: Random House, 1973), 11

famous. The most important link is Faulkner's first literary friend, Oxonian Phil Stone. First, Stone arranged that Stark Young and the adolescent poet meet. Later, a young Faulkner stayed in Young's New York apartment when working at Lord and Taylor's bookstore, where a fellow worker was Elizabeth Prall, later Mrs. Sherwood Anderson. What follows is a part of American literary history.[3]

Stark Young used Faulkner as a model for the young poet in his 1927 novel *The Torches Flare*. Therefore, before a great novelist made his mark, another north Mississippi writer drew upon him to create a character. Young, however, was quite a different literary figure. He was primarily a dramatist and a literary philosopher. From 1926 to 1934, he wrote four novels using his family, the McGehees, and a Mississippi setting, and he contributed to the Agrarian manifesto *I'll Take My Stand*, but his most revealing work is his last, *The Pavilion* (1951).[4]

His first and last novels, *Heaven Trees* and *So Red the Rose*, are portraits of plantation life in pre-Civil War and wartime Mississippi. The last, appealing to America's then-current appetite for historical fiction and interest in the war between North and South, became a bestseller and was made into a motion picture. Two years later (1936) came the more vital *Gone With the Wind*, and Young's effort was forgotten. His relatively muted and rather lifeless books do provide portraits of the ruling class in the Agrarian South, but aside from this passage in *The Pavilion*, his work lacks interest:

> Byron had something in him that was like nature itself…something immense, with its own urgency; something lucid and violent, and uncontrollable save through its own conflicting forces.… Against this force in him, Byron was forever hurling himself, and so kept his whole being hungry, dissatisfied, restless, and disdainful. It exposed him to himself, gave him a shameless secret candor, and left him an egotism with power but without a genuine consoling vanity. It made him in the common moments of life often impossible to admire. In times of great danger, great causes, of painting himself on great canvases…it gave him a superb and fatal heroism. It carried him along and left him solitary, weak and universal. (122)

Young could never find a way to dramatize such human chaos. He will be remembered as a defender of the old order, a skilled, sophisticated dramatic critic, and a sensitive translator.

The next writer, Tennessee Williams (1911-1983), was born in the Episcopal rec-

---

3   John Pilkington, "Stark Young," in James B. Lloyd, ed. *Lives of Mississippi Writers* (Jackson: University Press of Mississippi, 1980), 484-488. Blotner, 314-316.

4   Hubert McAlexander, Jr. "William Faulkner —The Young Poet In Stark Young's *The Torches Flare*," *American Literature* 43 (January 1972): 647-649. See the excerpt from *Thirty Years a Slave* in this volume to get another view of the McGehees as slave owners.

tory in Columbus, just south of the Cession, and spent part of his youth in the rectory in Clarksdale, Coahoma County, in the Delta part of north Mississippi. Like Faulkner, Williams bears the marks of his birthplace, but that is just one influence at the service of a great talent. His play *Cat on a Hot Tin Roof* is set in our region. In a "plantation home in the Mississippi Delta," the stage directions tell us immediately. In Brick, we watch what Young described in Byron — with touches of our region. Other plays, like the works of Faulkner, come out of some of the fury.[5]

The final writer, Katharine Sherwood Bonner McDowell, who signed her fiction Sherwood Bonner, is the earliest (1849-1883), and the most derivative in a sense, trying to please editors and make a name for herself. In 1873, she ran away to Boston from her home in Holly Springs, leaving her husband and infant daughter. Her life, therefore, became a feminist narrative. She attached herself to Longfellow, the most venerated American writer of his day, and secured a position as his secretary while he put together his *Poems of Places*. First writing newspaper articles, she began to write dialect tales, for which the public had a strong appetite developed by the literary magazines. In these she introduced her slave Gran'mammy as the main character. The tales were collected immediately before and after her death in *Dialect Tales* (1883) and *Suwanee River Tales* (1884). She also wrote other fiction, some a bit romantic, and a novel of sectional reconciliation, *Like unto Like* (1878). In many works, she quite naturally expressed a decided strain of feminism.[6]

5   Tennessee Williams, *Cat on a Hot Tin Roof*, Signet Ed. (New York; New American Library of World Literature, Inc., 1955), xiii.

6   See Hubert Horton McAlexander, *The Prodigal Daughter: A Biography of Sherwood Bonner* (Baton Rouge: Louisiana State University Press, 1980). The book was brought out in a new edition with an introduction that corrects some errors and comments on subsequent criticism (Knoxville: University of Tennessee Press, 1999).

Bishop Elias Cottrell (1853-1937), born in slavery and rising to the position of bishop, is a great figure of twentieth century North Mississippi. An aristocratic white woman used to talk about how "stately" he looked as he rode in his chauffer-driven limousine.

BISHOP ELIAS COTTRELL OF THE CME CHURCH

WILSON GOLDEN

Elias Cottrell was born into slavery on January 31, 1853, on a plantation near the thriving community of Hudsonville in the heyday of Marshall County — Mississippi's "Empire County." From birth, his eventful life was a studied contrast in black, white and tan. Young Elias was among the 17,439 slaves enumerated in the 1860 Marshall County federal census. We know from surviving photographs that he was light complexioned; contemporary accounts recall his blue eyes. Available sources support the fact that his mother was an African American named Ann Mull, although how and when she became enslaved is not known. Elias, age 4, and Ann, age 36, appear in the 1858 slave inventory of the estate of Thomas Mull, who died in Memphis in November 1857. By 1870, then again in 1880, Ann (or "Annie") appears in the Marshall County census as the wife of the black Daniel Cottrell. Rather than by the surname of his previous owner, Thomas Mull, the emancipated Elias appears in the 1870 Census as Elias Cottrell, having assumed the name of his father, Daniel Cottrell, a former slave of Benjamin Cottrell of Sylvestria plantation. While one memoirist identified Elias as the stepson of Daniel, who exactly fathered Elias may never be known.[1]

Still dominating American politics at Cottrell's birth in 1853 was the nation's "original sin" of slavery as the United States observed the 77th anniversary of its independence. Only three years earlier, leaders in the U. S. Congress had forged yet another Union-saving compromise over the expansion of slavery into new states and territories. The "peculiar institution" into which Cottrell was born so severely strained the American Union that by late 1860 Abraham Lincoln's election as president triggered America's tumble into its bloodiest conflict. By the conclusion of the Civil War's awful slaughter, an estimated 750,000 — fully 2.4 percent of the nation's 1860 population — would die and the legal enslavement of four million Americans rendered unconstitutional by the adoption of the

---

1   Federal Censuses, Ancestry.com and Find-A-Grave.com, Memorial # 37672742. In 1860, Marshall County ranked fourth in number of slaves among Mississippi counties, 20th in the entire nation. Slave names did not appear in the 1860 census since it was essentially a slave schedule showing only the owner's name and slave headcount in compliance with federal constitutional apportionment requirements. In the 1870 federal census, the first since the end of the Civil War and emancipation, Elias was listed as a 17-year-old mulatto living in Range 2 of Marshall County, one among eight children of Daniel (1815-1894) and Ann (born 1825) Cottrell; in addition to Elias, four other Cottrell children were listed as "mulatto," the other siblings as "black." Elias was the second oldest child and he and older brother Madison, age 22, were listed as mulatto. The six younger siblings ranged from ages 2-12, including two females. A white Cottrell family genealogy in the collection of Hubert H. McAlexander shows a family memoirist referring to "Uncle Dan, Bishop Cottrell's step-father."

13th Amendment. Mississippi journalist Hodding Carter Jr., writing nearly a century later, called the cataclysmic war "the nation's supreme tragedy, its character as Grecian as the columns" of Mississippi's antebellum mansions.[2]

The future bishop's era was a time of full immersion in the unfolding drama of the great American experiment in freedom and democracy, spanning the Civil War, a World War and the Great Depression, through 19 American presidencies, from Millard Fillmore to Franklin D. Roosevelt. His remarkable life of nearly 85 years began at the apogee of slavery and witnessed its abolition — then Reconstruction, the South's subsequent "redemption" and Jim Crow, the Great Migration of the early 1900s — 30s, and the earliest stirrings of what came to be known as the 1950-60s Civil Rights Movement. As a person of mixed race, from his birth, matters of race loomed large in Elias Cottrell's world. While he would later be heralded as a visionary and post-emancipation transitional race-accommodationist, his modest origins in rural Marshall County hardly foretold his future greatness. He later wrote of his "vivid recollections of conditions and feelings between the races in the days of slavery," yet in his later ministry and public life he "realized...that (his) mission was to the whole people."[3] Cottrell's adult attitudes were doubtless shaped by his pre-ministry life experiences and influences, beginning years before his birth when planter Benjamin Cottrell and a brother, Zadock Daniel Cottrell, acted on their strong belief in education by establishing both male and female academies in the early days of the community.[4] Later in life, the Bishop wrote warmly of Benjamin Cottrell, calling him "kind and conservative in his way of dealing with [the slaves], requiring them to keep the Sabbath, attend church service."[5]

Moreover, as often happens, Cottrell's rise from bondage to bishop was bolstered by timely mentorships. Tradition holds that a neighboring white farmer, Richard Hill Parham, and his former slave Berry Hill played this role for the precocious young Elias. Parham had relocated from Richmond, Va., to Marshall County in 1843, bringing along Hill and numerous other slaves. After the Civil War, the newly-emancipated Hill settled near his former owner and became a successful planter himself. Early on, both Parham and Hill

---

2   Hodding Carter, Jr., *A Vanishing America: The Life and Times of the Small Town*, ed. Thomas C. Wheeler (New York: Holt, Rinehart and Winston, 1964): 63.

3   Bishop Elias Cottrell, *An Appeal to the Citizens of Holly Springs, Marshall County, Mississippi, and to the White People in Particular* (hereafter "*Appeal*") (self-published brochure, ca. 1923, in the McAlexander/Marshall County Collection, Archives and Special Collections, J. D. Williams Library, The University of Mississippi): 1-2.

4   Hubert H. McAlexander, *Chalmers Institute 1837-1879* (privately published, 2015): 53-54.

5   Rev. R. Milton Winter, ed., *Amid Some Excellent Company* (Holly Springs, Miss: Spring Hollow Publishers, 2003): 257.

were impressed with the industrious Cottrell's ambition to enter the Methodist ministry. One biographer relates that Parham provided him with a house and land to farm, Hill with a horse for plowing. "After the day's work was done, the young Negro would build a fire of pine knots and, by their light, he studied." Parham also made books available to young Elias that had belonged to Parham's late brother, University of Mississippi-educated Rev. William Parham. With persistent devotion of his few spare hours to self-education, Cottrell eventually gained admission to Central Tennessee College in Nashville, where he was once again the beneficiary of a mentor—this time a Jewish rabbi who instructed him in Hebrew and Greek, important elements of a classic seminary education.[6]

After graduation from Central Tennessee in 1873, Cottrell was "converted" to Methodism at age 21 and licensed to preach in November 1875. Two months later, he was admitted on trial to the Olive Branch circuit in the North Mississippi Annual Conference of the Colored Methodist Episcopal Church in America (CME)[7] and ordained in Holly Springs in 1877 prior to becoming a deacon at Sardis. In 1878, he was ordained by CME's first bishop, William Henry Miles, as an elder at Verona in the Olive Branch circuit.[8] Cottrell's distinctive speaking style was significantly enhanced by his early mentor R. H. Parham, who at the beginning of Cottrell's ministry, had worked with him developing sermons that he subsequently delivered throughout his church circuit.[9] In 1878, it was noted that Cottrell "delivered what was considered the best sermon of the General Conference,"[10] and he soon moved from the North Mississippi to the Tennessee Conference, assuming the prestigious pulpit at Capers Chapel in Nashville. This call was followed in short order by assignments to Collins Chapel, Memphis; Mother Liberty Church, Jackson, Tenn.; and First Church, Nashville. Cottrell again moved from Nashville to the North Mississippi Conference, serving churches at Lamar, Byhalia, and Verona, then back to the West Tennessee Conference at Liberty Street Station in Jackson.

Cottrell began his family on January 1, 1880, when he married his college sweetheart, Catherine ("Kate") Davis of Nashville, the daughter of white, English-descended parents. There followed in 1881 the birth of a daughter, Mary Frances; by 1900, Elias and Kate,

---

6   Olga Reed Pruitt, *It Happened Here: True Stories of Holly Springs* (Holly Springs, Miss.: South Reporter Printing Company, 1950): 25-26.

7   "Colored" was changed to "Christian" in 1954.

8   Isaac Lane, *Autobiography of Bishop Isaac Lane, LL.D.: With a Short History of the C.M.E. Church in America and of Methodism* (Nashville, Tenn.: Publishing House of the M.E. Church, South, 1916): 163-64.

9   Pruit, *It Happened Here*, 26.

10   Lane Autobio, 163.

daughter Mary Frances, and an adopted daughter, Beulah (age 2), were living in Holly Springs. Throughout those early years of his ministry, Cottrell supported his family by farming when not preaching; then, in 1882, his fortunes turned when he was selected by the church's General Conference meeting in Washington, D.C., as its first book agent and editor of the CME Christian Index. His career steadily advanced with his 1890 election as the CME commissioner of education and finally, in 1894, to election and consecration as the CME's 7th bishop at the General Conference meeting in Memphis.[11] His tenure as principal CME bishop continued for 43 years, until his death in 1937, the longest period of service of a CME bishop up until that time.[12]

Elias Cottrell was the beneficiary of over 250 years of persistent—if uneven—efforts to nourish the spiritual needs of America's enslaved population dating to the introduction in 1619 of the slave trade at Jamestown, Va. Despite the inevitable "tensions and contradiction between the egalitarian potential of evangelical Christianity and the realities of slavery,"[13] the post-emancipation religious instruction of Southern blacks was provided in varying degrees by the principal white Protestant Christian denominations. The CME and other religious and educational efforts were undertaken by the Methodist Episcopal Church, the African Methodist Church, and the African Methodist Church, Zion.[14] Then, in 1866, the general conference of the Methodist Episcopal Church, South, organized its black members into separate congregations and conferences, from which the CME Church was established four years later by a group of black ministers and white sponsors. The CME Church thereupon set about to ordain its own bishops and ministers independent of the predominantly white parent group.[15] In Marshall County, the history of racial division reflected the prevailing attitudes among mainline Protestant denominations as part of the determined outreach to the newly-freed black population extended by white preachers of the North Mississippi Conference of the Methodist Church. An 1879 report posited that the colored population, "many...slaves of ignorance and superstition," was

---

11   Lane Autobio, 164. Following Catherine's death, in 1917 Cottrell married the much younger Alice Ellis of New Orleans. Over the next eight years they became the parents of Elias P., Jr. (1919-2005), Anna Edelweiss Evans (1921-1993), John William (1923-1999) and Florence Ethel (1925-1941).

12   Winter, *Amid Some Excellent Company*: 257, n. 2.

13   *Documenting the American South: The Church in the Southern Black Community* (Chapel Hill: The University of North Carolina, 2004) URL: http://docsouth.unc.edu/church/index.html.

14   Gene Ramsey Miller, *A History of North Mississippi Methodism 1820-1900* (The Parthenon Press, Nashville, 1966): 89.

15   C. H. Phillips, *The History of the Colored Methodist Episcopal Church in America* (Jackson, TN: Publishing House C.M.E. Church, 1925).

"in great need of the Gospel preached by those qualified to instruct them…" noting that "the prejudice which has long existed among them against our preachers is giving way."[16]

This perceived resistance was not reflected in the Bishop Cottrell's comments on his experience growing up in the Sylvestria church while he was still enslaved:

> I came along when master and slave worshipped in the same church and at the same hour preached to and ministered unto by white preachers. We rejoiced and praised God under the influence of the same ministers….born a slave, reared and owned by a Christian master, who took me in the white church at the age of five years, [I was] brought up, with my ancestors, under white religious influence. These colored people, in the days of slavery, were converted through the preaching and prayers of Southern white ministers, who took them by the hand and led them to the alter, wept and shed tears over them, imploring the lessons of God, and persuading these illiterate slaves to accept Christ as their personal Savior.[17]

Bishop Cottrell's ministry consistently focused on themes of positive, respectful, amicable cooperation. Earnestly pleading for harmony and Christian forbearance, he gently but persistently excoriated those bent on self-glorification.[18] Well into his ministry, at age 70, Cottrell concluded a particularly poignant appeal for racial understanding and forbearance regarding the proposed location of a new CME church in the Mississippi Industrial College area of Holly Springs: "I close with a prayer and a good wish for harmony and peace among the white and colored people of Holly Springs, Marshall County, Mississippi."[19] Similarly, nearly a decade later toward the end of his long life, Cottrell again addressed his experience in the Sylvestria Methodist Church of his childhood, following its total destruction by fire in the early days of the Great Depression, saying he felt:

> very sympathetically touched, remembering the early days of the intimate contact of the two races… for more than four score years…white and colored worshipped together in this church, both races ministered to by consecrated ministers of the Southern M. E. Church. These ministers…constituted the highest type of Christian brotherhood…[and] an unselfish service. Racial lines were not as

---

16   Miller, *North Mississippi Methodism*, 89. In general, the theology and polity of the CME Church fell well within the broader context of John and Charles Wesley's Methodism and mainline Protestant Christianity. The Methodist Episcopal Church, South, had been formed in 1844 following a split over the issue of slavery, not to be reunited until nearly 100 years later, eventually merging with the Evangelical United Brethren Church in 1968 to form the modern United Methodist Church.

17   *Appeal*, 9-10. The old log Sylvestria Church, constructed on land donated by Benjamin Cottrell, was regarded as "one of the landmarks of the Old South." Amid, 259.

18   "Bishop Elias Cottrell Pleads for Harmony," *Baltimore Afro-American Ledger*, December 17, 1910.

19   *Appeal*, 12.

rigidly drawn in the Methodist Church as today [1931]. Uppermost in the mind of the Christian ministry was the conversion of souls; with them it was not white, nor black souls. They prayed and wept over those dark skinned people as they did over their own race....I am sure the hearts of many of the colored people, namely those of the old settlers and their immediate offspring, feel deeply touched in the loss of old Sylvestria Church. Of course the majority of these old colored people had long since died.[20]

While ever "frank in speaking to both races" from lectern and pulpit, Cottrell meticulously avoided "stirring up...racial animus or antipathy," knowing such "would tend only to foment strife and intensify race prejudice...." It was his firm intention to "stay in the middle of the road—think, do, and live right" so as to avoid the "displeasure and scorn of the community." Speaking of his regard for the white citizens of Holly Springs and particularly the young white men, Cottrell observed "they are all aristocratic Southerners;.. blue-blooded Anglo-Saxons...[who] owned slaves,...most of them...no cruel barbarians, but [who] took good care of their slaves, loved and protected them,...the Anglo-Saxon usually bequeaths his wisdom and virtues to his offsprings."[21]

The 1905 founding of Mississippi Industrial College (MI), "the love of his heart,"[22] was without doubt the crowning achievement of Elias Cottrell's life as a minister and educator. The roots of MI date to a series of earlier developments, beginning with the 1866 founding of Shaw College by the Methodist Episcopal Church as an institution for black liberal arts education in Holly Springs. The Shaw charter authorized the establishment of a "normal" curriculum, and in December 1869, Mississippi's Reconstruction constitution for the first time mandated the establishment of a statewide system of free public schools. Almost immediately, the college offered and a sympathetic state government accepted the transfer of Shaw's department to serve as a state normal school. On November 15, 1870, students were admitted to the new State Normal School for Training Negro Teachers under the tutelage of principal/professor Gorman, graduating an impressive class of 26 at the end of the first year. To expedite the training of a cadre of teachers to staff the state's new common school system, each member of the state legislature was authorized to nominate one student whose declaration of intent to teach in the state's public schools for a minimum of three years earned a weekly allowance of 50 cents. In April 1873, the legislature responded to the new school's plea for more space by appropriating $10,000 for the pur-

---

20   Winter, *Amid Some Excellent Company*, 257-8, an account written by Bishop Cottrell as part of a column by local historian John M. Mickle published in the *Holly Springs South Reporter*, February 19, 1931.

21   *Appeal*, 3, 6.

22   Jessie J. Edwards (M.I. College Class of 1975 and president of the school's alumni association) commentary posted on Ancestry.com.

chase of the Turner Lane residence, located opposite the Marshall County fair grounds on West Street, but then in 1875, incongruously voted to terminate the student allowance. Five years later, a student-initiated fee of five cents per month was implemented to fund a reference library. The library eventually acquired over 3,000 volumes, largely through donations from local citizens.[23]

Over a decade after the 1890 closure of the Tougaloo State Normal School in Jackson, the state's outspoken racist governor, James K. Vardaman, in 1904 vetoed funding for the Holly Springs normal school, forcing its closure and leaving Alcorn State College as the only state-funded normal school for blacks.[24] In his successful 1903 campaign for governor, Vardaman, who had built a journalistic and political career as an avowed advocate of state-sponsored racism, focused on race as his central issue, favoring public schools for white citizens only. Vardaman asserted his belief in white supremacy, repeatedly advocating the closure of all black public schools and opposing public education for blacks "beyond the most basic moral instruction and vocational training because…blacks should remain in economic servitude and…education was unnecessary for the kind of work they would do."[25] He argued that since few blacks owned property and property taxes were paid almost exclusively by whites, funding allocations should be based strictly on property taxes paid. "When I speak of educating the people, I mean white people….the Negro is necessary in the economy of the world but...was designed for a burden bearer." This belief was reiterated in his January 1904 inaugural address and, true to his campaign pledge, the "Great White Chief" vetoed the first black education appropriation that came to his desk.[26]

In this environment, Elias Cottrell and the CME Church decided to establish Mississippi Industrial and Theological College "for the Negro youth of our state and all the states."[27] According to the school's successful 1979 National Register of Historic Plac-

---

23   *It Happened Here*, 92-93.

24   Edward Mayes , *History of Education in Mississippi. U. S. Bureau of Education Circular of Information No. 2, 1889* (Washington, DC: Government Printing Office, 1899). Alcorn was designated Alcorn State University in the early 1970s.

25   David G. Sansing, Ph. D., mshistory.K12.ms.us (2004) and sources cited therein. Isabel Wilkerson, in her seminal 2010 work on the Great Migration, said Vardaman frequently voiced support of lynching as a means of maintaining white supremacy, having once sardonically observed that the only effect of black education was "to spoil a good field hand and make an insolent cook." *The Warmth of Other Suns* (New York: Random House, 2010): 40.

26   Nannie Pitts McLemore, *The Progressive Era in A History of Mississippi*, ed. Richard Aubrey McLemore (Hattiesburg: University & College Press of Mississippi, 1973): 2: 34, 37. Vardaman's somewhat more forward-looking successor, Edmund F. Noel, argued in his losing 1903 campaign against Vardaman that "it was unconstitutional to discriminate against the Negro in the field of education." McLemore, 35.

27   David H. Jackson, Jr., *Booker T. Washington and the Struggle Against White Supremacy* (New York:

es nomination, "[t]he educational mission of the school was grounded in theological, vocational-technical, and musical training for black youth from preschool through college age." Established despite what Cottrell noted was "strong opposition to my efforts to found a school…under the shadow of an institution [Shaw] that had been on the ground" since 1866, M.I. College's mission, quite distinct from its sister Methodist institution just across Memphis Street in north Holly Springs, was to make practical and useful knowledge accessible to second — and even third — generation descendants of the sons and daughters of former slaves whose parents and most certainly grandparents were without formal education, many of whose illiteracy dated to slave code prohibitions. In the most basic terms, MI's mission was to lift post-emancipation generations from their almost universally-marginal existence as sharecroppers in rural cotton fields to some modest level of enjoyment as free people. Even if only to a limited extent in rural areas and small towns like Marshall County and Holly Springs, the movement away from an agrarian economy, overwhelmingly dominant since the country's original settlement by European explorers, was exploding all across America and the western world. Education, Cottrell believed, offered the breakout opportunity for his people to have a fairer shot at what would later be called the American Dream, led by "intelligent Negro preacher[s], with a better educated constituency, removed fifty years from a state of ignorance and superstition."[28]

Around the time of the founding of M.I. College, an understandably sensitive moment for Cottrell, he penned a letter to the editor of the local newspaper under the heading "A Correction by Bishop E. Cottrell" that addressed the apparently widespread rumor of racially-based "labor troubles." Writing with characteristic finesse, he vehemently denied that he had urged the town's "colored women not to cook, wash, and nurse, nor do any work unless the white people pay them better wages," speaking with the "courage of my convictions…to do right, and to fear nobody, nor condition of things.…" Cottrell then asserted his belief that "(s)mall wages are better than idleness,..the bane of society, whether white or black…," concluding with the proclamation that he "was born a slave and have earned every dollar I am worth by thrift, industry and economy." His rather amazing public testament was prefaced by an editorial comment that spoke tellingly of the tenor of the times: "Any reasonable person would consider that the bishop has too much at stake to antagonize…the dominant race, even if he has it in his heart to do, which we give him credit of not having."[29]

In addition to a cautious approach to the white community, Cottrell demonstrated

---

Palgrave Macmillan, 2008): 65; Mississippi Industrial College Catalog, 1907-08.

28   *Appeal*, 6, 7, 11.

29   Holly Springs *South*, November 5, 1903.

a deep personal commitment to fulfilling his dream, raising over $75,000 primarily from the state's black population and mortgaging his own home on one occasion for $5,000 and another for $3,000, significant amounts in his day. Acting in his capacity as head bishop under the aegis of the Mississippi Conference of CME, which he modestly described as "a little handful of a contingent coming out of the Southern Methodist Episcopal Church," Cottrell boldly launched his vision to provide 20th-century African Americans with liberal arts and industrial training, fostering an educated black citizenry empowered "to improve their homes and purchase land,…pay their taxes," living "in peace and harmony with the opposite race."[30]

Fittingly, Cottrell chose as the new school's site not only his hometown of Holly Springs, but a hillside literally across the street from the well-established and prestigious Rust College/University, which by then had been in operation for nearly 40 years.[31] He took understandable pride in the emerging campus, which eventually consisted of what he described as "four magnificent brick buildings whose architectural beauty and finish would not disgrace the campus of Harvard or Yale."[32] The new 120 acre campus, situated on land purchased from James W. Fant for $35,000, was first adorned by an impressive dormitory built in 1905, named in honor of Cottrell's wife, Catherine, incorporating part of the antebellum Mills-Potts-Fant mansion.[33] Classes began in January 1906 with kindergarten through high school level instruction and a trade school that taught such practical skills as farming, carpentry, and electronics. By the following May, enrollment had grown to more than 200 students, and to 450 by 1908.[34]

The distinctive styles of the early MI buildings, still evident in structures surviving in the 21st century, showcase turn-of-the-twentieth-century American architecture. Graceful Catherine Hall reflected strong Jacobean and Colonial Revival architectural details, as did Hammond Hall, built in 1907 as a second dormitory. Jacobean Revival architecture featured a distinctive "curvilinear parapet and single story portico," as contrasted with the 1910 Washington Hall, the school's principal classroom and administration building

---

30   *Appeal,* 7, 8.

31   Miller, *North Mississippi Methodism,* 89. Shaw College was originally named in honor of Rev. S. O. Shaw, a $10,000 donor to the construction of the first building. In 1882 the school was renamed in honor of Dr. Richard S. Rust, secretary of the Freedman's Aid and Southern Educational Society.

32   *Appeal,* 8.

33   Hubert H. McAlexander, *A Southern Tapestry* (Virginia Beach, Va: The Donning Company, 2000): 108. Town historian John M. Mickle attributed the original 120-acre site to the residence of Peter Walker Lucas (1796-1870). Amid, 155.

34   www.hillcountryhistory.org.

named in honor of Booker T. Washington, with a façade "accentuated by two projecting gable-roof pavilions…[and] a portico…situated between the pavilions with Doric columns and an entablature with balustrade." Carnegie Auditorium, built in 1923 with funds donated by the Andrew Carnegie Foundation, was a two-and-a-half-story brick structure on a raised basement plan with a centered fanlight. It remains today as one of the best examples of Colonial Revival architecture anywhere in Holly Springs.[35]

A highlight of the college's early years came when Booker T. Washington visited Holly Springs in October 1908. The town became the scene of a minor spectacle, a momentous occasion for Bishop Cottrell, Mississippi Industrial College, and indeed the entire State of Mississippi. During what the noted black educator and orator from Alabama's Tuskegee Institute described as "a cheerful journey through Mississippi," one news account reported that Washington was greeted by some 58,000 during his tour of the state, including an event in Jackson attended by several statewide officeholders, most significantly, Governor Edmond Noel, recent successor to the state's arch-racist Governor Vardaman. Speaking over seven days to packed crowds in arenas as diverse as an opera house combined with a roller skating rink, Washington's enthusiastic turnout attested to the appeal of his enormous biracial prestige, famously demonstrated in 1901 when he was a White House dinner guest of Theodore Roosevelt in the early weeks of his presidency.[36]

Coming down from Memphis by private Pullman tourist car to avoid Jim Crow segregation taboos, Holly Springs was the first stop of the seven-city statewide tour. After visits to the town's Baptist Normal College and Rust University, Dr. Washington and his party of 30 national and state dignitaries inspected the Mississippi Theological and Industrial College, as MI was still then known, followed by a reception and "elegant repast" across town at Cottrell's impressive home, located in the southwestern area of Holly Springs at the intersection of Boundary and Chulahoma Streets. The Cottrell residence, with its towers and turrets, was ebulliently described by a national publication as "one of the most beautiful homes owned by Negroes in any part of the country."[37]

An address at Rust College later that day was attended by a biracial audience estimated at 1800 of the region's citizens. Typically, on Washington's southern educational tours

---

35   M. I. College was one of the most important black colleges in Mississippi for many decades, until the end of segregation resulted in steadily declining student populations that led to its closure in 1982 following the cutoff of federal funding. During the 1990s, the Holly Springs Police Department and other businesses occupied some of the newer buildings, but all eventually abandoned the property. Rust College bought the buildings in 2008. See lostcolleges.com for a brief history.

36   Booker T. Washington, *The Booker T. Washington Papers*, ed. Louis R. Harlan and Raymond W. Sucock (Urbana: University of Illinois Press, 1981): 60-68.

37   Jackson, *Struggle*, 64-67; *The New York Age*, October 22, 1908 (digitalcollections.nypl.org).

during 1908-1912, his addresses touched on "the rapid progress of the Negro race in education, in acquiring land, in building up business, and in becoming financially independent and thrifty." In Holly Springs, Washington specifically "inquired of both white and colored people why it was the two races were able to live on such friendly terms." People of both races, he later reported, "gave almost the same answer…it was due to the fact that in Marshall County so large a number of colored farmers owned their own farms."[38] The value of self-sufficiency and entrepreneurship were dominant themes of Washington's message throughout his career, a mantra often reflected in Cottrell's own CME ministry and work as an educator. A subject of much dispute then, and continuing to the modern day, was whether rhetoric espousing the virtue and dignity of labor was primarily a pragmatic accommodation to the realities of the white-dominated post-Reconstruction Jim Crow South, or a genuinely felt—if overly optimistic—aspiration nurtured by idealistic and respected black leaders like Washington and Cottrell.

After 60 eventful years as an ordained CME minister, Bishop Elias Cottrell died at nearly age 85 on the evening of December 5, 1937, the victim of a heart attack that followed an eight-month illness.[39] As a testament to his dedication to his life's dream, at his death, Cottrell was still serving as treasurer and chairman of the MI board. Hardly a day had passed during all the intervening years since the turn of the century that the Bishop did not strive to build and expand and uplift this special place of learning in Holly Springs. From his deathbed, Cottrell had drafted what was to be his final message for delivery to the East Mississippi CME Conference, as ever, modest and apologetic for his inability to attend the meetings for the first time in many years. Although 84 years old at the time and constrained by strict doctor's orders due to his extended and ultimately fatal heart ailment, Cottrell voiced his lifelong commitment and hope that the conference should "…be harmonious and that brotherly love…continue" to "do the noblest work ever done…" in the denomination's history.[40]

Cottrell's funeral services were held in the Carnegie Auditorium at his beloved Mississippi Industrial College, highlighted by eulogies delivered by seven fellow CME bishops gathered from far and near — Holly Springs and Memphis, Cleveland, Kansas City, Texas, and two from Chicago. CME Bishop Joseph Lane's description of Cottrell's "magnetic leader-

---

38   Washington, as quoted in Hubert H. McAlexander, *Strawberry Plains Audubon Center: Four Centuries of a Mississippi Landscape* (Jackson, MS: University Press of Mississippi, 2008), 102.

39   The Holly Springs *South Reporter* (Holly Springs, December 9, 1937).

40   Elias Cottrell letter dated December 7, 1937 (presented two days after his death on December 5, 1937, to the 19th Annual Session of the East Mississippi Conference), as reproduced in M. I. College News, Number 11 (Jan. 1947) in the collection of the Ida B. Wells-Barnett Museum, Holly Springs, Mississippi, courtesy of Rev. Leonora Harris, Executive Director and Founder.

ship," written two decades earlier, might well have served as the Bishop's most fitting eulogy:

> As a preacher, Bishop Cottrell has but few equals. Argumentative and forceful, he delivers his message with great power. Aside from his mental powers, he has a very attractive personality. His greatest work is seen in the founding and establishing of the Mississippi Industrial College, at Holly Springs. He traveled, preached…and raised large sums of money for this work. Under his magnetic leadership the patronizing (CME) Conferences have done a remarkable work at Holly Springs.[41]

Following the services, Cottrell was interred in a nearby cemetery on the outskirts of Holly Springs, fittingly, the site of an old bone yard. The cemetery was later named Bishop Cottrell Memorial Garden in his memory.[42] From bondage to virtual sainthood, Elias Cottrell's life was by all measures characterized by courage, humanitarian dignity, and a firm commitment to accommodation, reason, and devoted service to God and humankind. As he once simply expressed in an open appeal to his beloved community, his faith was grounded in the unshakable belief that "God is with us, and we are going forward…and the right will win."[43]

> Author's Note: Throughout this article, the terms Colored, Negro, Black and African American are quoted or employed in describing people of African descent. Most modern writers use the term African American, but occasional use of the other terms is dictated by the context of historical discussions, as herein.

---

41   Lane Autobio, 164. Bishop Lane, Cottrell's admiring biographer, was not present to deliver a eulogy. In a Jefferson/Adams-like death coincidence, Lane died at age 103 on the morning of the very Sunday Bishop Cottrell died in the evening, Cottrell almost certainly unaware of Lane's having already died.

42   *Tapestry*, 124.

43   *Appeal*, 5.

Mississippi Industrial College campus
Southern Tapestry by Hubert H. McAlexander

Booker T. Washington and his blue ribbon academic committee visiting
Bishop Cottrell at his house in Holly Springs

Holmes Teer (1859-1938) was such a successful black entrepreneur that he became mythic.
Marshall County Historical Museum

THE MYTHIC HOLMES TEER

HUBERT H. MCALEXANDER

Holmes Teer has become a figure of mystery. That has happened in the effort to explain a wealthy black landowner in early 20th century Mississippi. Whitley Cocke, retired farmer and scion of landed Woodsons, used to tell the barber shop about Teer's finding a cache of gold, a discovery he made while digging a fence hole. That was the source of his great wealth.[1]

An essay by Dr. Lillian Wilson Stratmon, a Teer descendant, reports that he rode over the fields every day, changing clothing and mounts at noon. "Some say," she writes, "that he rode a white horse and wore a white hat." He always dressed in a suit. So he emerges as a mythic white-clad horseman riding over the landscape.[2]

Holmes Teer married Tennessee Freeman (1860-1941), from the same Woodson neighborhood. Her brother, Henry, became the second-wealthiest black landowner. There are many questions to ponder here. Among them, I have wondered about their surname. Did they take a version of "freedman"?

Dr. Stratmon begins her treatment by stressing Holmes Teer's mixed heritage. "A union between a young slave girl and her master" produced him. The photograph illustrating the essay reveals a handsome young man in a suit, stock, and vest, a dark visage with very regular Caucasian features.

The record of his rise can be traced in deeds. In 1893, he purchased "for cash in hand" his first tract of land, 250 acres on the northern bank of the Coldwater River six miles north of Holly Springs. By 1900 he had purchased all of Section 26 along the river, 640 acres. He was leasing to tenants. I know that some of them were sharecroppers. Eventually, he would own a 2,305-acre tract, a cotton gin and grist mill and a store building in Holly Springs. In 1905, he was appointed to the first board of Mississippi Industrial College, founded by his friend —another exceptional figure, Bishop Elias Cottrell of the Colored Methodist Church.[3]

By Tennessee Freeman, he had six children: Jesse, Eddie, Joseph, Mary Jane, Clara, and Lillian, the aunt for whom Dr. Stratmon was named. Holmes Teer encouraged all his

---

1   Telephone interview with Whitley Cocke, January 10, 2006.

2   Dr. Lillian Wilson Stratmon, "Teer, Landowner and Philanthropist," Holly Springs *South Reporter,* 1 June 2000.

3   Hubert H. McAlexander, *Strawberry Plains Audubon Center: Four Centuries of a Mississippi Landscape* (Jackson:University Press of Mississippi, 2008), 101-102, 170.

children to attend college; and he set aside funds for all relatives who wanted to enroll at Mississippi Industrial. He also freely lent money to many, some of whom never repaid him. He was the donor of the land for Isom Chapel and for the cemetery nearby, where he and his wife are buried.

Holmes Teer was the first black man in the county to have an automobile, a Model T Ford. His vast acreage was worked by 22 tenants, and he lived in a substantial house. Dr. Stratmon never saw her great-grandfather, who died in 1938. But, she writes, "I remember the running water, the indoor bathroom and the electric lights which were in a farmhouse a long distance from any city utilities. I also remember the two gas pumps, the many tractors, trucks, bailing machines, and other farm equipment."[4]

The outline of this story I knew growing up. My family had settled in 1836 two miles or so south of the Holmes Teer place. They had built a house there and established a plantation and nursery. Before 1900, my great-grandfather established a store and post office (with the postmark "Mack") in the plantation office. My great-grandfather, Ed McAlexander, married Minnie Jackson, with roots in the southwestern part of Marshall County. Her grandmother was Harriett Teer Jackson (1814-1902). She is buried in the family cemetery at Mack.

Teer is an unusual name. Harriett Teer Jackson was quoted as saying, "Well, I guess that Holmes Teer is kin to me." Then she would laugh in disparagement, daring anyone to take her seriously.

All my life, I have been interested in genealogy and local history. In 2004 I even took a trip to Pickens County, Ala. — where the Teers and Jacksons came from to Marshall and a "burned county" (one whose records had been destroyed) — to find what I could. There was little to find there. I knew that Harriet's husband, Wiley Jackson (1803-1877), had settled in the 1850s next to the Dean place near Chulahoma in Marshall County, and that he was buried in the Dean Cemetery (the name Dean is still used among his descendants). After his death, Harriet sold his land and moved to the household of a daughter near Mahon Station, not far from Mack. A few years later came the McAlexander-Jackson marriage.

So I've always been interested in the Jacksons and Teers. Not too long ago, I was going through the 1870 census gathering material for my 2015 book on the Chalmers Institute, when I came upon this entry for the Jackson household:[5]

---

4   Stratmon, "Teer, Landowner and Philanthropist."

5   Population Schedules of the 9th Census of the U. S., Mississippi, 1870. Marshall County, p. 420.

Jackson, Wylie 67 Male White born SC
Harriet 57 Female White born AL

Then came their daughter Elizabeth Ann and her husband, Bennett McCluskey, and their two sons.

Then this startling entry:

Teer, M. 40 Female Mulatto born AL Housekeeper

The mulatto housekeeper had been brought by the white family from Alabama, and she remained close by even after slavery ended. Who was her father? Was he Harriet Teer's brother, or her father, or her husband?

Then come the housekeeper's children:

Delie 17 Female Mulatto born AL
Mary 12 Female Mulatto born MS
Holmes 11 Male Mulatto born MS

There in the Jackson household was Holmes Teer. So Harriett Teer Jackson knew more than her listeners realized. Holmes Teer was probably close kin.

The Rake — David McAlexander (1836-1872)
Collection of Hubert H. McAlexander

The Rake's oldest son, Charles Alexander Wilson (1859-1954)
Courtesy Dorothy H, Miller

The Rake's Other Family

Hubert H. McAlexander

David McAlexander was a rake. That, everyone knew. He posed for an outrageous daguerreotype wearing a top hat and clenching a cheroot between his lips. I grew up looking at that portrait. When I was a teenager, an old neighbor, Mrs. Jessie Woodson Gibbons, confirmed my impression. Whispering that this was "graveyard talk," she told me that when Mary Stephenson married David McAlexander, her family "took to their beds." Because of my early historical bent, I knew that Mary's father, Maj. J.P.M. Stephenson, died five years later, in 1863. His will revealed that the money he left Mary was bequeathed in trust "as long as David F. McAlexander lives" (Marshall County Probate File #3294).

Digging up the gold that his own father, William McAlexander, had hidden during the Civil War, David made his heirs subject of a lawsuit (B[enjamin]. W[offord]. McAlexander, et. al., vs. Mary E. McAlexander, Chancery Case 800, 1872, filed at the Marshall County Courthouse in Holly Springs). To make matters worse for his repute, after the Civil War, David became a leader of the hated Republican party. He was on the 1872 ticket for tax assessor when he died. He was not buried in the Stephenson cemetery.

I had lived with all that, though my family never discussed those matters. A neighbor, Miss Martha Moseley of Strawberry Plains, did tell me that her grandmother classified the McAlexanders of Mack, our old family place, as "Stephensons — not McAlexanders."

In the fall of 1969, I went to the University of Wisconsin in Madison to finish my education. The next June, I married . Sometime after that, one day the phone rang in our little rental house. It was my grandfather's first cousin, then living about fifty miles away, where her husband was the city manager of a small Wisconsin town. She had seen my name in the phone book and wondered who I was. Her father had left Mississippi for Texas and then Oklahoma in 1890.

We drove over to see her. She was twenty years younger than my grandfather and very good-looking. She was eccentric — she had never fully unpacked her household, because someday they would go back to Oklahoma. Eccentricity, I was accustomed to, and I was especially interested in some fascinating things that her family had brought west. As she babbled on about whatever she wanted to talk about, she said of David McAlexander, her grandfather, "Well, you know that he had a child by a slave girl." What? My Mississippi family never ever talked about anything like that!

I eventually inherited the daguerreotype, and as I studied it, I would think of that information too.

Then, many decades later, I came to know Dr. Lillian Wilson Stratmon, who had written an essay on her maternal grandfather, the wealthy African American landowner Holmes Teer. I subsequently (about 2013 or 2014) learned that I was quite possibly kin to him. Much earlier, I had learned that at a 2001 symposium on black-white relations, Dr. Stratmon had said that her father was descended from the McAlexanders. I telephoned her. Yes, she said, that was true. As she gave me more details, I put them together with what I already knew.

Her paternal grandfather, Charles Alexander Wilson (1859-1954), was the son of a McAlexander and a slave girl. The rake David McAlexander had married Mary Stephenson in December of 1858. He was the youngest son of the wealthy planter William McAlexander and the last to marry. I realized that he was Charles Wilson's father.

So I scrambled to find out as much more as I could. The slave girl, whose name her descendants could not remember, married a Mr. Wilson, and her son by McAlexander took the Wilson name. In 2006, his 81-year-old granddaughter, Lillian Stratmon's first cousin, remembered him well. Charles Alexander Wilson was preternaturally bright, and his mother worked hard to send him to school. The granddaughter wrote me that "for his day and time, he was a so-called 'educated Negro.' He wrote and spoke quite perfectly, but with a Southern white man's drawl" (Dorothy E. Miller to HHM, 24 July 2006, in my possession). Charles taught school and later moved to Memphis and worked as a clerk at Cole Manufacturing Company. In retirement, he moved back to Holly Springs and lived to be 96 and a devoted correspondent with a highly-developed sense of irony.

I was reluctant to write this essay for the volume. The probable Teer connection I thought I had discovered was enough for me; and another case of racial mixing in one of my ancestral lines, resulting in the same descendant —Dr. Stratmon —seemed highly unlikely. But I must link it with other strange situations that I appear inclined to experience. I am proud of Charles Alexander Wilson and proud to be a probable kinsman of Dr. Stratmon. I realize that this quite complicated story of racial mixing only highlights a common occurrence in the slave-owning South, a phenomenon of our tangled web.

From *The Heritage News*, a publication of the Marshall County, Mississippi Genealogical Society, Vol. 20, Issue 2, June 2014, pp. 4-5. Reprint from *The South Reporter*, Holly Springs, Mississippi, April 14, 2011.

The Ben Ingram Story

Sue Watson

Adescendant of the late Ben Ingram Jr. is putting together a history of the trial and acquittal of her grandfather nearly a century ago.

Schyleen Ingram Qualls, the granddaughter of Ben Ingram Jr. was a guest speaker at a recent Holly Springs Rotary Club meeting, where she read from a book she is writing on the Ingram family. She described the events which took place in Byhalia in 1918 and her grandfather's acquittal by an all-white jury. Ben Ingram Jr., age 42, was charged with the murder of his neighbor, Green Brumley, with whom he had a long-standing dispute over property boundaries.

Prior to Ingram's shooting of Brumley, Brumley was heard in town, saying, "I am going to kill Ben Ingram." The black farmer Ingram, respected by blacks and whites alike, was tried and acquitted of the charges of murder in 1919.

Qualls was invited to speak to Rotary by Roy Ray after his wife Eleanor saw a letter to the editor from Qualls that ran in the March 17th edition of *The South Reporter*. Several Rotarians said it was the best program the club has ever had.

Qualls said Eleanor Ray helped her to find her first juror contact — Dan Gill, grandson of Ingram trial juror Gus Gill.

Qualls, who has interviewed family members about the incident and collected newspaper articles and other documents about the trial of her grandfather, read excerpts from her book, the first reading, she said, to Rotarians.

Several influential white businessmen — Maynard Nichols, the banker; W. D. Fitts of McCrary's Store; and J. L. Burrow Sr. of Burrow & Sons — hid Ben for three hours in the basement of Burrow & Sons store to protect him from Brumley, who was also in town in his buggy. These men and others, including men in the area like Sim Watson, Sye Bogan, Cal Matthews, Osborne Bell Sr. and Sam Richmond, later helped protect the Ingram family following Ben's arrest and throughout his trial.

Qualls's mother, Alfreda Ingram Moore, tells some of the story in the book, along with Robbie Ingram Warren, her aunt; Hubert Ingram, her uncle; and Clara Woods Adams, her cousin, and fourteen other people, most of whom Qualls interviewed in the early '70s. Qualls said she wanted to talk to people whose families played various roles in the saga — descendants of attorneys for the defense, witnesses at the trial, and especially of the twelve jurors. Several individuals have already contacted her and shared valuable information and photos for her book, which helps to give these wonderful and courageous people their place in history, she said.

"Photos really help to tell the story and are so valuable," she said. "So many of our grandfather's photos were lost when my grandfather's house burned in the '50s."

Qualls continues to talk with people who are helping her weave together the fragments of this phenomenal historic event in the history of Byhalia and Marshall County. "It is almost a singular, positive story of Southern justice," she said. "My grandfather grew up in very turbulent times," Qualls said. "He defied customs — saw everyone as equal — and was a dreamer."

Ben Ingram was a highly successful farmer and businessman who owned about 2,200 acres of land in the Byhalia area, 700 of which still remain in the family. The only thing Ben's family needed [from] the outside world was coffee, flour and salt. He planted orchards, ran a blacksmith shop, and had a miller's barn, a smokehouse, farm animals, cotton, and grain — everything needed by farming families. He had a Delco electric system and indoor plumbing for his home long before TVA provided services for the area.

He was one of the first men in the county, black or white, to own an automobile, Qualls said. Ingram's white friends helped him buy his first car in 1914, because dealers would not sell a car at that time to a black man. Thereafter, Ben Ingram had a standing order for a new car every year in Holly Springs.

Qualls said telling the story of her grandfather will open the door for others to talk about other successful black men in Mississippi during the era.

Some of Ben Ingram's successful contemporaries and best friends from Holly Springs included Dr. Lee McCoy (president, Rust College), Dr. Robert MacIntosh (a dentist), Jordan Brittenum (funeral home director), Holmes Teer (a prosperous landowner), and Robert Church, Sr., who established a black-owned bank in Memphis.

"My grandfather had close white friends and he seemed able to get along with anyone except for his neighbor, Green Brumley," Qualls said. She referred to the period of 1918-1920 as one of the lowest in the United States for African Americans. About 250,000 blacks left Mississippi in 1920, she said.

"The people in Byhalia grew up together and had good relationships around farming and supported each other," she said. "The town was not perfect, but people living there were moving forward. They took pride in keeping the Klan from completely controlling the area at the time."

Qualls's mother, Alfreda Ingram Moore, was born nine years after the 1918 incident. If Ben Ingram had been convicted of the murder or his neighbors had not protected him, Qualls said she would not be here to tell this compelling story about her grandfather.

Her mother tells part of the story:

"Papa had a rule never to answer the door after dark and never to go out after dark without a companion."

Robbie Warren Ingram, Qualls's late aunt, confirms that white friends hid Ben and then gave him a gun and ammunition; Ingram went on home to face his fate. Brumley came upon the Ingram farm on 309 South, near Isaac Chapel CME Church, where Ben and his wife, Ruth, were early members, and started shooting from his buggy at Ben, who was standing beside his house. Ben Ingram tried to get closer to Brumley and hid behind trees to evade gunshots. He had dropped the gun he was carrying on his way out of the house.

Several of the Ingram family went outside, risking being shot during the showdown. Brumley was shot and killed — Ingram sustained a gunshot wound to his leg.

People black and white from all over the area, about 500 in all, poured onto Ben's farm after the shooting to protect the family. Doc J. B. Bailey was called to the Ingram house to tend Ben's wound. Ben Ingram was arrested the next day. To protect him from being lynched, deputy sheriff Edgar Williams arranged a protective caravan and he was taken to a Memphis jail to await his trial.

During the weeks of the trial, many businesses around the courthouse closed, as people packed the square with horses and buggies. The courtroom was filled to overflowing. Blacks were not allowed to sit on a jury at the time or to vote.

During the trial, Ben's attorneys, Lester Fant, William Alexander Belk, Clyde Wright, and Lemuel Augustus Smith, argued that they had to let Ingram go or they would not be following the law. At the end, Ben Ingram testified, telling his story, "straight as a dime," from start to finish. He was taken out of the courtroom while the jury deliberated.

"People said, no matter what, they probably were going to hang him," witnesses told Qualls in her 1970 interviews.

"The family went back to Byhalia," Robbie Warren said. "The jury found Daddy not guilty. The whole house broke loose when they got the call. He came home the next day. People advised him to leave Mississippi, but he stayed until he died of heart failure at age 68."

Ingram died on Qualls's mother's 17th birthday, Jan. 9, 1944.

"And my mother has been the inspiration to write this book," Qualls said. "She is the youngest and only child still alive of Ben Ingram's 17 children and five nieces and nephews, which he and his wife Ruth reared."

Nearly 35 prominent men and women of all walks of life served as witnesses for the defense.

"I think it was who he was that saved him," Qualls said.

Qualls said once the book is published, she will put her energy into her dream of getting a major feature film produced. Then, she plans to set up a Ben Ingram Jr. Foundation in Byhalia that will build an educational center for children. She has already established a Ben Ingram's Scholars Program at Rust College.

"I want to share my grandfather's story because it turns conventional wisdom on its head and creates a space for us to view Mississippi and its people in a new and multidirectional light," Qualls said. "I am grateful to these people who did what they did. There were loving, compassionate, and great people in Mississippi then as there are now.

"It's important we embrace this as our collective history. We are not separate from each other. Whatever has been done to one of us has been done to all of us. We are not separate from anyone's suffering just as we are not separate from anyone's joy or triumph. It is important to consider human dignity. Perhaps there is something you or I will have an opportunity to do in our lives like the people of Marshall County did in 1918. Maybe 133 years from now, someone will say, I would not be alive if it were not for an act of courage or love by one of us. Wouldn't that be a blessing?"

WHITE LIES IN THE SOUTH

HUBERT H. McALEXANDER

A genealogical phenomenon encountered in north Mississippi is indicative of the entire South. Many people make their ancestors as distinguished as possible. The easiest way is by attribution of kinship, the precise degree usually never given. The general point was driven home when recently an historically-minded friend sent me a local 1946 obituary, written by a family member of the deceased.

The first thing that struck me as "off" was the spelling of the subject's name. The heading was Frank Leake Strickland. A final e had been added to the middle name. Leak descendants were still around, and I am such a longtime student of local history that I knew that locally the name had never had that e.

But let's begin the obituary:

> A gentle soul has gone from Strickland Place to join the saints preceding him in the mansion, prepared for him by his Savior. With one last — almost whimsical — smile toward his grief-stricken sister, watching over him, as she had all her life, he departed towards the kingdom awaiting all who humbled themselves as had this child of God.

Now that the reader has absorbed that, let it be known that I suspect that the writer of the piece was that sister.[1]

The subject of this peroration was Frank Strickland, who was mentally retarded. Whenever anyone stopped an automobile to give the steadily-walking old man a ride, he would say, "Perle's not a bit well, not a bit." Perle was his sister, Miss Perle Strickland, who married, rather late in life, a German — Gerard Badow. People in town remembered that she wore white in the wedding though she was almost sixty.[2]

What follows now is the obituary paragraph giving family history:

> The oldest son of William Matthew and Janie Leake Strickland and grandson of Col. Francis Terry Leake, Mississippi's largest ante-bellum Cotton Planter [capitalized as printed], after whom

---

1   Unsigned obituary of Frank Leake Strickland, Holly Springs *South Reporter*, February 28, 1946.

2   In his collection, *Civil War Women* (Lafayette CA: Thomas-Berryhill Press, 1991), the Reverend Milton Winter includes, as an Epilogue, the newspaper account of the grand wedding of Miss Perle, which took place October 2, 1926. Miss Perle's father, Maj. William Strickland, married his second wife, Miss Jane Leak, in 1867.

he was named, and a direct descendant of Walter Leake, the States's first Executive, Frank Strickland lived in Holly Springs all his life, having retired from active work with the *South Reporter* some years ago. He leaves his only sister Perle, her husband Gerard Badow, his sister-in-law, Mrs. Jacob L. Strickland and his only niece Ruth Strickland Weir of Louisville, Ky. and her son William.

Here one encounters more than usual inflation. Of course everyone of much prominence in the South was a "colonel." Miss Pearle's grandfather, Col. Francis Terry Leak (1802-1863) was an important planter whose plantation journal has been the subject of a recent literary hoax that received national attention (see the following essay in this volume entitled "Southern Hoaxes"). But Colonel Leak was the largest planter in Tippah County, which did not compare with adjoining Marshall County, much less the whole state.[3]

Further, Francis Terry Leak was not a direct descendent of the third governor of Mississippi, Walter Leake (1762-1825), the son of Capt. Mask Leake and Patience Morris of Hanover County, Va. Miss Perle's grandfather was a North Carolinian, son of another Walter Leak (1761—1844) and Hannah Pickett of Richmond County. The men named Walter — be it Leake or Leak — were probably cousins, so Miss Perle, by accident, was not as far off as most involved in Southern ancestry enhancement. But enhancement it was.[4]

The most interesting example of this practice is found in Stark Young's 1926 novel *Heaven Trees.* There he bases a character, Dr. George Clay, on a real person, Dr. George Gallatin Tait. But Young gives the character a readily known connection of distinction: "The renowned Henry Clay was his cousin" (42). Here is a striking reflection in fiction of what went on in Southern reality.

The actual Dr. Tait married, first, a Miss McGehee, of the revered family on which Stark Young draws for his two antebellum novels. In reality, this Miss McGehee was descended from Ann (Nancy) Scott. But in *Heaven Trees*, the narrator says this of the Scotts: "Grandmother McGehee's mother had been one of the Virginia Scotts, the sister of the mother of the great General Winfield Scott" (139). Stark Young just had to add that, but he gets a bit scrambled up—was General Scott's mother also a Scott? The excellent and thorough family genealogy has no indication of any connection.[5]

---

3   Joseph Karl Menn, "Large Slaveholders of the Deep South,1860," a dissertation (Ann Arbor: Xerox University Misrofilms, 1974), 2:1,163; 1,094-1,100.

4   Dunbar Rowland, *Mississippi* (Atlanta: Southern Historical Publishing Association, 1907), 2:63. James E. and Ida Huneycutt, *History of Richmond County, North Carolina* (1975), 90-91. The North Carolina branch had probably dropped the final e, for there seems no trace of it here.

5   Start Young, *Heaven Trees* (New York: Charles Scribner's Sons, 1926) and *So Red the Rose* (New York, Charles Scribner's Sons, 1934). Young is treated on 289-290 of the excellent McGehee genealogy — Jane N. and Ethel C. Woodall Grider, *McGehee Descendants, Vol. III* ((Baltimore: Gateway Press, 1991). The lines coming down from his grandfather Hugh McGehee are on 286-293. The Micajah McGeehee

The McGehees are, in reality, a distinguished Southern family. In a rather obscure line of the Jacksons (in my own family), the aunt of my great-grandmother Minnie Jackson McAlexander always said that her father, Wiley Jackson (1803-1877), was kin to Gen. Stonewall Jackson. Research does not show that. Is this enough evidence that the practice permeated the entire South? It did. There is no need for me to go on and on.

and Nancy Scott material is on 148-149.

Southern Hoaxes

Hubert H. McAlexander

From the *Flagpole*, Athens, GA, September 30, 2015

"Not this one too!" I groaned to my wife. "Why does every Southern hoax have to be centered in Marshall County, Mississippi!" Now, after years of brooding, I have decided to make my protest public.

The last straw is the Ben Affleck-Henry Louis Gates mess. Gates, a distinguished scholar of African American subjects at Harvard, runs a PBS television show called "Finding Your Roots." He had movie actor and director Ben Affleck as a guest. Affleck, I have learned, is a liberal who has been generous in creating a foundation in Africa. That, of course, I applaud. What I do not applaud is Affleck's asking Gates to suppress his discovery of a slave-owning Affleck forebear. This the world found out from Sony Wikileaks. For whatever reason, Gates did not include any slave-holding ancestor on the Affleck program.

On June 25, 2015, the *New York Times* and other newspapers carried the PBS announcement that the third season of the program had been suspended. The *Times* and others, in addition, found it significant that there was no mention of a fourth season.

Affleck is descended from the Georgia slaveholder that Gates discovered and from a number of slave-holding people in Marshall County. Various bloggers have easily found the Marshall County forebears. They are all people that I have long known about, and many other descendants are my friends. The key figure is Maj. James Henry Alexander (1814-1911), who lived in the southwestern section of my county near the village of Chulahoma. All of us white people from Southern backgrounds are descended from some slave-owning people. Get used to it. We are responsible for ourselves, not our ancestors.

This is only the latest attempt to deny and falsify my local history. I was born in 1939 in the old cotton town of Holly Springs, Miss., which had a fascinating architectural legacy and a scrambled, often false, sometimes mythic house-tour history. All my adult life, I have done research to find and establish historical fact. I had to correct Shintoist fabrications, sloppy research (or none), careless attribution, make-believe, and self-aggrandizement through ancestry. Most of this came from local sources. Now I have to face new examples inspired by political correctness, or misplaced or misunderstood liberal sympathy.

A couple of years ago, a scholar drawn to the "Behind the Big House Tour" in my town said that his forebears were slaves held by a man named Green, who owned 300. No one in my county owned 300 slaves. The largest owner, Dr. Weldon Jones, had more than 200; and no one named Green or Greene owned very many. This seems a new kind of Shintoism. At the least, it is a falsification of history. It was conveyed to me in an email from one of the tour's supporters.

Now we move to another kind of untruth, one that has its roots in getting attention from proximity to literary genius. Surely you can tell what is coming next. A few years ago, a professor at Emory University, then named Sally Wolff (later Wolff-King), presented a program at the Library of Congress claiming that William Faulkner had been a close hunting friend of Holly Springs man Edgar Francisco, had read that man's family plantation ledgers, and had mined it for his literary works. In the Washington audience was a cousin of the Franciscos, who warned Professor Wolff of the untruth of whole story.

Despite all contrary biographical evidence, she went right ahead and wrote a book based on this untruth. She was on public radio, and the book was discussed in the *New York Times*. As a student of local history, I had read the ledgers in my early research in local sources. As a college professor of American literature, I taught William Faulkner's works for fifty years. Wouldn't you think that I might have made a connection if Faulkner had used that dry, quotidian material?

During the subsequent controversy about the evidence upon which the book was based, a blogger with a local background interviewed local people. Though many asked not to be quoted, they discussed the ridiculousness of the claimed Faulkner friendship. One student of north Mississippi history — Jack D. Elliott Jr. — ended up publishing an expose in the *Journal of Mississippi History* — "Confabulations of History: William Faulkner, Edgar Francisco, and a Friendship that Never Was," Volume 54, No 4 [Winter 2012 —but not published until winter of 2015], 309-348). But that source is not National Public Radio or the *New York Times*, and Falsehood has a life that Truth can not match.

Many of the family emailed me, outraged about the false claim. But they are reluctant to brand the source a liar while he lives. The academic Faulkner website stopped all discussion of the matter because the book had been "peer reviewed." Thus we see secure academics close ranks in defense of sloppy work. Those academics owe the public an apology.

One wonders whether anyone cares about TRUTH any more. The least I can hope is that such people would at least let Marshall County, Miss., alone.

One Corner of Yoknapatawpha

James Seay

From the *Oxford American: A Magazine of the South*, Issue 86, Fall 2014.

During the autumn of 1929, when Faulkner was writing *As I Lay Dying* to the hum of the dynamo in the powerhouse where he was working the night shift, my father, some 20 miles away in Panola County, Miss., had another kind of dynamo in his head. He had retrofitted a 1927 Model T Ford with axle spacers and what were called "motor car" wheels that enabled it to run on a railroad. My father described his new creation as slow and noisy, the latter owing to poor alignment of railroad track and wheels. The tires had burned off his "T-Model" when the family home in Batesville caught on fire the year before, and he decided to convert it into a vehicle that he could take into the hunting grounds of the Tallahatchie River bottomland, or, as it was sometimes called, the Big Bottom.

This was the bottomland along the Tallahatchie River in Panola County, which is at the eastern edge of the Mississippi Delta and adjacent to Lafayette County, where Faulkner lived. By the time of my father's youth in the late 1920s, much of the timber in the Big Bottom had been cut away by lumbermen, my grandfather among them, but there were still some big woods remaining that were rich with game. The spur-line railroad (known as the Dummy Line by locals), on which timber had been transported from the Tallahatchie Bottom to the Darnell Lumber Company sawmill just outside Batesville, was soon to be abandoned, and my father could motor down to a hunting camp that he had established. At the end of the rail line there was a wye that would get him and his hunting pals turned around and headed back to town.

Though it is not likely that Faulkner was present to hear the new sound of my father's "T-Model" in the woods that year—he was working steadily on *As I Lay Dying* during the hunting season—Faulkner was in fact a regular in those very woods. Beginning as early as 1915 or so and continuing through the mid-1930s, Faulkner had come to hunt, and drink, with the hunting parties that Gen. James Stone, father of Faulkner's friend Phil Stone, held annually at a camp five miles from my father's camp in the Big Bottom. Faulkner would later draw on these experiences at Gen. Stone's camp in his creation of "The Bear" and other sections of *Go Down, Moses*, as well as in *Big Woods*. Each year Faulkner's fictional hunters "would drive away to Jefferson, to join Major de Spain and General Compson and Boon Hogganbeck and Walter Ewell and go on into the big bottom of the Tallahatchie where the deer and bear were." Major de Spain had a hunting camp in the

Tallahatchie River bottomland, limning the hunting camp of his real-life counterpart Gen. James Stone.

The Tallahatchie River serves as the northern border of Faulkner's fictional Yoknapatawpha County. On the map of Yoknapatawpha that he drew for *Absalom, Absalom!*, Faulkner identifies the location of Major de Spain's Tallahatchie River camp in the northwest quadrant of the county. On a later map, annotated for Malcolm Cowley's *Portable Faulkner*, Faulkner altered the "Fishing camp" designation of his earlier map to read "Hunting & fishing camp where Wash Jones killed Sutpen [*Absalom, Absalom!*]. Later owned by Major De Spain."

Faulkner's annotations identify this particular corner of Yoknapatawpha as the setting not only of *Absalom, Absalom!* but also "The Bear," as well as the short stories "Wash," "A Justice," and "Red Leaves." All of these works, with the exception of "Wash," hark back in one way or another to the time when Chickasaw and Choctaw Indians were still present in the region, both before and after the land cessions of 1830 and 1832 wherein they ceded their land to the federal government. Issues of land ownership, conflated later with issues of slavery, are fundamental concerns in the two short stories, though those issues are not expressed in the heightened moral register that Faulkner summons in *Absalom, Absalom!* and "The Bear." In the latter, the protaganist Ike McCaslin is so conflicted that he questions the right of even the Chickasaw chief Ikkemotubbe to have sold land to his grandfather. This vexation is deepened further by Ike's discovery in the plantation ledger that his grandfather fathered a daughter with one of his slaves and later fathered a child with that same daughter, neither of whom would he formally acknowledge as his child. Ike comes to regard the land as forever tainted by the injustice of slavery. He is profoundly aggrieved too by the destruction of the wilderness that has been home to the bear Old Ben and the primitive spirit that the bear represents.

Faulkner named his "apocryphal county," as he called it, after an actual river, the Yoknapatawpha, which was the Chickasaw name for the river that is now called the Yocona, a corruption of Yoknapatawpha. A further variation appears on an 1861 map I located at the U.S. Corps of Engineers in Vicksburg, Miss.. The river is identified as "Yoch na pata fa." Above it, and sited on the Tallahatchie River, is the now vanished town of Panola. My father's camp, General Stone's camp, and the confluence of the Yocona River with the Tallahatchie River were all within a radius of less than ten miles.

Faulkner's fictional county, according to notes Malcolm Cowley recorded after a conversation with Faulkner in 1948, "borrows scenes and features from three real Mississippi counties." If Faulkner cited those three counties, Cowley did not record them, but I am confident that one of them is Panola, if on no other basis than Faulkner's many visits to the Stone hunting camp and the identifiable "scenes and features" that may be observed.

Looking back on that time and place, John Cullen, a farmer and one of Faulkner's fellow hunters, says, "there never was and never again will be on this earth such a paradise for hunting dogs and men as the miles and miles of great virgin forests and jungles of the Big Bottom." Cullen, who collaborated with scholar Floyd Watkins on a book of reminiscences, *Old Times in the Faulkner Country*, recalls further that "a man could travel for miles under the open timber and never see a road. Ole Colonel Stone owned a good bit of land, the place where he built his camp." In his book *My Brother Bill*, John Faulkner also recalls the Stone camp: "By the time Bill was grown and began deer hunting, our timber [in Lafayette County] had mostly been cut. That's why he had to go to the 'Big Bottom' for his story....The Delta begins thirty miles to the west of us....It was here, just beyond Batesville at General Stone's cabin, that Bill first went on his deer and bear hunts and wild-turkey shoots."

Faulkner's visits to Stone's camp and the bottomlands of the Tallahatchie, it seems to me, exposed him to a milieu that, while not radically unlike the one in and around his Oxford, nonetheless extended and enhanced his sense of Yoknapatawpha's potential as a fictional ground. First there was his exposure, as a hunter going in and out of the woods on a log-train, to the dynamic created by the mechanical force of the lumber industry meeting the resistance of nature. Faulkner was especially sensitive to this tension. The character of that nature was near-primordial—dense virgin timber, swamp, canebrake, briar thickets, diverse wildlife—and it was on the verge of extinction: "that doomed wilderness whose edges were being constantly and punily gnawed at by men with plows and axes."

When I say that Faulkner was exposed to a somewhat different milieu here, remember that Panola County and the Tallahatchie Bottom are where the Delta merges with the hills, a landscape unlike that of the predominantly hill country in Faulkner's Lafayette County—and one bearing a slightly different cultural stamp. A liminal zone, if you will. A space betwixt and between, a state of transition and ambiguity. Panola County embraces both the Delta and the hills. In one direction the horizon seems limitless, in the other the hills begin closing in. To say that the one encourages expansiveness and the other clannishness is perhaps too reductive, but it begins to suggest possible tendencies.

Remember too that Faulkner's Oxford was, and remains, a university town and as such offered a degree of refinement that Panola County lacked. That is not to suggest that Faulkner's experience in Lafayette County was limited to town life. Again, these various differences were not profound in their every expression, but there were significant nuances and shadings, and Faulkner was keen on gradation—and ever alert to possible strategies for extending the dramatic reach of his Yoknapatawpha.

After my father told me of his motorcar and the proximity of his hunting camp to General Stone's camp, it occurred to me that I should try to find the site of the Stone camp and inquire among the locals concerning their memories of the place. Clearly Faulkner had found in the surrounding Big Bottom—in its larger history of slavery and in the immediate drama of its diminishment by ax and plow—one of his most resonant and compelling emblems of struggle and loss. Nowhere in Faulkner's fiction do we find a more plaintive rendering of what he called "the human heart in conflict with itself." In "The Bear," there is Ike McCaslin's plea, "Don't you see? This whole land, the whole South, is cursed, and all of us who derive from it…lie under its curse?…Don't you see?" Ike repudiates his heritage and retreats into a life of near penury in which "even if he couldn't cure the wrong and eradicate the shame…at least he could repudiate the wrong and shame, at least in principle." In *Absalom, Absalom!*, Sutpen, with his band of wild Haitian slaves, wrests from the wilderness a plantation, Sutpen's Hundred, and then goes on in his attempt to subjugate all around him as though the world were a slave quarters. And there is Quentin Compson's conflicted cry in *Absalom, Absalom!* when asked by his roommate at Harvard why he hates the South: "I don't. I don't! I don't hate it! I don't hate it!"

I wanted to locate the old Stone camp also because I was curious to learn more about my own family's investment in that part of my home county. My grandfather had cut and milled timber in the Tallahatchie and Yocona Bottoms (and hence was a villain, by implication, in Faulkner's indictment regarding the diminishment of the wilderness) and he later owned farmland there. With directions my father had provided and with the help of Panola County's chancery clerk, Brooks Vance, and some of the elders around Panola, I found the old campsite one spring in the late 1970s. As it turned out, the hunting lodge itself, or clubhouse, as the hunters called it, was still standing. It was in the middle of a big soybean field. In any direction you turned there were silos, John Deere tractors, and more fields under cultivation. Except for a big oak tree that had been left standing beside the house, the only thing that would suggest there was ever a woodland there was a line of trees that formed a horizon along the Tallahatchie River less than a mile away. The effect of the whole scene on my sensibilities was not unlike what I would have felt had I discovered one of the whaleships on which Melville's Pequod was modeled, the Acushnet, say, or the Essex, stranded somewhere in the whaling grounds.

I was aware too of another phenomenon having to do with literature and place. If I had never read Faulkner and you took me to this bean field and told me all about it and the clubhouse, which resembled the house of a tenant farmer more than a hunting lodge, I would nod and agree, but in truth it would be little more than just another bean field to me. When an author sets a narrative in motion around an actual place that we recognize, however, that place becomes invested with a kind of extra-reality, if the fiction has established a valid claim on our imagination. In addition to its own history, the place takes on that of the fiction as well. All this is by way of telling you something of the effect the sight of the old clubhouse and its surroundings had on me. For other readers that sensation might come in Pamplona, Yasnaya Polyana, the moors of Yorkshire, Birnam Hill (Birnam Wood, alas, like Tallahatchie's Big Woods, has also vanished—and not merely to Dunsinane gone), or wherever literary pilgrimages might lead. I cannot claim that my vision was of the intensity of Ike McCaslin's when he returned to the hunting camp for the final time in "The Bear," but perhaps I had a whiff of it: "The wilderness soared, musing, inattentive, myriad, eternal, green; older than any mill-shed, longer than any spur-line."

One of the old-time Panola County natives I talked with, Jim Hancock, remembered the days when he sometimes went for as long as two months without seeing anyone else in the Big Bottom. He was a trapper, and his trapping season usually began around the middle of November, after his father's crops were laid by, and extended until early February. During that time he worked alone out of a 10' x 12' tent, trapping mink, beaver, raccoons, and occasionally otter. Hancock told me he once trapped a white otter, which the game warden said was "a freak of nature, just like Babe Ruth." Born in 1904, Hancock was trapping regularly by 1923, and until his retirement 50 years later he was engaged in something related to the Tallahatchie Bottom, either trapping or logging or clearing land and farming it.

Though he knew who Babe Ruth was, Jim Hancock had never heard of William Faulkner. He did, however, remember the day that General Stone died in the clubhouse of the Stone hunting camp, which was near where he trapped and hunted and later worked in logging camps, one of my grandfather's included. He said somebody came and told him that old Gen. Stone had died in the clubhouse—that they had been drinking and gambling all night and he had died that morning and that the camp cook wouldn't go back in the house as long as the general was in there dead.

At one time General Stone owned some 2,000 acres in Panola County, most of it in the Tallahatchie Bottom. His father had begun acquiring land when he settled there in the mid-1850s. There were also considerable land holdings on Stone's mother's side of the family. Her great-uncle Potts is reputed to have owned 100 square miles of land along the Tallahatchie River. Potts's sons, Theophilus and Amodeus Potts, known as Buck and Buddy, owned the land on which General Stone's hunting camp later stood. (A Potts family member was a partner with my grandfather in ownership of a parcel of that same land in later years.) They served Faulkner as models for his characters Uncle Buck and Uncle Buddy, the former of whom was Ike McCaslin's father, and it was his entries in the plantation ledger that led Ike to his realization concerning his grandfather's treatment of his slaves.

Gen. Stone was born James Bates Stone, his middle name most likely in honor of Rev. J. W. Bates, for whom the town of Batesville was named. Stone's birthdate is listed as 1856 in *Biographical and Historical Memoirs of Mississippi* (Chicago, 1891), but his tombstone in Batesville's Magnolia Cemetery is marked 1854. (It is a stone's throw, so to speak, from my family's burial plot.) After graduating from Kentucky Military Institute, Stone entered law school at the University of Mississippi, though he withdrew after a few months. Dan Ferguson, former mayor of Batesville, who knew both the Stone and Faulkner families, told me that Stone "read the law" in order to qualify for the bar, a not-uncommon method of self-education.

In my youth I visited Ferguson's farm with his son Danny for horseback riding and camping trips. In later years I learned that the farm had been a part of the Stone landholdings in Panola County and that the dilapidated log house where Danny and I sometimes found shelter from the rain was Stone's birthplace.

Danny once found a silver flask in a hidden crevice of the house. I'd venture a guess that someone was maintaining a private stash for drinking on the sly. A fondness for strong drink ran in the Stone family. And, as I've mentioned, drinking was one of the main draws at Stone's camp, along with the gambling and hunting. Jim Hancock noted that he heard that Stone had been drinking heavily during the night before his death. *The Panolian* of November 26, 1936, carried the announcement that "while on a hunting trip at his lodge west of town Monday morning about 10:30, seated in a chair, Gen. James Stone, age 83 years, passed peacefully to the Great Beyond." This would have been the Thanksgiving hunt. A month later, at the Christmas hunt, one of his sons, James Stone, Jr., died also. According to the Panolian, the cause of death was a heart attack, but one of my grandfather's former associates, Selwyn Shuford, told me that the younger Stone had been drinking all night and was found face down in a pool of water surrounding the artesian spring outside the lodge.

As for further potential effects of alcohol, one of my father's most vivid memories of his hunting days in the Bottom was of the time that hunters from the Stone camp came to his camp late one night with a corpse:

> While we were camped at the Fuller Field one winter, an ice storm covered the earth. Some people from Sardis [a town in Panola County near Batesville] were camped in the old Stone clubhouse. One night about 12 o'clock midnight some of them came to our Fuller Field camp with a corpse loaded on a mule-drawn wagon. They had been drinking corn likker, the man had put his lips to a poison bottle of it, and died. They wanted us to haul the corpse to Batesville and send it on to Sardis. The rails over the bridge were coated solid with ice, and the only way for us to cross it was for one of us to go ahead of the "T Model" and clear the ice from the rails.

The man undoubtedly suffered poisoning, immediate or accumulative, from moonshine that had been distilled through an automobile radiator, a not-uncommon distilling process, but one that resulted in toxic whiskey, owing to the lead residue in the radiators.

The automobile radiators were cheaper than copper stills, and irresponsible or ignorant moonshiners sometimes resorted to the cheaper method.

Whether General Stone and Faulkner were present at the Stone camp on that particular hunt, I do not know (nor am I suggesting that Faulkner drew on that experience in creating the Bundren family's travails in conveying Addie Bundren's corpse by mule wagon to be buried near her family in *As I Lay Dying*; mule wagons were more common than FedEx is today). But the drinking at the Stone camp was legendary, and Faulkner of course had a lifelong battle with alcohol. Dan Ferguson jokingly told me that he saved Bill Faulkner's life. He said that General Stone once brought Faulkner into Batesville from the camp and asked him to get Faulkner a cure for the hiccoughs. Faulkner mentions the hiccoughs incident in a letter (undated) to his agent's assistant.

> I am now working at a story which the POST should like. I am sorry I didn't see you again [in New York]. I got into my usual drinking gang [at the Stone camp] and drank pretty hard for a time after reaching home [from the trip to New York], was taken sick, quit drinking, had hiccoughs for forty-eight hours, and as a result I am expecting to be notified that I have permanently ruined my stomach and must live from now on upon bread and milk.

Ferguson said that General Stone told him he would have brought Faulkner into town sooner but Faulkner "had been down there drunk for two weeks." Ferguson went to Will Cox's drugstore, but Cox was out of town, so Ferguson had to call a druggist in nearby Como to come to Cox's drugstore and fix a "secret" remedy. Faulkner lived to tell the story, though he recast it considerably. In "A Bear Hunt," published in the *Saturday Evening Post* in 1934, the character Lucius Provine is cured of his hiccoughs in an encounter with Chickasaw Indians who have been led to believe that Lucius is a revenue agent investigating their moonshine whiskey—making operation.

Stone established his first law practice in Batesville in 1880, and he was engaged in farming and business interests as well. His newspaper notice in an 1891 *Panolian* states that his law practice embraces the "Circuit and Chancery Courts of Panola and adjacent counties and in the Supreme and Federal Courts of the State." Stone often rode alone on horseback to get to these various courts of law, the locations of which were distant enough that he sometimes had to make camp overnight. It is said that he claimed John Wilkes Booth once stumbled into his camp. True or not, the narrative impulse and sense of adventure evidenced there were undoubtedly aspects of General Stone's character that enthralled the young William Faulkner and contributed to his creation of Major de Spain.

Soon after Stone's notice appeared in the *Panolian*, he moved with his family to Oxford. Among other considerations, there was the fact that the Federal District Court met there. Stone had served as general counsel to the railroad in Batesville and would later serve in the same position in Oxford, hence the title general, according to some accounts. He retained ownership of his lands in Panola until financial difficulties forced him to begin selling land in order to pay drainage taxes. But he continued to maintain his hunting camp there.

In addition to Stone's hunting camp, the Dummy Line railroad and other features of the logging operations provided Faulkner with images for the vanishing wilderness of *Go Down, Moses,* in which "the diminutive locomotive and its shrill peanut-parcher whistle" could occasionally be heard by the hunters as it carried the cut timber out of the Big Bottom. (Before the Dummy Line was abandoned by the logging company, and before my father had his motor car, the distant whistle of the logging train served as a geographical marker for my father and his fellow hunters, in addition to their compasses.) Major de Spain had arranged with the lumber company for the hunters to ride the train to a stop near the camp in the same way that General Stone had an agreement that allowed him and his hunters, including Faulkner, to catch rides to and from an official stop near the clubhouse. I found an entry in the Panola County chancery records in which General Stone deeded 16/100 of an acre to Batesville Southwestern Railroad Co. in 1911. This would have been the land required for what was designated as Stone Stop, which consisted of a small building used for storage beside the railroad. According to my father, one of the train conductors was Jim Stone Moseley, named in honor of General James Stone.

The log-line junction, Hoke's, which figures prominently in "The Bear," was undoubtedly modeled on the junction and sawmill that Darnell Lumber Company operated in Panola County just west of Batesville, about 11 miles from the Stone camp. Faulkner and his fellow hunters came from Oxford to Batesville and then loaded their camp supplies on the log train at Darnell's for the journey to Stone Stop. From there they would go by mule wagon to the clubhouse.

The old Chickasaw and Choctaw Boundary, which divided the lands of those two nations, still serves on Panola County land maps and chancery records as the northeast boundary line of the tract of land on which the clubhouse was situated. The Chickasaws, according to federal treaty makers, described the boundary line as follows:

> Beginning at the mouth of the Oak-tibby-haw and running up said stream to a point, being a marked tree, on the old Natches [Natchez] road, one mile southwardly from Wall's old place; thence with the Choctaw boundary, and along it, westwardly through the Tunica old fields, to a point on the Mississippi river about 28 miles by water, below where the Saint Frances River enters said stream on the west side.

The white surveyors who came along after those land cessions of the early 1880s employed a similar method of description; that is, one based on existing landmarks and without any apparent concern that those landmarks might shift or disappear over time. Their determination of the beginning of the boundary in a document of field notes from the General Land Office, dated October 16, 1836, reads as follows (with misspellings preserved):

"Boundry Line Between: The Chickasaw and Choctaw Cessions in Mississippi biginning at a point on the East bank of the Mississippi River directly opposite the house where a Mr. Philips once lived which is situated in the town of Helena in the state of Arkansaw. Set large post and erected mound as per instructions." They then trekked through briars, cane, and swamp for their survey.

If you begin at the point across from where a Mr. Philips's house was situated, and on the Mississippi side of the river where the mound was erected, and make your way along the old Choctaw-Chickasaw Boundary for about 27 miles, you'll come to the site of the Stone hunting camp: Section 32, Range 2 E, Township 28. The structure, as of this writing, has fallen into a state of disrepair, and in fact is flooded, the tragedy of which I will address later.

I would like to tell you the name of the person who held the original patent on that tract of land, but I am unable to do so. Most likely it was a Choctaw Indian, for the tract lies on the Choctaw side of the boundary. I can tell you the names of a number of Chickasaw Indians—Shana, Untishetubbe, and so on—who marked their Xs and received a pittance for sections of land on the other side of the boundary in this immediate area. Many of those sections were later owned by General Stone (and some subsequently by my grandfather), in addition to his ownership of the clubhouse tract. The Panola County Chain of Titles goes back only to 1862, and the Department of the Interior was unable to help me find the patent. It would not have surprised me, though, if they had told me that the original patent on the clubhouse tract was held by Ikkemotubbe. He was the Chickasaw chief, you'll recall, in Faulkner's fictional account, from whom Sutpen got his 100 square miles, Sutpen's Hundred, "for money or rum or whatever it was."

And so Faulkner's chancery would read Ikkemotubbe, Sutpen, de Spain, and finally the name of the fictional Memphis lumber company to whom Major de Spain sold the timber rights in "The Bear." Actual lumber companies began arriving in the Big Bottom around the time Faulkner indicated in "The Bear," the late 1880s. Before they arrived, however—and at approximately the same time the fictional Sutpen came storming in, the early 1800s—a more sympathetic figure passed through and was so taken with the unspoiled quality of the place that he later wrote an account of one of his experiences there. The traveler was John James Audubon, and in one of his essays he gives directions for finding "the Swamp" so that students of nature could visit and observe its "rare and interesting productions: birds, quadrupeds and reptiles, as well as molluscous animals, many of which…have never been described."

Audubon's essay concerns a panther hunt. In the course of one of his rambles, he chanced upon a squatter's cabin on the Coldwater River (the Coldwater joins the Tallahatchie less than ten miles west of where the Stone clubhouse and my father's hunting camp were located). Audubon was so engaged by the handsome pelts on the wall and the squatter's descriptions of the area's wildlife that he asked the squatter to be his host and guide for a few days. The next morning while they were feeding the hogs, the squatter told Audubon of a large panther that had been ravaging his livestock: "The Painter, as he sometimes called it, had on several occasions robbed him of a dead deer; and to these exploits the squatter added several remarkable feats of audacity which it had performed, to give me an idea of the formidable character of the beast." Audubon was fascinated and offered to assist him in hunting down the animal. After gathering enough neighbors and dogs for a hunt, they charged off into the swamp. There follows an enthusiastic report of the hunt and the wilds through which they travelled, the upshot of which was the death of the panther. Afterward the hunters made camp, killed a small deer for their meal, and sat around telling tales, singing, and passing the flask.

The problem with regard to attacks on livestock was a common one in the region. Not only were there panthers, but bears posed a problem as well. And in addition to preying on livestock, they would ravage stands of corn. One such example is contained in a letter posted by Edward Neilson from his plantation Bearsden, which was within 10 or 15 miles from the hunting camps of Stone and my father: "Tallahatchie, 30th of July 1861.…I think we will make corn enough to do us if the bear do not eat it up. In the last three or four days several have commenced upon it and they are destroying it very rapidly."

Posted the next day: "This evening about sundown just as I was going to supper I heard Griffin shoot down in the corn field and call for the dogs. I got my bear knife and went to him in a hurry. He was setting old Jimmy [the name of his gun] for a bear and while he was at it, one started to come over the fence close by him. He shot him on the fence and he rolled over inside but got up and got outside. We put the dogs after him and he went about 150 yards in the cane and stopped for a fight. I gave Griffin the knife and I took the gun. It was dark when we got to him. He ran one of the dogs right up to me and I shot him [the bear]. The dogs all seized him and Griffin gave him the knife. He caught Venus after he had been knifed twenty times and got her down when I gave him a blow on the head with the barrel of old Jimmy which knocked him down and made him let her go. I never saw a bear stand as much knifing. It took at least fifty blows and they well aimed to make him lay still. I do not know how bad Venus is hurt. It was so dark I could not tell. The bear was very large and in good eating order. He was destroying our corn very rapidly."

Before reading this account, I had at times wondered if Faulkner's rendering of Old

Ben and the bear's capacity to survive for so long what the hunters mounted against him was perhaps a tad hyperbolic. One of Old Ben's paws is mutilated from a trap in the distant past, he has been assaulted by countless hounds, and at the time of his death it is found that he has collected fifty-two slugs under his hide over the years. (Readers will recall that Moby Dick carried the remains of broken harpoons from previous encounters with whalers. And it is reported that the whale Mocha Dick, the probable model for Moby Dick, had numerous rusty harpoon tips beneath his skin.)

Neilson's hunt involves a relatively short time and distance. His bear went only 150 yards from the fence before he stopped to fight Venus and the other dogs. In contrast, the climactic hunt for Old Ben is of long duration and distance. Granted, those conditions are in the service of dramatic effect, but Faulkner's drama is in fact consistent with the reality of many bear hunts. Among the papers from my uncle Damon Page's archives is a letter that a man who farmed in the Tallahatchie Bottom wrote to one of my uncle's in-laws, a Mr. Prince. Besides being faded and difficult to read, the letter is compromised by misspellings and inconsistent punctuation, but it will serve to confirm further Faulkner's accurate sense of the duration and rigor of typical bear hunts. It is posted from "South Panola Co Mississippi, September the 30th 1867":

> I will tell you of our hunting excursions we lost our start dog last spring and could not dance a lick until the last weak Mr Clinton and myself cut out last weak up to ascues bluff [probably near Askew, which coincidentally is my father's birthplace, in the northwest corner of Panola Co.] in search of beare dogs. succeeded in getting too fine start dogs, we went out yesterday late in the evening started one at the back of our field & killed it, tell Caleb we got him up a tree about 1/2 mile south east of of the east end of Pennsylvania Avinew [a joke], it was then in the knight three miles from home and in a half Aire [hour] from there home. we could not strike our trail consequently we had to cut our way through to the open woods. we got home at ten Oclock last knight all well. we ran three [two words illegible here], we went again this morning & had 3 more chaces & killed two Clinton killed one & I killed one. Major Dickens was with us today the last race was after one of those that don't climb trees he was a whale, they are getting very saucy & catching hogs by the whole sale and even wallowing in my cotton field but [end of page] but I think these new dogs will make them sit farther. tel Caleb they are eaqual to Old Red and both young. tell Caleb also that Clintons three Pups is whales & they will make the bear set farther when they get grown. Mr Prince I have nothing of interest to wright as you have already seen but I thought Caleb might bee interested some in my hunting tale as he knows the ground and could appreciate a portion of it at least.

When Ike McCaslin goes into the wilderness to try to get his first look at Old Ben, he realizes after a time that even though he has left his gun behind he is still tainted by civilization. He must relinquish everything if he is to see the bear. He hangs his watch and compass on a bush, leans his snake stick beside them, and pushes on into the Big Bottom, which Faulkner described earlier as "the same solitude, the same loneliness through which frail and timorous man had merely passed without altering it, leaving no mark nor scar, which looked exactly as it must have looked when the first ancestor of Sam Fathers' Chickasaw predecessors crept into it and looked about him...." Ike gets lost, comes upon the old bear's tracks, its imprint distinguished by the trap-maimed paw, and follows to where the bear is waiting, appropriately, beside the watch and compass. The boy and the bear study each other briefly across a small glade before the bear fades back into the wilderness to await its symbolic fate. The fate of the bear, of course, is the fate of the wilderness itself, for the bear, as Faulkner once suggested, is the spirit of that wilderness.

During the late 1880s word got around that the Southern forests could be had for relatively low prices (most of the farmers regarded the timber as an obstacle), and speculators, usually from outside the South, came with a fury to buy up or lease large blocks of timber. By 1900 the sawmills in Mississippi had doubled, and four years later the state ranked third among lumber-producing states. In *Mississippi Harvest*, Nollie Hickman reports that in 1925 lumber output from these virgin forests reached an all-time high of slightly more than three billion board feet. For me the most dramatic illustration of how much timber all of this involves is found in old topographic maps that indicate woodland by green shading. Arrange them in a stack in chronological sequence—they are updated periodically—and flip through from past to present. You can read a good portion of the history of the area in terms of a steadily diminishing green shade.

As I have mentioned, my grandfather cut and milled timber in the Tallahatchie and Yocona Bottoms for many years. One of his smaller mills, called a groundhog mill, was along the route to the Stone camp, and I am confident that Faulkner and his fellow hunters knew of it. Like the wilderness, that mill too has vanished. In fact, one of the large lumber companies in Memphis (not unlike the fictional Memphis lumber company to whom Major de Spain sells the timber rights in "The Bear") sent a representative to Panola with an offer to buy my grandfather's entire lumber business. My grandfather declined, and within a month his main sawmill and lumber yard containing thousands of board feet of prime hardwood lumber were nothing but ash. Not exactly like the big guns sent to kill McCabe when he refused to sell his brothel in Altman's movie *McCabe and Mrs. Miller*, but close. That is, my grandfather was not shot, but he never fully recovered financially from the fire, his business being uninsured.

I don't have the sense that my grandfather had available to him the assurances of protection from loss in the lumber business in Panola County—or that he would have availed himself of those assurances, given the probable cost. (It is not apples and oranges to note that General Stone lost virtually all of his land in Panola County, owing to the fact that he could not pay drainage taxes. Apparently he was not insured against losses in other ventures.) Before the mill fire my grandfather had another uninsured loss—a huge float of hardwood timber on the Tallahatchie River near Belmont above the hunting grounds. He didn't own a spur-line railroad, so his crew skidded the cut timber from the woods to the banks of the Tallahatchie and rolled log after log into the current. Downstream was a log boom that my grandfather and father had constructed, with the plan of catching the timber and then hauling it to their main sawmill nearby. As they waited at the boom, the Tallahatchie began to rise unexpectedly. My father said he looked up as the timber came around the bend of the Tallahatchie and the churn of foam created by the head logs of the float was like froth on a giant mad-dog's mouth. The timber broke through the boom and spread itself for miles downstream in the flood. Farmers later would pull their mule wagons up to my grandfather's sawmill with choice hardwood logs marked by metal die on one end with my grandfather's signature S. "Hey, Mr. Seay, can you mill this up for me?"

There was no strict evidence linking the Memphis lumber company with the fire, but one of the locals said that on the day before the fire he saw two Brazilians lingering on the Batesville town square. How he dreamed up the Brazilian identity—or thought he could distinguish a Brazilian from, say, a Bedouin or an Inuit—is a mystery. But local lore rules, and in that lore the story of hired Brazilians setting fire to my grandfather's mill and lumber yard is as firm as any in Faulkner's fiction.

The tract on which General Stone's camp was situated is currently listed in the Panola County property records as held in a revocable living trust by an owner who lives out of state. That person and other family members, some residing in Mississippi, have evidenced little interest in the Stone clubhouse except to the extent that profit could be had by selling its artifacts online. When I learned of the online offerings—doors, fireplace bricks, and the like—I was outraged that the clubhouse had been stripped bare. I could not countenance the thought that my home county would possibly be left without a visible trace of Faulkner's sojourns there. I flew to Mississippi from North Carolina and summoned the help of a friend in Batesville, Kenneth Brasell. We drove the 60 miles to New Albany, Miss., where a relative of the owner had the artifacts in his garage. I told the man I wanted to buy the whole lot. I do not know if he was sensitive in any appreciable way, prior to my visit and conversation with him, to the idea of provenance and how that might best be honored. I won't attempt here to parse the concept, pro or con, of private ownership of items invested with historical or literary significance. All I knew was that I wanted to insure that each artifact found a habitation that would honor the connection with Faulkner's achievement, and in my mind it was fundamental that the first site should be in Panola, my home county and an indisputable corner of Yoknapatawpha.

After consulting with Kenneth, I made an offer and we bought all of the doors, some bricks, and a window frame with empty glass panels. Together we donated one door to our

Batesville public library, and divided the remaining items. I donated one of my doors to the University of Mississippi Museum in Oxford. I am still looking for appropriate sites for the other door and the window frame.

The family apparently bought the land in order to put it in the federal wetlands program and collect money while the land reverts to whatever growth will establish itself. Fair enough, but I seriously doubt their dedication to ecology and anything but profit, given their advertising the artifacts of the clubhouse on eBay. Beaver dams now create flooding that has put the clubhouse in a state of desuetude. My hope had always been to initiate restoration of the clubhouse in my retirement years and seek registration with the National Register of Historic Places. But by the time I learned of the family's stripping of the clubhouse and its flooding, it was too late for anything other than the recovery of those remnants I've described.

I recently drove out Dummy Line Road—the foundation of which is the Dummy Line railroad that afforded Faulkner and his hunters access to General Stone's hunting camp and on which my father hauled back to town a corpse in his motorcar when the world was covered in ice—and got as close to the site of the clubhouse as possible in a four-wheel-drive pickup with the idea of walking the remaining distance—as a trespasser, I assume—but the thick growth and briars and danger of cottonmouth moccasins turned me back.

When I first discovered the clubhouse in the 1970s, I knelt down beside the artesian spring and cupped water in my hands to drink. Even then, after centuries of flow, the spring delivered a stream of water as thick as your wrist. The cold, deep earthiness of the water, with its tincture of sulfur, seemed to me an apt distillation of all that the land had borne, both the real Panola and its fictional corner in Faulkner's Yoknapatawpha. Old Ben's blood, Venus's blood, gunpowder, the spoor of Jim's Hancock's white otter, Audubon's crayon, Sutpen's fury, the ash of my grandfather's mill, the last breath of General Stone's son in that same artesian spring, Major de Spain's ink on the lumber company's lease, the frail purchase of my father's motorcar wheels on the Dummy Line, the rumor of Brazilians, Faulkner's footsteps and shadow. It was all there, blent in an alchemy of dream.

After Old Ben has finally been hunted down and Major de Spain has sold the timber rights to the Memphis lumber company, Ike catches a ride on the log train at Hoke's and heads into the Big Bottom a final time, thinking along the way of what the train has come to mean:

> It had been harmless then. They would hear the passing log-train sometimes from the camp; sometimes, because nobody bothered to listen for it or not….But it was different now. It was the same train, engine cars and caboose, even the same enginemen brakeman and conductor…yet this

time it was as though the train (and not only the train but himself, not only his vision which had seen it and his memory which remembered it but his clothes too, as garments carry back into the clean edgeless blowing of air the lingering effluvium of a sick-room or of death) had brought with it into the doomed wilderness even before the actual axe the shadow and portent of the new mill not even finished yet and the rails and ties which were not even laid; and he knew now what he had known as soon as he saw Hoke's this morning but had not yet thought into words: why Major de Spain had not come back, and that after this time he himself, who had had to see it one time other, would return no more.

The McCorkle House in the 19th century
Hubert McAlexander, *Southern Tapestry*

Appendix One:
Truth in Dealing
with the Past

Hubert H. McAlexander

From the Holly Springs *South Reporter*, Pilgrimage Edition, 2005

I wrote the following treatment of one of the Cession's earliest and most significant houses in 2004. It was published in the Pilgrimage Edition of the Holly Springs *South Reporter* the next spring. This is an article on an historic structure based on scrupulous research, though there are no notes in a newspaper version. I grew up in a town with a remarkable architectural legacy, celebrated by an annual house tour and an inaccurate presentation of history by many of the ladies involved.

Laboring under that kind of falsification for years, I made contact with my close friend Charles Nunally Dean (1927-1983) about 1954 and that began a setting-of-things-straight that has lasted to this day.

The history of the Crump Place, the oldest intact structure in north Mississippi, begins when Samuel McCorkle, pioneer land agent and a leading speculator in the newly opened Chickasaw Cession, laid claim to the eastern half of the block of land now bounded by Gholson Avenue, Memphis Street, and Chulahoma Avenue. During the "Flush Times," in the year 1837, he constructed a fine residence, the finest that the fledging village of log structures had yet seen.

Fortunately, invoices for McCorkle's residence survive to tell us just what he originally had built and even how he furnished his residence. The list of building supplies includes 19 window frames and 10 door frames, one mantle at $25, one mantle at $8, one "fine mantle" at $20, one "common mantle" at $10, two "small mantles" at $5 each, one "Fine Fancy Door finished" at $50, and four Presses for $301. The cost for this full list of materials was $867.49. Another bill for purchase and delivery of 3,820 bricks from Whitfield, Bledsoe, & Co. was paid in full on January 11, 1838.

On Aug. 9, 1837, McCorkle purchased a "mantle Glass," for his parlor, from Nelson Chambers & Co., probably a Memphis business. Another bill of lading is for hauling 1,611 pounds for furniture: one large box and two tables, one bedstead, post & carpet, bed rails, one truck, two boxes, one bureau "at Peden Shop," one bedstead, three beds, and "two little Tables at Pedens if the wagon will hold them if not, don't take them." The Peden establishment must have been in Memphis. But on Jan. 5, 1838, the McCorkles did purchase from Hatchell & Norfleet, Holly Springs cabinet makers, a trundle bed.

Samuel McCorkle (1795-1850), born in North Carolina, had come west in youth, married his wife America (who was born in Mt. Sterling, Ky.) and settled in the 1820s in Paris, Tenn., where he established himself as a surveyor and was eventually appointed land commissioner of the Twelfth Tennessee District. McCorkle was among the first to realize the economic opportunities offered by the 1832 Treaty of Pontotoc, by which the Chickasaws ceded their north Mississippi domain of six million acres to the United States government. In 1835, he and a group of Paris friends founded the Pontotoc Land Company, a speculating concern, and McCorkle lived briefly in Pontotoc, Miss. (where the government land office was located) before moving to Holly Springs. One of the 20-man partnership led by William S. Randolph to lay out and sell a settlement at "the holly springs," McCorkle was one of the founding fathers of our town. In 1837, at the time he was building his fine residence, he established the Holly Springs Real Estate Banking company on the south side of the square.

Samuel and America McCorkle had one child, Catherine (1825-1894). After completing her education locally at Sylvestria Female Academy, Kate McCorkle was married in 1842 by the Episcopal rector to Charles G. Nelms, an attorney. Eldest of three sons of Presley Nelms and Anne Ingram of Anson County, North Carolina (all of whom eventually settled in Mississippi), Charles Gallatin Nelms (1815-1862) was the first to move south, perhaps influenced by his first cousin Eben Nelms Davis, who had settled on Strawberry Plains plantation five miles north of Holly Springs in 1837. Charles Nelms was practicing law in the village by the next year, and after he married, he and Kate lived with the Mc-Corkles.

The fall of 1849 issued a year of deaths for the Nelms and McCorkle families. Charles Nelms' brother, Dr. Joseph Presley Nelms, and his family had only recently come south when they lost their son Eben. The following March, Dr. Nelms' wife died and was buried beside her child in the Nelms lot in Hillcrest. Then in the fall of 1850, Samuel McCorkle too was buried beneath a fine monument in another hurriedly purchased lot. By this time, the Nelmses had all moved to DeSoto County, where Dr. Nelms had resumed a bachelor existence, having given over the care of his daughter Mary (or Mollie, as she was always called), to his brother and sister-in-law, who were childless and now living at their plantation, Norfolk.

Mollie Nelms divided her youth between Norfolk plantation, Holly Springs, and two distant boarding schools. In 1858 and 1859, she was enrolled at Nazareth Academy in Bardstown, Ky., after which she was sent to a fashionable finishing school in Philadelphia

— Madame Chagerey's French School. By the time of the 1860 census, Mollie was living with America McCorkle. Soon they were joined by America's daughter and Mollie's aunt, Kate McCorkle. Charles G. Nelms had raised a company, the DeSoto Rebels, of which he was colonel, and marched them off to the front.

Kate left Norfolk and came to Holly Springs, where the three generations of women spent the war. It was a sad time. Wounded at Shiloh on April 7, 1862, Colonel Nelms died a week later in Corinth. His body was brought home to rest next to Samuel McCorkle's beneath still another fine monument. When Grant's army occupied Holly Springs in the fall, 200 soldiers bivouacked on the McCorkle grounds, and their officers were quartered in the residence. The three women were allowed to go to the dining room only after the officers had dined — and eat what was left. But worse than the indignities suffered was the fear of the possible explosion of the Presbyterian church up the street, which the Federal Army had filled with munitions. When General Earl Van Dorn made his daring raid on Grant's supply base on December 20, he spared the church, and probably the McCorkle residence as well.

After the war ended, the house saw happy times again, as a social center for the charming young Mollie Nelms. On Tuesday, October 2, 1865, at 12 o'clock in Christ Church, she married Edward Hull Crump, lately a Confederate officer under the command of John Hunt Morgan. A scion of the Hull-Crump connection of Fredericksburg, Va., which had begun removing to Marshall County as soon as the Chickasaw lands were opened to settlement, Edward was the son of William Crump and his wife, Ann Hull, who followed the rest of the connection and lived at Tuckahoe plantation near Holly Springs. After the wedding trip, Mollie Nelms Crump moved with her husband to his farm near Hudsonville. Here three children were born to the couple — John in 1868, Kate (named for Kate McCorkle Nelms) in 1870, and Edward in 1874.

In late summer of 1878, Holly Springs was struck with an epidemic of yellow fever. Edward Hull Crump took his wife and children to an uncle's plantation and gathered his two stricken brothers from Holly Springs. John Mickle, a cousin and noted local historian who fled the town in the carriage of his grandmother Jane Hull Minor, always remembered going by the Crump farm: "They were lifting Major Brodie Crump out of an ambulance at the gate of his brother Edward H. Crump, near Hudsonville, as we passed, and, in a hack behind were Mr. and Mrs. William Crump. I never saw the gentleman again." All died, Edward last. Putting on the mourning that she wore for the rest of her life, Mollie Nelms Crump returned to the farm with her children. It was a hard-scrabble existence, and her son Edward never forgot his mother's courage and strength during those years.

After inheriting land in Tunica and DeSoto counties five years later, Mrs. Crump moved her family into Holly Springs. America McCorkle had died in 1879, and upon the

1885 death of Dr. Francis W. Dancy, a widower with whom Kate McCorkle Nelms made a second marriage, Mollie Crump and her children moved into the McCorkle house with her aunt. Upon Kate McCorkle Nelms Dancy's death in 1894, Mollie Crump inherited the property. She lived there until her death in 1940. Over the decades, it became known as the Crump Place.

All of the McCorkle and Nelms furniture remained: the carpets, the silver and china, the large portrait of America McCorkle. A photograph by Lem Johnson taken in 1901 shows the house much as it would have been when Samuel McCorkle built it. Mrs. Crump and her yard man moved about the place every morning tending the garden, where Mrs. Crump grew the finest roses in Holly Springs. Like many a Southern house, the Crump Place continued to shelter several generations. Upon the death of Mrs. Crump's daughter Kate Crump Butler in 1902, her three orphaned daughters came to live with their grandmother "Danny" Crump. It was probably then that Mrs. Crump added a bedroom and small sewing room at the west end of the front facade. Still later in the 20th century, four generations lived in the house.

By that time, the house had become known through the region as the childhood home of Mollie Nelms Crump's youngest son, Edward (1874-1954). Removing to Memphis in 1894, with little except the clothes on his back and his good connections, E.H. Crump became a wealthy man and a political leader with enormous influence. He held numerous elective offices, including mayor of Memphis and United States congressman. But he is remembered best as the man who came to control Tennessee politics and became a power in the National Democratic Party. He had a steadfast love and concern for Holly Springs. He was always ready to lend a helping hand to old friends, and he is credited with saving the town by dispatching the Memphis fire department to a terrible fire on the town square in 1951.

The house passed out of the Crump family in 1962. The new owners, Mr. and Mrs. Randolph Holt, added the room at the end of the east facade and enclosed the long L-shaped back gallery. In the 1970s, Roger Wood and his wife, Jane Sibley Lester, purchased the Crump Place from the Holts and added a greenhouse in the back court.

In a great stroke of good fortune, the Crump Place was purchased in 2002 by David Person, an attorney based in San Antonio and London. Person, whose family left Holly Springs in 1907, had deep Marshall County roots. He descends from two notable early attorneys, Judge James Lockhart Totten (1803-1866), speaker of the Mississippi House of Representatives, and Judge James Fisher Trotter (1802-1866), United States Senator, justice of the state supreme court and professor of law at the University of Mississippi. Judge Trotter is one of the two Marshall countians included in the Mississippi Hall of Fame. On still another line, Person's great-grandfather Logan Walker once owned Airliewood.

With the aid of Chelius H. Carter, local preservation architect, David Person has returned the oldest portion of the Crump Place to its original state and feeling. The long back gallery now restored, the whole structure repainted Mrs. Crump's "Colonial Yellow" and filled with the Empire and Victorian furniture that marked old Holly Springs, the Crump Place once again reflects the indigenous fabric and texture of our town.

Appendix Two:
Plantation Names
in the Cession

John M. Mickle (1860-1942), the historian of old Marshall County, lists the following plantation names in one of his newspaper columns ("The Pines, Landmark of Civic Importance," in Robert Milton Winter, ed., *Amid Some Excellent Company* [2003], 203-204):

Snowdoun	Govan family, between Lamar and Salem
Woodlawn	The Dabney Minor family, same location as above
Greenwood	The Hull family, same general location
Woodcote	Judge Alexander M. Clayton, Lamar
The Lodge	Charles Thomas, off Highway 7 toward Lamar
Sylvestria	The Cottrell family, south of Hudsonville
Tuckahoe	William Crump, just east of Holly Springs
East End	John Hull, across the road from Tuckahoe
Athenia	William Lumpkin, four miles south of Holly Springs
Galena	Will Henry Coxe, east of Chulahoma

To that list, we add others that were found later and as we put together this book.

Marshall County

Sunnyside	Wall-McPherson, just north of Sylvestria
Happy Hill	Robert B.Alexander, just south of Holly Springs
Groveland	Richard Hill Parham, on the Tennessee line
Strawberry Plains	Eben Nelms Davis, north of Holly Springs
Edgewood	Dr. Nazareth Leggett, near Hudsonville
Oakland	Peter Scales at Hudsonville
Prospect Hill	Rufus Jones, near Tallaloosa

Oak Grove	Mallerb Jones, five miles west of Tallaloosa
Woodlawn	John Wooten, five miles west of Tallalosa
Wildwood	Dr. Willis Monroe Lea, west of Holly Springs
Caledonia	William Blanton Lumpkin, near Lumpkin Mill
Morro Castle	William Blanton Lumpkin, south of Holly Springs
Hazelwood	Olin Hamlin Lumpkin, near Moro Castle
Greenwood	Alfred Brooks, west of Waterford
Luconia	Green Pryor, between Chulahoma and Wyatt
Hickory Park	Volney Peel, near Laws Hill
Hedge Farm	Robert Raiford, north of Victoria
Percalpa	Albert Quarles Withers, near Victoria
Valleyside	Eaton Pugh Govan, near Lamar
Oak Hill	Hugh Davis, near Michigan City

TIPPAH COUNTY (NOW BENTON COUNTY)

Gothic Hall	Harrison Patton Maxwell, near Salem (now extinct)

PONTOTOC COUNTY

Fairview	Patrick Henry Fontaine, near Pontotoc
Lochinvar	Robert Gordon, south of Pontotoc
Stony Lonesome	Joel Pinson, south of Pontotoc

LAFAYETTE COUNTY

Orange Hill	Alexander H. Pegues, Woodson's Ridge
Solitude	L.Q.C. Lamar, near Abbeville
Oak Hill	Jacob Thompson, south of Oxford
Fairview	Dr. Robert Otway Carter, northwest of the Tallahatchie
Cotland	Carter brothers and sisters, five miles west of Oxford
Oak Grove	Washington Price, north of Yocona on the Delay Road
Cedar Hill Farm	Yancey Wiley, near College Hill
Jasmine Farm	David Scott Tankersley, near College Hill

DESOTO COUNTY

Lodockery	Alfred Dockery, near Hernando
Raw Head and Bloody Bones	Dabney Herndon Hull
Forest Grove	Gen. J.C.N. Robertson, three miles from Hernando

TATE COUNTY

McGehee's Gate	Abner Francis McGehee, three miles south of Senatobia
Silverton	John Oliver Meriwether, four miles east of Senatobia

PANOLA COUNTY

Hollywood	John Scott McGehee, four miles east of Como
Ivy Cottage	James Blanton McGehee, near Como
Wallace Park	Col. Thomas Wallace, a mile from Como
Tait House	Dr. George G. Tait, Como
Palmetto Place	Thomas Jefferson Taylor, six miles southwest of Como
Twin Stairs	Col. Norfleet Ruffin Sledge, Como
Egypt Place	William David Sledge, Mastodon
Monthalia	Edwin Coleman, west of Como
Dreamland	Eliza Jane Smith Pope

TUNICA COUNTY

OK Plantation	Sterling Withers, on the Mississippi River
Alterra	Campbell Mangum
Beaver Dam	Sterling Owen
Bowdre	Penn Owen

COAHOMA COUNTY

Elkhorn	George and Levin Dickerson, Friars Point
Cedar Mound	Alex Kerr Boyce

Eagles Nest	James Lusk Alcorn, 7 miles northeast of Clarksdale
Matagora	Col. David Moor Russell
Honey Hill	Charles Grimke Bobo
Halcyon	Andrew Jackson, Jr.
Rena Lara	John P. Richardson, 12 miles west of Clarksdale
Woodmere	John Wesley Baugh, 9 miles southwest of Clarksdale
Prarie Plantation	William J. Oldham
Mound Place	James Lusk Alcorn, on Yazoo Pass
Magnolia	Capt. E. A. Lindsley
Red Bud Springs	Dr. Van Easton
Arcadia	J.W. Cutrer, north of Tutwiler

Bolivar County

These names are taken from a valuable history of Bolivar County, compiled by Florence Warfield Sillers in 1948. It was reprinted by the Reprint Company, Publishers, Spartanburg, S.C., in 1976.

Hollywood	John Crawford Burrus, near present town of Benoit
Sunnywild	James F. Stokes, near present town of Gunnison
Doro	Charles Clark
Glenwood	George W. Gayden, on Lake Beulah
Waxhaw	John Cousar Kirk, near town of Rosedale
Rosedale	Col. Lafayette Jones
Leesland	John Venable Lobdell
Elery, then later Ingleside	Edward McGehee
Sunnywild	Miles H. McGehee, 8 miles above town of Rosedale
Perthshire	George Guildford Torrey
Woodlawn	Joseph Sillers
Moss Side	Daniel W. Cameron

ACKNOWLEDGEMENTS

In putting together a book of this sort (of what sort you may ask), one incurs many debts. I am happy to acknowledge them here.

For aid in typing and formating, Eve Bondurant Mayes, Patricia McAlexander, and my old student and now master formatter Albert Dixon have been indispensable. Gary Doster has contributed in numerous ways. For supplying or preserving historical materials or suggesting historical context, I am grateful to Sylvia Seymour Akin, Terry Baker, Patsy Moore Bogen, Richard B. Burnett, Paul Calame, Chelius H. Carter, Mary Jane Calame Chotard, Vadah Cochran, Henry Dancy, Charles Nunnally Dean, Lester Glenn Fant III, Martha Teel Fant, Jennifer Ford, Peggy Heard Galis, Anne Razey Gowdy, Thomas S. Hines, Richard C. M. Houston, Eugene Banks Lanier, Lucie Lee Maynard Lanoux, Patty Povall Lewis, Willie Mallory, Thomas Kincaide McCraw, Mark Miller, Martha V. Moseley, Edward G. Parham, Taylor Pointer, John Hays Pritchard, George Banks Ready, James H. Robertson, Dean Hugh Ruppersburg, Chesley Thorne Smith, Lemuel Augustus Smith III, Lilian Wilson Stratmon, Netty Fant Thompson, Dr. Robert E. Tyson, Sam Varner, Joseph E. Winston, and Sterling Withers. My brother and sister, Charles C. McAlexander and Betty Brown McAlexander Powell, have contributed so much and in so many ways over the years. For the final proof reading in Athens, I relied on the intelligent scrutiny of Wilson Golden and Patricia McAlexander.

Of course, I am obligated to Bobby Mitchell, Anne Percy, Sue Watson, and James Seay for allowing me to reprint their efforts. I am fortunate to have persuaded Jack D. Elliott, Jr., and Wilson Golden (my student at Ole Miss in 1966, who went on to a legal career in Mississippi and the nation's capital) to write essays for the volume. Native Mississippians with many generations behind them, each brings particular training and talents to the task. Dr. Lucius McGehee of Memphis, also an author, has Mississppi roots and interests that go back far, as does the Rev. Milton Winter.

Three people have played central, though mostly hidden, roles in this book. Over the years of our shared interest in the Marshall County past, Bobby Mitchell and I have worked together on manifold projects. My old friend Will Lewis of Oxford has kept me supplied with tantalizing Lafayette County material that has led to the writing of many essays. Sledge Taylor of Como is the only person I've known who leaves mud on his stairway and has represented this country in China and in Germany. We have numerous connections (finding more and more as the book grew), and he is responsible for many essays. Our friendship is one of the great benefits of this book.

Luckily, because of the vision and generosity of my old friend Ruff Fant, the manuscript fell into the hands of Nautilus Publishing Company in Oxford, Mississippi. Founded by Neil White, the company has quickly become the primary publisher of northern Mississippi. Neil has proven sympathetic to this project, and within the house, Sinclair Rishel has handled the manuscript with great care to produce the handsome volume you hold in your hands. At the end, Le'Herman Payton designed the wonderful cover.